Quality Service Pays

Quality Service Pays

SIX KEYS TO SUCCESS!

HENRY L. LEFEVRE

*Sponsored by the American Society for Quality Control
Quality Management Division*

QUALITY PRESS
American Society for Quality Control
Milwaukee, Wisconsin

QUALITY RESOURCES
A Division of The Kraus Organization Limited
White Plains, New York

Copyright © 1989 American Society for Quality Control

All rights reserved. No part of this work covered by the copyrights hereon may be reproduced or used in any form or by any means—graphic, electronic, or mechanical, including photocopying, recording, or taping, or information storage and retrieval systems—without written permission of the publisher.

First printing 1989

Printed in the United States of America

Quality Resources
A Division of The Kraus Organization Limited
One Water Street, White Plains, New York 10601

Library of Congress Cataloging-in-Publication Data
Lefevre, Henry L.
    Quality service pays : six keys to success! / Henry L. Lefevre.
    p. cm.
    Bibliography: p.
    Includes index.
    ISBN 0-527-91629-3
    1. Service industries—United States—Quality control. 2. United States—Manufactures—Quality control. I. Title.
HD9980.5.L36   1989   89–10447
658.5'62—dc20   CIP

Contents

Preface vii

1. Six Keys to Quality Service 3
2. *Key 1:* WHAT IS QUALITY SERVICE ALL ABOUT? 11
3. Know Thy Customers 23
4. Know Thine Own Business 39
5. Steps to Quality Excellence 55

6. *Key 2:* UNDERSTANDING SAMPLING 67
7. Sample Plans and the Service Sector 81
8. Military Standard 105D—The Basics 89
9. Military Standard 105D in Action 99
10. Dodge & Romig Sample Plans 113
11. Continuous Sampling 123

12. *Key 3:* MASTERING THE BASIC TOOLS 137
13. Trend Charts 141
14. Variation in the Service Sector 157
15. Control Charts for Variables 175
16. Control Charts for Attributes 191
17. Capability Studies 215
18. Choosing the Right Process or Product 227
19. Efficiency and Problem Solving 241

20. *Key 4:* UNDERSTANDING AUTOMATION 253
21. Computer Basics 257
22. As Literacy Approaches, Questions Multiply 267
23. Database Quality Control 277
24. *Key 5:* INVOLVING PEOPLE 289
25. Keep People Involved 301
26. *Key 6:* KNOWING WHERE AND HOW TO USE THE OTHER KEYS . . 315
27. Quotable Quotes 337
Index 351

Preface

Quality departments in the service industries are like orphans waiting for adoption. Almost everyone proclaims their right to live. Few, however, want to acknowledge their legitimacy or pay for their maintenance. Many service industries have hired consultants from manufacturing as "foster parents," in order to gain insight into raising baby quality assurance departments. To date, however, few have been willing to sign lifelong contracts for the infant departments' nursery care. Why is that a problem? Because service sector quality control has been an infant for over 20 years and promises to remain one for another 20.

The Quality Management Division, formerly the Administrative Applications Division, of the American Society for Quality Control is the designated midwife for service sector quality. I have been a member of that organization since 1968 and was chairman during the 1975–76 fiscal year. For the last 20 years, dedicated members have valiantly tried to wean and nurture service sector quality control. Others have tried to throw it out with the bath water.

THE WEANING YEARS

Governmental agencies were leaders in the field of service sector quality; Dr. A. C. Rosander has been working in this field since World War II. Some of his exploits are documented in his recent books *Washington Story*[1] and *Applications of Quality Control in the Service Industries*.[2] Were it not for Dr. Rosander, the Quality Management Division might have abandoned the service industry side of its charter and become solely a management services division.

The banking industry also made major contributions toward recognizing the need for service sector quality. Eugene Kirby and Bill Latzko were pioneers in this area. Although much of Kirby's work was not published, he did document some of his ideas in "Quality Control in Banking,"[3] which appeared in the 1975 Yearbook of the Administrative Applications Division of the American Society for Quality Control.

Bill Latzko, the 1985–87 chairman of the Administrative Applications Division, is another "quality in banking" pioneer. He is also a prolific writer; many of his publications are identified in the bibliography of his recent book *Quality and Productivity for Bankers and Financial Managers*.[4]

WHY HASN'T QUALITY SERVICE TAKEN HOLD?

The question "Why hasn't quality service taken hold?" is not an easy one. The Quality Management Division of the American Society for Quality Control, and its predecessor, the Administrative Applications Division, have been trying to answer it for over 20 years. They have come up with a few answers and many questions. One of their biggest problems involves answering the question "What is service quality?"

In this book, "service quality" includes both quality in service industries and quality in the service sector of manufacturing companies. Service industries like hotels, fast-food outlets, insurance companies, governmental agencies, hospitals and banks are not noted for their high-volume manufacturing operations. There are, however, some jobs common to both the service and manufacturing sectors; the control of raw materials is one. In addition, most manufacturing organizations have clerical operations and use computers. These activities involve either service quality or administrative quality control and fall under the service sector umbrella. Formal attempts to bring quality to these areas, however, are limited.

This book identifies many tools that have been used to improve quality in the service sector; it also identifies many people and companies who have been able to use them.

WHY ME?

"Service-industry and administrative quality control" is an art striving to become a science. I have assisted in transitions like this since World War II.

My first assignment of this nature was in the Army Air Force Weather Service. At that time, weather forecasting was more art than science. By now, it is more science than art, although the artistic element will never disappear.

My entry into the field of quality control began when I was a chemist working for Union Oil Company; my skills were fine-tuned during my tenure as a manufacturing engineering supervisor for the Aerojet General Corporation. At Aerojet, my main function was to keep the quality control engineers from inadvertently shutting down the plant.

While with Honeywell, I helped computerize their quality control function and learned that computers, when properly used, can save the company an enormous amount of time and energy. When misused, however, computers can perpetuate disasters.

At the Coors Container Company, working with Ed Schrock, I delved into the mysteries of Statistical Quality Control. I found a need for quality control on the service side of this company. The idea was good but its time had not yet come.

Prior to getting directly involved in service quality, I became active in the Administrative Applications Division, now the Quality Management Division, of the American Society for Quality Control. Here, I learned the elements of administrative and service industry quality.

Upon going to work for the Air Force, I got my feet wet in service quality; I also learned to swim. At the Air Reserve Personnel Center and the Air Force Accounting and Finance Center, I developed skills in internal audits, objective personnel evaluations, attribute sampling, continuous sampling, streamlined funds forecasting, database quality control and other tools appropriate for service industry and administrative quality control.

During my 40-plus years working with quality control, I have learned a lot—and am still learning. Much of my accumulated knowledge is documented in this book in the hope that others can learn from my past successes and failures.

Much can be learned from reading. Even more can be learned by applying the concepts.

STATISTICS FOR NONSTATISTICIANS

In writing this book, I simplified many complex statistical concepts; those that could not be simplified were left to more rigorous statistical texts. Technical material in this book was written for managers and technicians, not statisticians and professors.

Steps required to solve problems in the text are shown in detail; a good illustration is more helpful than pages of directions. When faced with your own analysis, run through these problems. Then analyze your own data. Solving a problem when the answer is given usually minimizes confusion.

Most of the examples in this book come from my observations. During a 40-year career in both manufacturing and service industries, I survived extensive exposure to subjective decision-making, fruitless witch hunts and professional wheel-spinning contests. I also studied the articles and books of masters in the field like Bill Latzko, Eugene Kirby and Dr. Rosander. I learned from them.

I trust the reader will benefit from reading about the disasters and successes I have described. It is better to learn from the errors of others than to make the same mistakes yourself.

Many names and places have been changed to protect the innocent as well as the guilty. You, the reader, may know both.

HENRY L. LEFEVRE
Denver, Colorado

REFERENCES
1. A. C. Rosander, *Washington Story* (Greeley, CO: National Directions, 1985).
2. A. C. Rosander, *Applications of Quality Control in the Service Industries* (Milwaukee, WI: ASQC Quality Press, 1986).
3. Eugene Kirby, "Quality Control in Banking," *Administrative Applications Division of ASQC Year Book,* 1975, pp. 53–57.
4. William J. Latzko, *Quality and Productivity for Bankers and Financial Managers* (Milwaukee, WI: ASQC Quality Press, 1987).

Quality Service Pays

Chapter 1

Six Keys to Quality Service

Holding the keys to quality service—and knowing how to use them—is like having access to the U.S. Mint. These keys open the doors to success in service industries and the service sector of manufacturing companies. Without them you can't gain access to the winner's trophy room.

Why is service sector quality control so important? Some say it's because the need is so great. Since World War II, product quality has received a lot of attention—as if it were industry's favorite son. Service quality, on the other hand, is treated like an illegitimate relative with tattered tennis shoes and patched-up clothes.

Poor-looking relatives with questionable heritage can control billions of dollars; so can service sector quality. Consider the budgets allotted to secretarial support, filing, data entry, customer service, consumer relations, computer operations, database management, sales, quality control, manufacturing engineering, purchasing and design. These parts of industry represent the service sector; they require many of the same skills as service industries like banking and insurance. Providing poor quality in the service sector is like fielding a "sand lot" team in the World Series play-offs: it gives the company a bad name and hurts profits. Quality service pays.

Here are the keys to quality service that are identified in this book:

1. Knowing what quality service is all about (Chapters 2–5)
2. Understanding sampling (Chapters 6–11)
3. Mastering the basic tools (Chapters 12–19)
4. Understanding automation (Chapters 20–23)
5. Involving people (Chapters 24–25)
6. Knowing where and how to use the other keys (Chapter 26)

The first five keys open individual doors. The sixth is the key to the safe. Without it, the others are useless—unless you have enough dynamite to blast through a foot of hardened steel. Knowing is not enough. You need to apply your knowledge.

KEY 1: KNOWING WHAT QUALITY SERVICE IS ALL ABOUT

The first key is understanding the nature of quality service. Without this background, you will be like a missionary trying to talk cannibals out of having you for dinner when you can't even speak their language.

Quality service involves attitudes, timeliness, proper tools, quality product and customer satisfaction. If you take care of the first four elements, customer satisfaction is assured—as long as you have a product the customer wants, readily available at a reasonable price. Attitudes, timeliness, proper tools and quality products are covered in Chapter 2.

With limited resources, you can't maintain equal control over all of the keys. As a consequence, you need to know which keys to emphasize. This can be achieved by determining:

- Who are your customers?
- What do they want?
- Do they mean what they say (or think they said)?

These elements are covered in Chapter 3. They apply to services and administrative quality control. They also apply to the manufacturing sector.

Knowing your customers, however, is not enough; you also need to know your business. Chapter 4 provides some insight into this objective. Techniques of value include:

- Tours of duty in the trenches
- Management By Wandering Around (MBWA) tours
- Open rap sessions
- Presidential audits
- System audits
- Cost analyses

Another part of quality service includes knowing the difference between evaluating and controlling quality. Some managers feel they are controlling quality when they measure it and then bellow for improvements. There are better ways. Some tools for evaluating and controlling quality are introduced in Chapter 5.

KEY 2: UNDERSTANDING SAMPLING

Some people worry if part of the work isn't inspected. They are like compulsive housekeepers who dust the furniture four times per day in fear that neighbors might drop in. Examples of compulsive workers include:

- Managers who edit every letter that crosses their desk—then edit again, after changes have been made—then edit a third time to make sure the changes were correct
- Travel desk supervisors who inspect every voucher even though their review may cost more than the total payment
- Fast-food-chain managers who try to check the quality of every meal their outlet sells
- Payroll supervisors who check every time card before authorizing payment

These examples are typical, but they only skim the surface. With a little thought, you can come up with dozens that apply to your work situation. When used properly, statistical sampling can benefit productivity and quality at the same time. When used improperly, however, it can create more problems than it solves.

Chapter 6 stresses the techniques used in taking a sample. There's more to it than looking at whatever strikes your fancy; your sample should represent the entire population.

Chapter 7 provides a brief rundown of sample plans used in the service sector. What should you sample? What sample plans are available for guidance? Should you use internal or external audits?

Chapter 8 introduces Military Standard 105D; it includes some insight into how it works as well as its advantages and disadvantages. Terms and abbreviations used by the standard are also defined.

Chapter 9 goes into the actual use of Military Standard 105D. Examples are provided to supplement the material.

Chapter 10 introduces the Dodge & Romig sample plans; they are a viable alternative to Military Standard 105D. The Dodge & Romig plans are particularly helpful when the expense of accepting substandard work is high or the average outgoing quality must be known. Examples are included to clarify details.

Chapter 11 presents a simple approach to continuous sampling based on sample plan CSP-1.[1] Here too, examples are included to clarify details of the plan. I have used CSP-1 to control quality in a clerical environment, and it worked.

KEY 3: MASTERING THE BASIC TOOLS

There are many tools available to help evaluate and control quality. Chapter 12 introduces you to a few of them. More details, however, are contained in subsequent chapters.

An old Chinese proverb says, "One picture is worth more than a thousand words." Trend charts are a lot like pictures; they help you determine where you've been and where you are apt to go if you make no adjustments. These charts are used extensively for service sector quality analysis. Instructions on how to design and interpret them are included in Chapter 13.

The transition from trend to control charts requires an understanding of variation. Chapter 14 provides this background with sections on sources of variation, measures of variation, histograms and Multi-Vari analysis.

When you observe variation, is there an identifiable cause, or is it random? Chapters 15 and 16 help answer that question in the process of discussing control charts for variables (Chapter 15) and control charts for attributes (Chapter 16).

Once the service sector became comfortable with control charts, capability studies started showing up; managers wanted to know how much to expect from groups and individuals under specified working conditions. Chapter 17 explains capability studies for both groups and individuals. Then problems are worked out to clarify the calculations and illustrate their use in the service sector.

There are times when it is necessary to compare processes or products. As an example, if you are going to purchase 5000 typewriter ribbons, it's important to select the brand that's best for your company; the lowest price may not provide the proper answer. You may also want to compare alternate clerical procedures, different ways of calculating travel pay, techniques for preparing entrées in a fast-food outlet or the procedures used by motel employees for preparing rooms. These comparisons can be made by running simple experiments; popular approaches include control charts, Ends Tests and the Tukey-Duckworth Test. All are simple and powerful. All have limitations. All three are covered in Chapter 18.

In the service sector, quality is important; so is efficiency. Chapter 19 covers tools for improving both, including

- Pareto charts (potential payoff comparisons)
- Flow charts (interrelationships within a process)
- Why-Why diagrams (process evaluations)
- Ishikawa diagrams (variables contributing to a problem)
- Cross-Functional Analysis (redundancy evaluations)

KEY 4: UNDERSTANDING AUTOMATION

To many people, computers are austere, argumentative, unbending robots that never make mistakes. To most data processing professionals, computers are friendly servants that are never moody, do what they are told and provide challenges. Chapter 20 starts the discussion of automation with a little history and a road map of what's to come.

Computer programmers and analysts have developed their own technical jargon, called Computerese. Chapter 21 explains the common computer terms and provides an introduction to computer literacy. It is difficult to negotiate with analysts if you don't understand the language they speak.

Chapter 22 goes further into automation by responding to these questions:

- Will it pay for itself?
- What services are available?
- Are commercial computer programs handy?
- Who should program your computers?

Most administrative, clerical and service organizations use computer databases. Some of these electronic file cabinets, however, are treated like 20-acre, hutchless rabbit ranches; the contents are hard to confine and difficult to control. In addition, they proliferate until they've used up all the allotted space. Chapter 23 provides insight into their supervision and control.

KEY 5: INVOLVING PEOPLE

People involvement can make the difference between success and failure. The Japanese often get people into the act via groups called Quality Circles. Many companies in the United States attempted to copy the better parts of these programs. Some were successful; others found the Circles completely unsuited to their operations. Some of the strong points and weaknesses of Quality Circles and other participative management programs are addressed in Chapter 24. They are not panaceas but they often help, especially when given strong support from the top.

How do you give a participative management program staying power? The art of involving people often benefits from motivational campaigns like Quality Circles and other team programs. Many have been successful for a time. They seldom last, however, without the astute use of objective personnel evaluations.[2,3] Obvious support from the top is also critical. These topics are addressed in Chapter 25.

KEY 6: KNOWING WHERE AND HOW TO USE THE OTHER KEYS

All the theory in the world is of little value if it is never applied. Chapter 26 covers applications, stressing government, banking, insurance, hospitals and the service side of manufacturing companies. Success stories often contain guideposts that can be used by others.

SUMMARY

This book provides many leads. It is easy to brush them aside with the comment "They don't apply to me; my operation is different." Everyone's operation is different! Most of the tools discussed in this book, however, can be adapted to the needs of different areas. Innovative leaders will find ways to use them in service industries and in the service departments of manufacturing organizations. Others will play it safe and fall behind.

The final summary is contained in Chapter 27 under the title "Quotable Quotes." When looking for a catchy phrase you can't remember, look there first.

FOOD FOR THOUGHT

Review a copy of your company's organization chart. Then answer the following questions:

1. How many of the employees have service functions?
2. How many work on nothing but production?
3. How much work in the service sector has to be done over because of poor quality?

Based on your answers to the above questions, estimate how much money your company would save by improving service sector quality and productivity by ten percent.

REFERENCES
1. Kenneth S. Stephens, *How to Perform Continuous Sampling (CSP)* (Milwaukee, WI: ASQC Quality Press, 1979).
2. Henry L. Lefevre, "Quality and Quantity in Productivity," *Nationwide Careers,* December 5, 1984, p. 7.
3. Henry L. Lefevre, "Integrating Quality and Quantity," *ASQC Technical Conference Transactions,* May 20–22, 1980, pp. 624–627.

Chapter 2

Key 1: What Is Quality Service All About?

In 1878, Margaret Wolfe Hungerford wrote, "Beauty is in the eye of the beholder." Ms. Hungerford is not well known these days, but her perception of beauty is widely quoted in the English-speaking part of the world. She is also paraphrased. The *Quality Control Supervisor's Bulletin*, for example, says, "Quality is in the eye of the customer."[1]

Quests for quality and beauty are eternal and evasive. Once you think you have found them, perceptions change. As an example, the beauty of snow used to draw my family from the warmth of Sacramento to the mountains near Lake Tahoe every winter. After an hour of making snowballs, though, the reality of the cold soaked in and the kids clamored for the warmth of Sacramento. Perceptions of quality are also flexible. W. Edwards Deming emphasized this when he said: "We shall learn that impressions of quality are not static. They change."[2]

If quality is so evasive, is it an attainable goal or a budget-busting dream with no conceivable payback? Many executives in both the manufacturing and service sectors agree that quality does pay. Variables they use to measure the payback include lower costs, good savings and improved productivity. The following quotes illustrate these points.

Lower costs

James E. Olson, president of American Telephone and Telegraph (AT&T), said, "Quality will cost us less money and better meet the needs of our customers."[3] The president of AT&T should know; his job depends on containing costs and maintaining profits.

Savings

Robin L. Lawton, president of Innovative Management Technologies, Inc., supports the savings theme. Lawton wrote about initiating a quality improvement program for an accounting organization. They "identified systematic invoice errors causing over $750,000 per year in unnecessary costs." In another case, he writes about a customer service organization that "identified a declining trend in quality of service which threatened business survival."[4]

Productivity

Another service company executive, Subhash C. Puri, director at Agriculture Canada, stresses the interrelationship between quality and productivity: "Productivity and quality are completely intertwined—a neglect of one jeopardizes the other."[5]

Quotes from these service-sector executives support the contention that quality in the service area contributes to corporate profits. Quality pays; quality service also pays.

WHAT IS QUALITY SERVICE?

The ASQC/Gallup Survey of 1985 checked public opinion to determine why consumers thought services were poor.[6] Service industries in the survey included auto repair, banking, insurance, government, hospital and airline. Those experiencing problems with services reported the following:

Reason given	Percent	Author's interpretation of problem category
Work not done right	39	product
Too slow	30	timeliness
Too expensive	20	pricing
Indifferent personnel	20	attitude
Unqualified personnel	12	product
Lack of courtesy	10	attitude
Unspecified poor service	10	unknown
Lack of personnel	5	timeliness
Poor scheduling	4	timeliness
Reservation problems	2	product
Poor food	2	product
Miscellaneous	11	unknown

I interpret these findings as saying that defects of products, timeliness and attitude were the most prominent categories of problems identified by the survey. In this case, defects are identified as failure of services or products to meet customer expectations.

Writing about the quality side of Disneyland, Lee Branst came up with similar data.[7] Favorable guest comments received by the company included the following:

Comment	Author's interpretation of comment category
Cleanliness	facilities
Friendliness	attitude
Courtesy	attitude
Good show	product

Although not mentioned in the article, the worst shortcoming at Disneyland might be the long lines (timeliness). The last time I visited the park, long lines were the one thing that bothered me.

Charles D. Zimmerman III, vice-president of United States Fidelity and Guaranty Company (USF&G), had a different list for his company:[8]

Item	Author's interpretation of item category
Fitness for use	product
Ability to replicate	product
Timeliness	timeliness
Adherence to specifications	product

Here we are working with the company's perceptions rather than those of the customers. As a consequence, a different definition of defects might be used. My preferred wording is "A defect is a characteristic that doesn't conform to requirements such as drawings, standards or specifications." A frown is an attitude defect if there is a requirement for a smile. A misspelled word is a product defect if there is a spelling requirement. A late delivery is a timeliness defect if there is a timeliness requirement. Products or services with one or more defects are called defectives.

My interpretation of these lists puts most service quality characteristics into five categories:

1. Attitude
2. Timeliness
3. Tools and facilities
4. Product
5. Customer satisfaction

IDEAL QUALITY SERVICE

If you want to see outstanding quality service, look at the TV ads of a well-known fast-food chain. They start with a beautiful young girl smiling at a customer as she takes an order. By the time the customer gets money out of his wallet, appealing food appears from nowhere. The work area is spotless stainless steel. Workers, shown in the background, are merrily doing their jobs. The customer wanders off to a clean table, takes a comfortable seat and then savors a delectable feast. Its quality matches meals you serve at home.

Let's look at the different features of this ad.

- *Attitude.* All employees in the ad are feeling great. No one got up on the wrong side of the bed. No one had a hangover. Everyone was motivated and charming. Camelot had come to earth for one brief moment.
- *Timeliness.* The entire meal was made from scratch in less than a minute; the props personnel must have helped with the cooking.
- *Tools and facilities.* Tools and facilities shown in the advertisement were squeaky clean. Shining stainless steel was everywhere, looking as if it had never been used. Uniforms were spotless. The kitchen could pass a "white glove" inspection without prior warning. The aura of cleanliness was everywhere.

- *Product.* After looking at the ad, it would be difficult to associate the food chain with warmed-over burgers, cold fries and warm malts. The viewers might even forget times they were snarled at, were overcharged, or were talked into unwanted extras.
- *Customer satisfaction.* Even the customers become part of the act. In such an ideal environment, how could they help but show approval.

The following pages cover these quality categories in more detail.

Attitude

The ASQC/Gallup Survey shows that dissatisfaction with indifferent workers is common for the service industries—especially with hospitals and government offices. Discourtesy also causes many complaints; hospital employees were the worst offenders.[6]

Disneyland overcomes most attitude problems by selective hiring and by thoroughly educating their employees. According to *Quality* magazine, "Walt Disney did not want a carnival or amusement park atmosphere, so no one was hired with that type of experience."[7] A good part of the formal employee training is conducted at "company universities that are located at Disneyland, Walt Disney World and the movie studio in Burbank, California.

The United Services Automobile Association (USAA) is also attitude conscious. The company has a need for prompt, polite and accurate customer service. According to Rebecca Lee Huls, USAA works on the concept that "each customer likes to believe his or her problem is the most important one we handle, and we agree."[9] To ensure they provide the right information in a friendly manner, USAA monitors the calls of some of the customer service people. Although the workers select which calls will be monitored, this practice proves useful to both the operator and the company. "Recorded phone calls help identify incorrect responses, unpleasant voices, and a variety of attitude problems. Playing the calls back often shows employees the difference between how they think they act—and how they REALLY act."[9]

During the 1970s a Colorado aerospace firm had a switchboard operator who snarled when she answered the phone. I hated to call the company. The operator seemed tired of her job and unhappy with the world in general. Technically, she may have been an outstanding telephone operator, but she seemed to have an attitude problem. Because of this, the quality of her service was poor.

How could this problem have been overcome? The company could have given her lessons in voice control or transferred her to a different assignment. Workers having frequent contact with customers should appear friendly. The impression they create can have a significant impact on sales.

Some companies do train their phone operators to use their voices more effectively. I have an answering machine, and when a caller hangs up without saying anything, an employee of the phone company cuts in with a recorded message. For months, the operator's voice was harsh and raspy. Recently, however, there has been a vast improvement. The voice still belongs to the same operator, but the tone is much more pleasant. Employees with exposure to customers should have their demeanor, vocal inflections and attitudes scrutinized. If there is a problem, correct it.

Common attitude problems in the service sector include the following:

- A "customers don't count" attitude makes most buyers unhappy. Few shoppers want a clerk to hover; most, however, expect some attention. As an example, I recently went shopping for a suit. The first shop had a $150 outfit that looked like it fit my needs. I didn't buy because the clerk kept wandering off; he also failed to answer my questions promptly. Later, however, I bought a $300 suit from another store. The clerk who made the sale had a better attitude; he also sounded more knowledgeable about his product. The suit I bought may or may not have been worth the extra price—but the quality of the service kept me satisfied.
- A "know-it-all" attitude also turns off customers. As an example, many people pay more for computers than they should, because some stores with the best values have clerks with the worst attitudes. No one wants to be brow-beaten by sales personnel, just because they don't know the difference between hardware and software. Clerks with good attitudes accept customer shortcomings and help select what is best for the buyer.
- A "we're the good guys" attitude can cause difficulties, too. This problem often shows up when working with vendors. In the old days, it was customary to assume that vendor problems should be resolved by the vendor, with no assistance from the buyer; suppliers were the bad guys. The current trend is to acknowledge that vendor problems hurt buyers as well as sellers. Many vendor problems are the result of poor communications between the two. The more vendors know about the product, how it will be used and what it interfaces with, the more responsive they can be to the buyer. This example highlights the fact that quality service is not limited to service industries; it also applies to the service sector of manufacturing companies, including their

purchasing departments. With the possible exception of a self-sufficient hermit in Tibet, everyone is involved with service.
- An "I'm the expert" attitude hampers communications. As an example, computer programmers and analysts with this attitude seldom ask the right questions. When they think they know everything, they make assumptions about what the user wants. As a consequence, the finished computer program may fit the programmer's idea of what is needed without coming close to the user's actual requirements. Similar problems occur when Purchasing doesn't ask Manufacturing the right questions; or Design doesn't talk to Marketing; or Sales doesn't talk to Production.
- The "you're the expert" attitude is the opposite of the "I'm the expert" attitude; both create problems. It is not unusual for managers to give too much freedom to computer analysts and programmers. After all, "they are the experts." This approach results in the development of computer programs that appear perfect to the computer people but useless to the user. Then, each blames the other.
- "Grumpy" attitudes extend beyond the service sector. One shop supervisor in an aerospace company was so unpleasant that the manufacturing engineers refused to work with him. Eventually, a new engineer decided to put up with the verbal abuse long enough to find out what the problem was. Persistence payed off. The engineer helped the supervisor solve a technical problem that had been bugging him for months. Once the supervisor found an engineer who was willing and able to help him, his attitude toward engineers improved. Quality service paid.

As these examples illustrate, the benefits of quality service are not limited to service industries. Quality service shows no matter where you work.

Timeliness

Problems with timeliness ranked second among customer complaints listed in the 1985 ASQC/Gallup Survey; it was most obvious when government employees were involved, although insurance companies and banks had timeliness problems too.[6] Poor timeliness in the extreme is cited by Richard K. Dobbins.[10] Dobbins was scheduled to fly to Vancouver, Canada where he planned to visit Expo '86; the flight was canceled. For compensation the airline provided a four-hour bus ride to Vancouver that included mix-ups at the border; an unplanned fast (no food was provided during the delay); loss of approximately four hours of time; a $6.25 refund. Customs personnel said that two other flights had been canceled during the previous two weeks. It is not likely that many of these customers used the same airline on their next trip.

Rosander[11] divides timeliness into the following categories:

- Time to order a service
- Waiting time before service can be performed
- Service time
- Post-service time
- Repeat-service time

Time to order a service can involve reaching the right person by phone. Some military hospitals have this problem; I have had to dial 30 times before getting access to Central Appointments at the Fitzsimons Medical Center.

We all get tired of waiting in line. Have you ever walked out of a bank or store because the lines were too long? When people walk out, they are unhappy and many unhappy customers don't return.

A typical service-time problem can occur when you get your car fixed. I spent ten weeks getting a new gas tank on my Rambler; nothing happened until we called the company's headquarters.

Post-service time can involve waiting in line to pay your bill; some cashiers take forever.

Repeat-service time often occurs when the service wasn't performed properly. Improperly repaired automobiles, faulty calculations and typographical errors are typical.

Other examples of timeliness problems follow.

- One of the engineers at a West Coast aerospace plant was very accurate. Unfortunately, he was also very slow. By the time he came up with answers, most of his problems had been solved by someone else; production couldn't wait forever. As a result, he missed several promotions he might have won had he been more prompt.
- The data processing department in a government agency had a 12-month backlog. Even minor changes in format took months. As microcomputers became available, many departments developed their own programming skills and bypassed the professional programmers. Had the organization been more responsive, it might have grown with the agency instead of barely holding its own.
- A quality assurance branch in the Air Force was responsible for preparing statistical reports for field offices. Many of their findings, however, were not used by the recipients because the branch was

taking more than two months to acquire and analyze data coming from the field. By then, the information had little value.

Tools and Facilities

Tools and facilities have a major impact on customers' perceptions. With fast-food operations, for instance, appearance and cleanliness are critical. In some other service areas customers look for "state-of-the-art" equipment. Examples showing the effect of tools and facilities on customer satisfaction include the following:

- Greasy-spoon restaurants have a bad reputation. Flies buzz around the food, empty tables are full of dirty dishes and the cooks' aprons look like they were broken in by car mechanics. In most of these places, I wipe the eating utensils before using them. I might even walk out; no one wants a stomachache. Most greasy-spoon joints I frequented as a teenager survived because they were located near schools. In those days my classmates and I would eat almost anything rather than walk more than a block or two.
- Accounting offices are expected to have state-of-the-art computer equipment. Those using hand-written ledgers and low-paid clerks have refused to enter the age of automation. For some mom-and-pop operations, the old way of doing things may be justified since automation should pay for itself.[12] In some organizations, however, failure to automate reflects a resistance to change more than anything else.
- Computer organizations that still use keypunch machines are not state-of-the-art. Keypunch machines are data processing equipment used to punch holes in computer cards—those sacred forms that are not supposed to be "spindled, folded, punched or mutilated." Some payroll checks and bills still come from these sources.

Product Defects

Quality in the service sector has much in common with quality in manufacturing. Both services and products should be free of defects. It is difficult, however, to monitor or improve a service until you have determined what "defects" you should be looking for. Chapter 3 shows how customer surveys can help identify what is meaningful to the buyer.

Chapter 17 shows how capability studies can help make standards and specifications more objective.

The following list is supplied to stimulate your thinking. It identifies a few typical ways of measuring the level of defects in the service sector.

- *Typists:* Percentage of pages with no errors
- *Fast-food servers:* Cold burgers per 100 served
- *Data-entry clerks:* Errors per 1000 keystrokes
- *Computer programmers:* Errors per 100 lines of code
- *Hotel staffs:* Percent of room audits that identify missing items (soap, towels, tissue, etc.)
- *Motel staffs:* Rooms meeting checklist requirements per 100 rooms serviced
- *Travel clerks:* Errors per 100 travel vouchers
- *Supervisors:* Errors per 100 timecards
- *Managers:* Evaluations-on-time per 100 due
- *Auto mechanics:* Complaints per 100 cars serviced
- *Bankers:* Errors on service charges per 100 entries
- *Loan officers:* Corrections required on loan transactions per 100 loans processed
- *Apartment managers:* Percentage of renters making complaints
- *Bank managers:* Lost accounts per 100 customers

W. Edwards Deming[13] published additional suggestions for measuring quality service. You, however, are the best judge of your own requirements. Talk to your customers and evaluate their comments. Many of them will be happy to tell you what they expect. They may even help you develop lists of what to measure.

Customer Satisfaction

Customer satisfaction is covered in detail in Chapter 3.

SUMMARY

Combine ideal attitudes, perfect timeliness, the best available tools and good facilities with a service that is free of defects. Then, customer satisfaction usually follows. As W. Edwards Deming has said: "A system

Key 1: What Is Quality Service All About? 21

of quality improvement is helpful to anyone that turns out a product or is engaged in service."[14]

Well-planned quality improvements pay for themselves; quality service pays.

Food for Thought

Make a list of ten ways of measuring quality service in your company. If you work in manufacturing, concentrate on the service side of your operation. If you are a manager, have your subordinates make similar lists and compare them.

REFERENCES
1. "Quality Is in the Eye of the Customer," *Quality Control Supervisor's Bulletin,* November 25, 1987, p. 3.
2. W. Edwards Deming, *Out of the Crisis* (Cambridge: Massachusetts Institute of Technology, 1986), p. 167.
3. "James E. Olson on Quality, Cost, and Customer Satisfaction," *Quality Progress,* July 1985, pp. 32–36.
4. Robin L. Lawton, "Creating a Customer-Centered Culture," *ASQC Quality Congress Transactions,* May 4–6, 1987, pp. 430–435.
5. Subhash C. Puri, "A Plan of Excellence for a Regulatory Agency," *ASQC Quality Congress Transactions,* May 4–6, 1987, pp. 619–624.
6. John Ryan, "ASQC/Gallup Survey Results Revealed," *Quality Progress,* November 1985, pp. 12–17.
7. Lee Branst, "Disneyland—a Kingdom of Service Quality," *Quality,* February 1984, pp. 16–18.
8. Charles D. Zimmerman III, "Quality: Key to Service Productivity," *Quality Progress,* June 1985, pp. 32–35.
9. "Control Charts for Service Companies," *Quality Control Supervisor's Bulletin,* November 25, 1987, pp. 1–2.
10. Richard K. Dobbins, "Service Quality: When Friendly Skies are Canceled," *ASQC Quality Congress Transactions,* May 4–6, 1987, p. 417.
11. A. C. Rosander, *Applications of Quality Control in the Service Industries* (Milwaukee, WI: ASQC Quality Press, 1985), pp. 226–227.
12. Henry L. Lefevre, "A Computer in Every Office," *The Press,* July 1982, pp. 6–13.
13. Deming, *Out of the Crisis,* pp. 183–247.
14. Deming, *Out of the Crisis,* p. 183.

Chapter 3

Know Thy Customers

Starting a service company with no knowledge of the potential customers is like swimming in the Gulf of Mexico with a broken leg, a bleeding cut and no shark repellent. Neither risk-taker can keep above water very long.

Julie MacLean, quality manger, Marketing and International Sector for Hewlett-Packard, supports this contention when she says: "Quality products and services are those that meet or exceed customer expectations. A company's definition of quality MUST be customer driven."[1] W. Edwards Deming adds support by saying, "Quality should be aimed at the needs of the consumer, present and future."[2]

In order to aim at the needs of customers, however, you must know who the customers are, identify their needs, and keep in touch with them. One of the lessons brought out by *In Search of Excellence* was "the excellent companies are better listeners."[3] Is this obvious? Thomas J. Peters and Robert H. Waterman, Jr., imply that the answer is no: "Despite all the lip service given to the market orientation these days . . . the customer is either ignored or considered a bloody nuisance."[4]

WHO ARE YOUR CUSTOMERS?

Warren L. Nickell, in his article on quality in marketing,[5] defines a customer as "the recipient of any of your work . . . (both inside and outside the organization)." In other words, your customer is anyone benefiting from your services—directly or indirectly. Philip B. Crosby has a similar approach. He asks the question, "Who is our customer inside the company?" Then he answers himself with, "It could be another department, the president, or whoever receives the result of our work."[6]

As an example, suppose the service you provide is entering data into a computer database. The head of the department responsible for the database is one of your customers. If you enter the wrong data, the department head's reputation will suffer. Members of your chain of command are also your customers; they pay for your services. If you make an error, they look bad. In addition, individuals using the database are your customers. They make decisions based on the assumption that the data they get from the database is correct. If it is faulty, their decision may be wrong. Poor quality often has a ripple effect; one instance of poor service may hurt many people.

It's nice to stress the need to know your customers, but what do you do when 95 percent of your sales go through a distributor? Industrial Solid State Control, Inc. (ISSC) had that problem.[7] They solved it by using a set of pressure-sensitive registration labels with serial and model numbers of the product on them. When the product was shipped, the top label was removed exposing the bottom label which had the company's logo and telephone number. Then the distributors knew who to contact when prompt assistance was needed. Information from the label and the purchase order was added to a computer database enabling ISSC to keep track of shipments going to each distributor. When the distributor shipped a module, the second label was removed and returned to ISSC; the additional information was added to the database. Then customers and distributors had access to a comprehensive database holding information they needed whenever field service was required.

Proctor & Gamble improved its customer contacts by putting a toll-free number on its packaging. During one year the company received 200,000 calls on this line. Many of the calls were complaints. Others, however, were suggestions. Company executives valued these calls so much that they had them summarized for monthly board meetings.[8]

WHAT DO CUSTOMERS WANT?

If you are a secretary, your boss is your first customer. It is relatively easy to determine what bosses want—just ask. Bosses are usually happy to tell you, although their wish list is not always attainable. As an example, they might want error-free typing with no corrections even though their handwriting is illegible and your typewriter was built during World War II.

Determining customer requirements takes extensive research; depending on intuition can be risky. As J. Stephen Sarazen says, "Customers, after all, perceive quality in their own terms." He also implies that exceeding customer requirements can be very profitable by adding, "To be successful, companies have to embrace 'customer enthusiasm.' 'Customer enthusiasm' can be defined as 'exceeding the customer's requirements or expectations to the extent that they are so excited about our products and services that they become an extension of the sales force.'"[9]

Walter J. O'Brien[10] emphasizes the risks of assuming that customers think like you do by comparing white and brown eggs. According to O'Brien, people in the United States generally prefer the white eggs; people in England usually prefer the brown.

Anticipating the needs of the customer is not an easy task. C. M. Welch[11] supports this belief with the story about a company that developed the "perfect" dog food; it gave dogs shinier coats, whiter teeth, and better breath. The problem, however, was that they forgot to bring their customers into the act; dogs hated the stuff.

Service industries have to be particularly careful when evaluating customer needs; their problems are different from those of the manufacturing sector. Differences cited by Carol A. King,[12] president of The Qualityservice Group, include those listed below.

- Services are intangible.
- Services are perishable.
- Services involve complex delivery systems.
- Services are often time-sensitive.
- Customer involvement is unpredictable.
- Customer standards are hard to identify, often involving customer preference and even moods.

W. Edwards Deming[13] indicates the problem is also complicated by the changing perceptions and evolving judgments of customers; at times, these judgments take years to formulate. Although it is difficult to pinpoint the needs and desires of the buyer, it is still necessary. Few companies can afford to develop the "perfect" service that no one wants.

TECHNIQUES FOR DETERMINING CUSTOMER NEEDS

Because of the importance of determining customer needs, a variety of tools are used for the task. They include:

1. Face-to-fact contact
2. Correspondence
3. Toll-free hot lines
4. Surveys

Face-to-Face Contact

Some companies, like those specializing in temporary help, have to work very closely with customers. Many of them work face-to-face, developing detailed job descriptions based on the customer's specific needs. One job description may call for a typing speed of 80 words per minute with less than one error per page. Another may call for two years' experience with an IBM-PC word processor using specific software. Once customer needs are known, the agencies send out temporary personnel who have been tested to ensure they have the skills that were requested. Companies working with these agencies should have a thorough knowledge of their requirements. They must also make sure these needs are translated into workable specifications. In other words, they must be careful with what they request; that is what they will probably get.

The Walt Disney Company's face-to-face program is called "cross utilization."[14] It involves having their executives put on theme costumes and take over customer-contact jobs for a full week. These jobs range from selling hot dogs to parking cars. That way, they get to feel the pulse of the organization. They also get direct feedback from the customers without the screening that usually occurs when information passes through multiple layers of management.

The face-to-face approach is similar to Management By Wandering Around. Executives at the Adolph Coors Company used the technique extensively before the management style was christened with such an upbeat name. When Bob Mornin was president of the Coors Container Company, he took frequent tours of the facility; he talked to everyone he met from the janitors to the executive vice-presidents. Bill and Joe Coors, who were running the Coors Empire, also made unannounced tours of the work areas. Their visits, however, were less frequent; they had more territory and more companies to cover.

Correspondence

Joe Girard, an outstanding car salesman mentioned in *In Search of Excellence*,[15] used just about every gimmick he could think of to keep in contact with his customers. As an example, he sent out over 13,000 cards per month as thank-you notes, Happy-New-Year's cards, Happy-George-Washington's-Birthday cards and many other innovative excuses for keeping in touch. Frequent contacts like these kept the buyers coming back. This exposure also encouraged customers to bring their problems and ideas to him. In the end, both paid off. According to *In Search of Excellence*, Joe Girard sold more new cars and trucks per year than any other salesperson for eleven successive years.

Unsolicited correspondence from customers also helps identify their needs and peeves. Writing takes time and effort on the part of the buyer. As a consequence, the feedback you get generally comes from people who are either irate or very happy with services they received. Their input is helpful but seldom representative of the entire population.

Toll-Free Hot Lines

Toll-free hot lines are a good way to solicit customer information with minimum effort on the part of the buyer. As mentioned before, the Proctor & Gamble hot line gave the company a chance to make around 200,000 customer contacts per year.[8] The ISSC hot line helped that company track shipments, identify product performance, expedite response to customer inquiries and correlate field-failure data with in-house testing results.[7]

With hot lines, you have an excellent chance to solicit information from the callers. Will they give more details? Can they identify individuals and products involved? What made them happy or unhappy with the service? Phone calls, however, should be handled with care and diplomacy. Unhappy customers can escalate the problem and haul you to court if not satisfied with the treatment they receive. Are all complaints justified? No! but even the unjustified calls should be taken seriously.

A small number of callers use customer service lines to attack anyone who will listen. This happened on a government toll-free hot line that was established to disseminate information on the Survivor Benefit Program. One individual made many calls verbally attacking whoever answered. This abuse continued until the department manager intercepted a call and set the caller straight. Unreasonable callers, however, are uncommon; most of them are honestly seeking assistance. Most callers deserve to be heard.

Customer feedback should be cherished; don't allow this valuable information to die in the files of the marketing department. Distribute customer comments and acknowledge them promptly. In addition, send copies of customer correspondence and summaries of customer calls to the quality assurance organization. That way, trends can be analyzed and the results can be sent to company presidents and vice-presidents.

In most service operations, unsolicited customer contacts are not enough; surveys are also needed to help identify customer requirements.

Surveys

Surveys are popular for measuring customer satisfaction, and customer satisfaction is a key to success. Jeffrey W. Marr, at Walker Research, the nation's 14th largest marketing research firm, supports this claim when he says, "The firms that are known to measure customer satisfaction are usually market leaders."[16]

Sources of surveys include departments within the company, market research companies, newspapers, magazines, trade organizations, chambers of commerce, governments and universities. Subjects surveyed range from "Was there service with a smile?" to "Rate our performance on a scale of one to ten." The possibilities are limitless.

The advantages of "freebie" surveys include price and depth. General-interest surveys are often available for little or nothing; some cover a broader area than most small service companies can afford. Additional information on "freebie" surveys is covered by C. M. Baumback,[17] M. I. Mandell[18] and others.

A typical set of gratuitous surveys was reported by the *Denver Post*.[19] They included the following information of value to banks and other financial institutions:

- A survey of 300 heads of households in Denver showed that 38 percent had left their primary financial institution in the past year or planned to do so in the next 12 months; 27 percent of those who planned to change cited poor service as the reason.

COMMENT: The customer turnover cited above is very high. What is the customer turnover for your company? If you don't know, maybe you need to find out. The price of ignorance can be failure.

- A study by Strategic Solutions, a bank marketing firm, showed that 66 percent of those unhappy with their bank's service claimed to have received rude, impersonal or poor service; 27 percent cited errors by their bank; 7 percent objected to their banks being slow or unresponsive.

COMMENT: Rude, impersonal or poor service as well as errors, poor timeliness and unresponsiveness are possible in any industry. How is your organization doing?

Public information of this type, found in newspapers or other publications, can help almost any service organization. The percentages may be different from company to company and from one area of the country to another. The basic information, however, can be used. Poor service is costly; quality service pays.

Surveys made for a single company are more expensive than the "freebie" kind. Their value, however, should be greater; they are designed to provide information specifically needed by that organization. When the data is not available elsewhere, the cost may be justified.

According to M. I. Mandell,[20] these are the steps that should be taken when starting a survey:

- Define the problem.
- Determine the objectives.
- Determine which type of survey will be used.
- Test the sample design.
- Develop the questionnaire.
- Train the interviewers.
- Conduct the survey.
- Supervise the interviewers.
- Analyze the data.
- Prepare the report.

Types of Surveys

After defining the problem and determining the objectives of the survey, it is necessary to choose the type of survey. Each has its advantages and disadvantages.

Tabletop customer surveys[21]

Have you ever filled out a survey card found on a motel desk or a fast-food restaurant table? If so, you were more quality oriented than most.

Customer survey forms found in fast-food restaurants might ask for comments about the food, the employees, the store's cleanliness and the atmosphere. They might also ask marketing questions such as:

1. What did you buy?
2. Where did you buy it?
3. What attracted you to the establishment?

The customer survey form at the motel might ask for information about the front desk, the sleeping accommodations, the bathroom and the restaurant. It might also have space for additional comments.

Most customer survey forms are brief. Even then, few people fill them out. If the forms were longer, marketing and quality assurance people would probably get even fewer responses. Feedback is hard to obtain; if you don't ensure that your customers have something to gain from being cooperative, you get little response. When they benefit from filling in the forms, they are more apt to cooperate.

The American Society for Quality Control (ASQC) had an excellent method of getting survey forms filled out at their 41st Annual Quality Congress (AQC) in Minneapolis. They asked attendees to submit completed questionnaires in exchange for their conference transactions. The implied linkage was effective—2200 transactions were handed out; 1984 survey forms were received.[22]

Fast-food chains and motels that are serious about getting feedback might consider starting their own lottery. Each individual returning a questionnaire could be eligible for the drawing. The drawing prize from a restaurant could be lunch for two. For a motel, it could be a free weekend at any unit in the chain. Winners should get enough publicity to encourage others to enter on the next round.

Advantages of tabletop surveys include the following:

- They are relatively inexpensive.
- They can spot some trends.
- They can spot some major problems.
- They can give you fast feedback.
- They can be answered at the customer's leisure.

Disadvantages of tabletop surveys include the following:

- Their sampling errors are large.
- They can mislead you.
- Their data shouldn't be extrapolated.
- When they are used, conclusions should be supported by other sources of data.

Mail questionnaires

When surveys and questionnaires are sent by mail, response rates under five percent are fairly common.

One organization enclosed a quarter with their questionnaire. Just about everyone accepted the money. Some responded to the questionnaire because they felt guilty about pocketing the quarter without giving something in return. This technique worked on me the first two times; since then, I quit answering them. Gimmicks shouldn't be overworked.

Publishers of some technical magazines have potential customers fill out questionnaires in exchange for free magazine subscriptions. Summaries of this information are of value to the magazine's advertisers.

Lew Zwissler of the Management Analysis Company sent questionnaires on "QA programs for research and development" to 1000 *Quality* magazine subscribers.[23] Although the audience was quality oriented, only 122 people or 12.2 percent of the recipients answered. Someone less astute than Zwissler might be tempted to assume that the people who responded gave an accurate representation of the entire population. They might even use the data to calculate confidence level, sampling error and other interesting statistics. This, however, can be risky. As W. Edwards Deming has written, "Every statistician knows the perils of drawing conclusions from incomplete returns, even if 90 percent of them come back."[24] With mail surveys, a 90 percent return in unusually high.

Advantages of mail surveys include the following:

- The cost is low.
- They are considered confidential.
- They can be answered at the customer's leisure.
- Some surveys can go out with the monthly bills, eliminating the need for postage.

Disadvantages include the following:

- Response rates are usually poor.
- Sampling errors are large.
- Long surveys often get few replies.
- Vague questions can't be explained.
- Cash customers may not be on the mailing list.

Phone surveys

According to Charles A. Aubrey, II,[25] phone surveys can accurately measure customer attitude. He also says, "Quality Control can be kept at a near perfect level since the interviews are conducted from one centralized location and a field supervisor is able to listen in on any interview to assure it is being correctly conducted." Unfortunately, however, 10 to 20 percent of the customers contacted don't complete the interviews and approximately 5 percent of U.S. households have no phones.[25] Those customers who refuse to be interviewed or have no phone may have significantly different ideas from those who participate. In addition, interviewers may influence the answers—intentionally or unintentionally.

Phone survey response rates are best when the interviewers have pleasant voices and friendly personalities. In addition, those scheduling the phone surveys get more cooperation from interviewees when the calls don't interrupt dinner or an important football game. To some, phone interviews are similar to high-pressure sales pitches. If they are not performed with finesse, interviewers may get dubious responses. A. Randall Evans[26] notes: "Customer inquiries characterized by a sense of urgency draw . . . hasty and shallow responses."

Advantages of phone surveys include the following:

- More information can be obtained.
- Vague questions can be explained.
- They can be monitored by supervisory personnel.
- They yield 80 to 90 percent response rates.[25]
- Samples can be random.
- Prompt feedback is possible.

Disadvantages of phone surveys include the following:

- Expenses are high.
- Callers require training.
- Phone numbers for a representative number of customers are not always available. Some customers pay cash and the company may not

have their phone numbers. These customers should, however, be included in a representative sample.

Personal interviews

Personal interviews are a helpful but expensive way of identifying specific customer needs. Many personal interviews are conducted in shopping malls. Others are conducted by customer research companies within their own facilities. In the latter case, the interviewees are often paid for time taken to express their opinions.

Frank Caplan[27] looks at personal interviews as "potentially the most effective information-gathering technique." He notes that the personality and capability of the interviewer can generate a "They really do care!" response. He cautions, however, that the presence of the interviewer can influence the interviewees. He adds, "The design and control of the interview process and the selection and training of interviewers must be very carefully accomplished to ensure success of the program." Unless the company has employees skilled in personal interviews, it is often preferable to have a professional survey team help design the questionnaires and ask the questions.

Taste-testing is a specialized case of the personal interview. Here, the testers are usually asked to show preference between two unmarked samples of food or drink. Celestial Seasonings in Boulder, Colorado, uses this technique for evaluating marketing approaches as well as new products. The interviewees are usually picked from nonprofit groups that have shown an interest in raising funds; their organizations receive checks based on the number of participants they provide.

Advantages of personal interviews include the following:

- You can get more information.
- You can use more props to explain your ideas.
- Interviewers can get information from facial expressions and body language.
- You can develop a better relationship with the customer.

Disadvantages of personal interviews include the following:

- They generally cost more.
- Interviewers require more training.
- Responses may be influenced by the interviewer.
- Interviewees don't always mean what they say.

Problems Associated With Surveys

A common problem associated with surveys is the difficulty of eliminating bias. Bias refers to an inaccuracy,[28] a systematic error[29] or anything tending to influence one in a particular direction.[30] If you had the wisdom of King Solomon and the statistical skills of Dr. Deming, you could control bias within reasonable limits. But you could not eliminate it. Why? Because of sampling errors, misinterpretations, inconsistencies and aging data. Poor dissemination of the information may also reduce the value of a survey.

Sampling errors

With tabletop surveys as well as unsolicited phone calls and correspondence, there is little or no attempt to select random samples. You take what you get. The sampling errors can be quite large. In some cases, you can identify serious problem areas and spot trends, but it is risky to extrapolate the findings. Most opinions you get are from customers with strong feelings; they are not from the general population.

Unless you give the customer a reason for replying, the mailed questionnaire isn't much better. The few who respond may or may not represent the entire population. Use care when extrapolating the data. When the sample doesn't represent the entire target population, you have a sampling error.

When Zwissler wrote about using 1000 subscribers to *Quality* magazine for a survey of who had QA programs for research and development, he acknowledged two biases but considered them acceptable.[23] He writes: "Companies that have employees that are subscribers of *Quality* would be expected to have a higher probability of having QA programs. Also, questions and errors may have been returned by a higher percentage of subscribers with an interest in the application of QA to R&D." As long as these biases are acknowledged, the results of the survey have some meaning. Users, however, should not assume that the results are representative for the population of "all companies with R&D functions."

The importance of taking a representative sample is emphasized by an analysis made by Jack West, quality assurance manager for Command and Control Divisions, Westinghouse Electric Corporation. West surveyed attendees at the 40th Annual Quality Congress (AQC) in Anaheim, California and compared their responses with those shown in the 1985 ASQC/Gallup Survey. According to an article in *Quality Progress*,[31] "Differences between the public at large and the quality professionals at the AQC are evident in several areas." With the general public, for example, the most common rating for warranties was "very important" (at the top of the scale). With AQC attendees the most common rating for warranties was "not important" (at the bottom of the scale). When evaluating the service quality of local governments, about seven percent of the general public gave them the top rating of 10; less than one percent of the AQC attendees gave governments a similar rating. The differences in these results would normally be attributed to sampling error. In this case, however, the object of the analysis was to measure variations in the judgments of two specific groups.

Inconsistencies

Evaluation of survey responses has a lot to do with the value of a survey; inconsistencies between what customers say and what they mean must be addressed. As an example, Don Burr, when he was chairman of People Express, was quoted as saying, "coffee stains on the flip down trays [in the airplane] mean [to the passengers] that we do our engine maintenance wrong."[32]

Another inconsistency involves differentiating between what is important to customers and what influences their selection of service companies. Jeffrey W. Marr[32] indicates that passenger safety is ranked as "most important" among airline passengers. Passengers, however, don't necessarily rank safety very high when selecting an airline; they consider most U.S. airlines safe.

Aging data

Survey data ages and eventually loses its value. As Peter Drucker observes,[33] "Every knowledge eventually becomes the wrong knowledge. It becomes obsolete . . . . Knowledge has to progress to remain knowledge."

Customer preferences change with time. My youngest daughter illustrates this concept. As a teenager, she would spend hours convincing me that she needed money to pay for some service or product she "couldn't live without." Once her campaign for getting money from daddy was successful, she would go out and buy something entirely different; something she hadn't even thought about at the time she was asking for the money.

Dissemination of survey information

Unless the results are used, time and money put into surveys are wasted. Marr[32] emphasizes this point: "Collecting and analyzing data won't have much impact unless findings are regularly discussed and acted upon." He also says that "the internal quality assurance administrators should regularly receive customer input so that internal quality systems can be developed to promote the quality aspects that are most important to customers."

SUMMARY

Know thy customers. This involves

- Identifying them
- Determining what they want
- Evaluating the quality of information you receive from them

If you know who your customers are, you can survey the right people. If you know what your customers want, you can stress the right services. If you know the limitations of survey data, you can avoid being sandbagged.

Aging data, biases, inconsistencies and sampling errors should all be considered before you commit major resources based on customer feedback. Otherwise, you may waste your funds on the wrong products and services.

FOOD FOR THOUGHT

1. Make a list of three people you serve (bosses, co-workers, customers, etc.).
2. Develop a list of five questions to ask concerning your service to them.
3. Use the list of questions to get feedback on your performance.
4. Work on the shortcomings and build on the strengths identified by your "customers."

REFERENCES
1. "Quality Is in the Eye of the Customer," *Quality Control Supervisor's Bulletin*, November 25, 1987, pp. 3–4.
2. W. Edwards Deming, *Out of the Crisis* (Cambridge: Massachusetts Institute of Technology, 1986), p. 5.
3. Thomas J. Peters and Robert H. Waterman, Jr., *In Search of Excellence* (New York: Warner Books, 1984), p. 193.

4. Peters and Waterman, *In Search of Excellence*, p. 156.
5. Warren L. Nickell, "Quality Improvement in a Marketing Organization," *Quality Progress*, June 1985, p. 46.
6. Philip B. Crosby, *Quality is Free* (New York: McGraw-Hill, 1979), p. 289.
7. Don Humer, "Tracking Field Performance," *Quality*, June 1985, p. 40.
8. Peters and Waterman, *In Search of Excellence*, pp. 193–194.
9. J. Stephen Sarazen, "Customer Satisfaction is Not Enough," *Quality Progress*, December 1987, p. 31.
10. Walter J. O'Brien, "The Customer: A Global Profile," *Quality Progress*, February 1986, p. 24.
11. C. M. Welch, "Why the Dogs Didn't Like the Dog Food," *Quality*, November 1984, p. 86.
12. Carol A. King, "Service Quality Assurance is Different," *Quality Progress*, June 1985, pp. 14–18.
13. Deming, *Out of the Crisis*, pp. 167–168.
14. Peters and Waterman, *In Search of Excellence*, p. 167.
15. Peters and Waterman, *In Search of Excellence*, pp. 157–158.
16. Jeffrey W. Marr, "Letting the Customer Be the Judge of Quality," *Quality Progress*, October 1986, pp. 46–49.
17. C. M. Baumback, *How to Organize and Operate a Small Business* (Englewood Cliffs, NJ: Prentice-Hall, 1985).
18. M. I. Mandell, *Advertising* (Englewood Cliffs, NJ: Prentice-Hall, 1974).
19. Mark Tatge, "Poor Service Costly For Banks," *Denver Post*, August 2, 1987, sect. G, pp. 1, 5.
20. Mandell, *Advertising*, p. 212.
21. Charles A. Aubrey, II, *Quality Management in Financial Services*, (Wheaton, IL: Hitchcock Publishing, 1985), p. 88.
22. Shirley Krentz, Manager of Conferences and Exhibits, ASQC, telecon, December 11, 1987.
23. Lew Zwissler, "QA Programs for Research and Development," *Quality*, April 1985, pp. 34–35.
24. Deming, *Out of the Crisis*, p. 223.
25. Aubrey, *Quality Management in Financial Services*, p. 82.
26. A. Randall Evans, "Customers Grade Quality," *Quality*, March 1984, pp. 35–36.
27. Frank Caplan, *The Quality System* (Radnor, PA: Chilton Book Company, 1980), p. 224.
28. Ellis R. Ott, *Process Quality Control* (New York: McGraw-Hill, 1975), p. 35.
29. Richard S. Burington and Donald C. May, Jr., *Handbook of Probability and Statistics With Tables*, 2d Ed. (New York: McGraw-Hill, 1970), p. 134.
30. *Webster's Third International Dictionary* (Springfield, MA: G&C Merriam, 1976).
31. "Quality Practitioners Express Their Opinions," *Quality Progress*, January 1987, pp. 66–70.
32. Marr, "Letting the Customer Be the Judge of Quality," pp. 47–48.
33. Peter F. Drucker, *Managing for Results* (New York: Harper & Row, 1964), pp. 118–119.

Chapter 4

Know Thine Own Business

Managers who don't know what's going on are like climbers in the Himalayas with no map, no guide, no compass and little chance of survival. There's the possibility that they might stumble on Shangri-La, but the odds are poor.

Many managers believe they know what is going on because they study the reports received from subordinates. Without direct feedback, however, the chance of being sandbagged is greater than any knowledgeable manager should risk. As Kaoru Ishikawa phrases it,[1] "Nothing can supersede actual knowledge obtained through firsthand experience."

Common techniques for "knowing thine own business" include:

1. Tours of duty in the trenches
2. Management By Wandering Around (MBWA) tours
3. Open rap sessions
4. Presidential audits
5. System audits
6. Cost analyses

The first four of these tools help protect managers and executives from having information screened before they get it. Few people want to look bad in front of the boss. As a consequence, some subordinates "beautify" reports, screening out the bad news before forwarding data to the executive suite.

System audits provide in-depth information about what is going on in the company—they are excellent for supplementing the executive's own observations. Information obtained through these audits, however, should agree with conditions that are actually seen. If major discrepancies exist, the reasons should be explored.

Cost analyses are critical; without them, managers are like rowboat captains in the middle of the Pacific Ocean, on a cloudy day, without a compass; even if they know where they want to go, they don't have much chance of getting there.

TOURS OF DUTY IN THE TRENCHES

Disneyland uses "cross utilization"[2] to keep their executives in touch with the customers and the working staff. For a full week, the bosses don theme uniforms and head for the action. They sell tickets, dish ice cream, peddle hot dogs, load rides, park cars, drive the monorail or take over any of the "on-stage" jobs that make the entertainment come alive. This experience puts them back in contact with the park customers whom they are trying to please. It also refreshes their memories about what it's like to be "one of the troops." This way, they get firsthand experience as well as feedback from the regular staff. Training in the trenches and at the work stations has been used by well-run companies for decades. When I was at the Union Oil Company, now called Unocal, promising engineers started out in a two-year training program before taking on engineering assignments. They rotated through numerous nonengineering positions, getting firsthand knowledge of what was going on in the trenches.

Scions, like the Stewarts at Union Oil[3] and the Coors brothers of the brewing empire, performed routine jobs before taking over executive positions in their companies. They learned what was going on at the "worker" level. They also made contacts that would help them throughout their careers.

MANAGEMENT BY WANDERING AROUND

Early exposure to the workings of a company is not enough; frequent refresher courses are needed. Just because the doctor took your pulse ten years ago doesn't guarantee that it is still OK. "Hands on" management is still needed.

Management By Wandering Around (MBWA) describes a practice used by "hands on" managers for decades. Bob Mornin used it when he ran the Coors Container Company. Bill and Joe Coors also used it extensively when the Adolph Coors Company was growing rapidly.

MBWA sounds simple. All you do is wander around and keep in touch with troops. Peters and Austin, however, say: "MBWA ain't as easy as it may sound! Doing it well is an art. However, it is an art that can probably be learned."[4] In *A Passion for Excellence,* they break it down into the elements of listening, teaching and facilitating.

Listening

Listening is also an art that can be learned. According to William B. Martin,[5] Associate Professor of Hotel, Restaurant and Travel Management at California State Polytechnic University in Pomona, there are five ways to become a better listener:

1. *Stop talking.* (It is difficult to hear anyone else if you drown them out.)
2. *Avoid distractions.* (Don't be preoccupied with the pearls of wisdom you plan to drop when they shut up.)
3. *Concentrate on what the other person is saying.* (That way, you learn more and also encourage the speaker.)
4. *Look for the "real" meaning.* (This is particularly true when listening to subordinates. It is difficult for them to be frank when you work in the executive suite and they work in the typing pool.)
5. *Provide feedback to the sender.* (Putting what you think they said in your own words helps reduce misunderstandings. If that isn't what they meant, they can say so.)

Teaching

"Teaching" as referred to in *A Passion for Excellence*[6] means explaining the boss's priorities, not telling people what to do. It is often difficult for troops in the trenches to identify the wants, desires and priorities of the upper echelon. Where MBWA is skillfully practiced, however, the workers have a chance to ask. When employees think management is giving production the top priority, they tend to stress production on the job. They try to type faster, analyze information quicker, input computer data more rapidly and expedite purchase orders. When they believe that management is quality oriented, they may sluff off on production and stress doing everything right the first time. When they believe that management wants a good balance of quality and quantity, they strive for a good balance.

Facilitating

According to William J. Latzko,[7,8] more than 85 percent of the detectable errors are management controllable; under 15 percent are worker controllable. A typical management-controllable error would occur when a typist has an archaic typewriter that stutters. Stuttering typewriters make multiple impressions for a single keystroke, requiring that the error be corrected or the letter rewritten. Management can correct this problem by providing better equipment. Management, however, can't correct a problem without knowing that it exists. That is where MBWA comes in. By "wandering around," management is more apt to become aware of the problem. Then they can facilitate its resolution by ensuring that a request for more acceptable equipment is approved.

A large number of management-controllable errors result from workers having equipment, procedures, designs, tooling or facilities that are not compatible with error-free work. Inadequate training also falls into this category. Management can't correct these problems unless they know about them. Who is responsible for keeping management informed? The worker? The manager? Both?

MBWA helps fill the information void. By touring the workplace, managers can see for themselves. At the same time, workers have the opportunity of speaking up. If the employees have the opportunity of requesting assistance from a "wandering" manager and fail to do so, their problems become worker controllable.

Facilitating, however, is not a cure-all; it must be accomplished with caution and finesse. When practiced indiscriminately, it can demotivate intermediate subordinates and cause workers to be censured for speaking up. A manager who waves a "magic wand" and solves a problem several levels below can undercut the chain of command. To avoid this possibility, managers should delay action until they have discussed the problem with those responsible for the area; it is important to have the overall picture. High-level facilitators should also ensure their sources of information are protected. Executives don't want to undercut intermediate-level managers—nor do they want to expose their sources to retaliation.

OPEN RAP SESSIONS

Open rap sessions are similar to MBWA but they require even more finesse. The president of the Syntex Corporation used to eat breakfast in the company cafeteria twice a week.[6] At first, few workers dared sit with him. In time, however, a few venturesome souls took advantage of the chance to exchange ideas with the president and found there were no repercussions. For 20 years, the president's table was a place for getting information to and from the chief. Bill Moore of Recognition Equipment had a similar arrangement;[6] it was called "Biscuits With Billy."

The key to informal meetings is the development of trust between the workers and the upper echelon. Without trust, communications become one-sided; workers listen and answer direct questions but seldom volunteer information. As an example, the commander of an Air Force agency had monthly meetings with members of his command; he used the occasions to brief both military and civilian subordinates. He told them of past accomplishments and future plans for the organization; he also recognized select employees for outstanding work. Then he opened the meetings for questions. One subordinate, who was having a frustrating time trying to process purchases through the base procurement organization, used this forum to air his problem. The commander responded by asking a staff member to look into it but nothing ever happened. In addition, the subordinate was thoroughly chewed out by his boss's manager for not carrying the problem through channels. (He had tried.) From then on, only entry-level personnel and die-hard chance-takers were willing to ask for help; a valuable source of feedback dried up.

PRESIDENTIAL AUDITS

Presidential audits provide a more formal method for determining what is going on in the trenches. Ishikawa[1] speaks of the presidential audits in Japan where the president actually leads the audit team. Staff and consultants frequently come along for support, but the president is in charge of the show.

Steps Ishikawa recommends for the presidential audit include the following:

1. Determine the scope of the audit. What will be covered?
2. Have the units to be audited submit an exploratory report describing their quality control system.
3. During the morning of the audit, have question-and-answer sessions

between the president, his audit team, and the people being audited. They generally cover the following material:

- Policies and objectives for controlling quality
- Results including processes used to obtain them
- Current problems
- Policies and objectives for the future
- Suggestions for the president and his staff

Data must be submitted to substantiate any claims made in the report.
4. During the afternoon, the audit team generally visits the workplaces including the research, development, prototype operations, purchasing, quality control, marketing and office functions.
5. The final session of the presidential audit usually involves remarks and suggestions of the audit team.
6. An audit report is generally prepared with suggestions for improvements. Then, the audited organizations must indicate how they plan to take corrective action and prevent recurrence of the discrepancies.

SYSTEM AUDITS

Most system audits in the United States are similar to the presidential audits of Japan. The main difference is that the president is not physically present. System audits help managers know what is going on, but in a less direct way. Although this information is based on the observations of others, it still helps management check the pulse of the company.

System audits are generally designed to identify system weaknesses and improper practices. Although few executives in the United States are directly involved in audits, their support of the function and their reviews of the results are vital.

According to Caplan,[9] system audits were developed to give management and others a measure of how closely accounting procedures were being followed. Now, they also identify system weaknesses and improper practices; they verify that the system is actually working.

Steps used in most system audits include

- Determining who will do the audit
- Selecting the area to be audited
- Scheduling the audit
- Auditing

- Reporting the results
- Specifying corrective action

Who Should Audit?

Most organizations have personnel dedicated to the audit function. When I was at the Coors Container Company, audits were considered a secondary function; almost all of them were performed by one individual. At Aerojet General Corporation, we supplemented the regular auditors with engineers and specialists familiar with the area to be audited. At Fort St. Vrain, Public Service of Colorado supported their auditors with consultants and experts outside the company. With most organizations, the auditors are accompanied by supervisory personnel from the area being audited. This practice reduces the risk of having conflicting stories about what occurred during the audit.

Customer-centered audits[10] use typical customers on the audit team; the object is to identify what satisfies and what dissatisfies the customer. Less sophisticated users frequently identify things overlooked by those involved with the service. Customer-centered audits, however, belong in a class by themselves. They are important and should be considered, but they are not system audits.

Areas to Be Audited

When audits are used to keep top management informed, top management often determines which areas will be audited. Some companies try to audit each area of the company every year. Others concentrate on areas critical to the success of the company or areas where the manager is having problems and requests help. An alternative is to stress areas where the cost of poor quality is high or the trend shows it is getting worse. Information on the cost of poor quality is contained at the end of this chapter. Information analyzing trends is covered in Chapter 13.

Scheduling Audits

Caplan[9] favors scheduling audits a year at a time and announcing them by November 1. Scheduling, however, should be loose enough to permit extending audits when unexpected problems are detected. Adjustments should also be made when the manager of a troubled department requests help.

Some organizations prefer having unannounced audits. This is particularly popular in areas where fraud or theft is possible. It has been my experience, however, that most surprise audits are conducted by outside agencies like bank examiners and corporate audit groups. Internal auditors generally find they get better cooperation when audit plans and schedules are discussed with the organizations to be audited.

Auditing

Most system audits involve checking activities against the procedures, standards and specifications. Checklists are generally prepared before the audit to ensure that important areas are covered and critical questions are asked. The scope of the review can expand, however, when problems surface during the audit.

When auditors run across problems beyond their expertise, they generally have access to specialists who can be called on for temporary help. When situations require interpretation, supervisors of the area being audited usually provide assistance. This procedure also helps supervisors understand requests for corrective action that are called for in the subsequent audit reports.

Reporting Results

Reports after the audit generally document deviations from the procedures and standards; they also recommend corrective action. In many instances, the corrective action involves correcting shortcomings; in others, it involves improving the procedures and standards. If the corrective action has been completed by the time the report is prepared, the report should document what was done.

Audit reports should help good operations look good and help substandard operations improve. When outstanding work is identified during an audit, it should be documented.

For maximum value, audit reports should go to the chief executive officer (CEO) and all other managers down the chain of command. Without executive support behind audits, they accomplish very little. When executives receive copies of system audits, they have one more source of information about what is going on at the worker level. Audits help executives know their business. As Ishikawa[11] says: "I strongly urge the institution of QC audits by the top. The CEO or the person with the highest authority may be responsible, otherwise it is essentially meaningless."

Corrective Action

Some audit teams negotiate corrective action details with management of the area being audited before the audit report is issued. Others give the audited area more time to develop their plan of action. Corrective action, however, should specify what will be done, by whom and when. Then, members of the auditing organization follow up to ensure that the promised action takes place. In addition, subsequent audits should review the areas to be corrected to ensure that the improvements were permanent and effective.

System audits are applicable to all areas of a company, including the service sector. Don't overlook this useful tool just because you manage a service operation.

COST ANALYSES

The cost of poor quality is usually significant for any service organization. Here are a few examples:

- According to H. J. Harrington,[12] "An audit of the Aid to Families with Dependent Children in the Washington, D.C., area indicated that 55 percent of the households receiving aid were not eligible under government ground rules." In this case, the cost of poor quality was paid by the taxpayer.
- According to Frank Scanlon of The Hartford Insurance Group,[13] "17 to 25% of all the paperwork is being reprocessed due to errors." He also observes, "Errors in Accounts Receivable can impact profits, e.g., undercharging errors are seldom brought to the company's attention whereas overcharges usually are."
- William J. Latzko[14] says, "It is estimated that banks spend approximately eight percent to ten percent of their sales or operating income on quality costs, and that 25 percent to 40 percent of the bank's labor costs are associated with quality costs."

The above figures show that the cost of poor quality is high. It is unfortunate, however, that many executives are unaware of its magnitude or importance. Results of the 1987 ASQC/Gallup Survey[15] show that many executives have little knowledge of how much poor quality costs their companies. Almost half (44 percent) estimate the cost of quality at less than five percent and 27 percent admit they don't know.

The admonition "know thine own business" includes knowing what quality costs. Armed with this knowledge, executives can initiate corrective action; without it, they are tilting at windmills like Don Quixote, or in blissful oblivion like Rip Van Winkle.

When setting up a quality costs system, it is customary to divide costs into the following categories:[16]

1. Prevention
2. Appraisal
3. Internal failures
4. External failures

Prevention Costs

Although prevention dollars should be spent wisely, money used to keep errors from happening usually results in reduction in the total quality costs (prevention plus appraisal plus internal failure plus external failure costs). Why? Because few organizations spend enough money in this area. Money spent preventing errors usually results in reduced total error costs because the total number of errors is reduced.[17] Good prevention can be expected to have a favorable effect on appraisal, internal failure and external failure, the other three elements of the quality cost package.

Prevention costs include better training, tools, equipment, systems and knowledge to do the job right.[17] According to Caplan,[16] they also include the costs of planning and administering the quality system, determining customer requirements, performing quality and reliability studies, devising new process designs and performing process capability studies.

Appraisal Costs

If you can't prevent errors, the next priority is to catch them before they do more damage. That's where appraisal costs come in. Harrington[17] emphasizes the importance of early error detection by showing where the estimated cost of correcting a computer programming error during internal test (internal failure) is 20 times the cost of correcting it during the design/code phase. In addition, he estimates the cost of correcting a programming error that slips through to the customer (external failure) as costing 80 times as much as correcting it during the design/code phase.

Appraisal costs involve all elements of inspection including preparation, testing, review of test data and reporting it to management. Caplan[16] identifies other appraisal costs, but many of them are limited to manufacturing or government contract operations.

Internal Failure Costs

Internal failure costs occur when errors are detected before the product is delivered to a customer outside the company. A typing error that is caught by the manager is an internal failure; the resulting costs include retyping the letter, reediting the letter, stationery and ribbons, wear and tear on the typewriter or word processor and overhead associated with these expenses. Of these, the cost of reediting may be the most significant. Intangible failure costs associated with the typing error include

- Loss of confidence in the typist if the error is caught by the typist's boss
- Loss of confidence in the typist and the typist's boss if the error is caught by someone higher up in the company
- Reduced promotion potential for everyone involved if the manager or executive catching the errors inflates the importance of error-free typing

Other internal failure costs found in the service sector include

- Engineering changes due to faulty designs if caught before the product leaves the company
- Cleaning up databases due to data-entry errors
- Discarded food due to poor cooking
- Computer time for rerunning programs due to data-entry errors
- Reinspection and retesting after work was found defective
- Lost discounts due to slow payment of bills
- Overtime caused by projects falling behind schedule
- Frustration and resentment of managers and their subordinates (an intangible cost)

External Failure Costs

Customers are your final inspectors. Errors and defects caught by them can be very expensive. In *Quality Customer Service*, William B. Martin says:[18]

"The lifeblood of any company is repeat business. Expanding the customer base is vital. This means companies not only have to attract new clients or customers, but also must keep existing ones. Quality customer service helps make this happen. . . . Satisfied customers not only come back, but they also bring their friends." Imposing on the people you serve by overburdening them with final inspection does not create satisfied customers.

Armand V. Feigenbaum, president of General Systems Company, was credited with saying, "Today, when a customer is satisfied with quality—when he likes what he buys—he tells 8 people. When he is dissatisfied, he tells 22."[19]

External error costs are hard to pinpoint; they are also very high. Typical external error costs include public relations costs for soothing irate customers; the cost of identifying and correcting the core problem; and the costs associated with product liability:

- The ever-rising cost of liability insurance
- The cost of legal advice—either internal or outside the company
- The cost of lawsuits (even those that are won can be expensive)

The costs of external failure can escalate

With most service companies, external failure involves anything that makes the customer unhappy. For the worker, the cost of external failure can range from being corrected to being fired. For the company, the cost of external failure can range from upsetting one customer to losing a major lawsuit. A hypothetical example of escalating external failure follows:

> Tillie Jones was a talkative teenager who worked for a department store during the Christmas rush. Tillie, however, preferred talking to friends over serving customers. This poor selection of priorities raised the ire of an impatient customer who was not willing to suffer in silence. As a consequence, Tillie received a lecture on the quality of her service. At this stage, the cost of poor quality was a verbal reprimand.
>
> Having a short fuse, Tillie talked back; the quality problem escalated and so did its price. Tillie's supervisor was upset by Tillie's attitude and fired her on the spot.
>
> Upset by the scene she helped create, the customer tore up her charge card and vowed never to return to the store. She also embellished the event enough to make it prime-time material. Then she discussed it during her weekly bridge club meeting. As a consequence, the store lost three more customers.
>
> Other members of the club enjoyed the tale so much they added details of

their own. The problem got out of hand; what seemed a minor incident created problems for many people.

With a little imagination, the story could have been turned into a first-class travesty. The costs of poor quality service can be high; they seldom stop with the initial event.

The following are real-life examples of how problems with poor quality services escalate:

- The gas tank on an American Motors Rambler developed a leak and the car was taken to the shop for repairs. There were no spare gas tanks in town, so the repair shop ordered one. Three weeks later, the car was still waiting for the replacement tank. In desperation, the owner called American Motors' headquarters and bemoaned her plight to everyone she could get on the phone. Within a couple of days, two gas tanks arrived in Denver. One was in response to the irate call to Headquarters. The other may have been in the pipeline all along. In all probability, the career of someone in the company's customer service organization took a big step backward before the dust had cleared.
- People working for the federal government associate the term "escalation" with "congressionals." Congressionals are complaints coming out of Washington. They are generated when individuals think they are getting a runaround and write to their congressional representative asking for help. In many cases, the complaints are minor. Getting the runaround, however, is a serious matter to many people. They are willing to go to the top to get attention; they escalate. The cost of congressionals varies. In some cases they merely disrupt the activities of the organization that responds. In other cases, entire agencies can suffer. All congressionals require prompt answers; you don't want to keep dignitaries waiting. If *they* are not given quick, quality responses, they can reduce the agency's funds and impede promotions. Even the brass at the top may suffer.

Repercussions of poor service come from many unexpected sources. Politically astute individuals work on the assumption that everyone they contact is a potential boss or knows a member of Congress. This approach works well for everyone. It ensures that all customers get the best possible service. It also keeps unsuspecting individuals from getting sandbagged. Here are some examples of this rule in action:

- In hospitals, doctors and their spouses are very influential. More than one admissions clerk has been fired for failing to provide quality

service to a doctor's mate. The quality of service that may be acceptable to the average patient, or even a doctor, may be totally unacceptable to the doctor's spouse.
- Military Generals' spouses fall into the same category. Many of them are unofficial Inspectors General. Although high-ranking, they are hard to spot; they seldom wear uniforms.
- In many organizations, secretaries carry the rank of their bosses. It isn't unusual for a manager's secretary to give directions to that manager's subordinates. In these organizations, the secretaries become quality control inspectors and auditors specializing in format, style, grammar and spelling. They are monitoring the quality of service in a limited and specialized area.

Legal action and the cost of poor quality

Some of the most traumatic external error costs come from legal action; extremely unhappy customers often sue. The expenses of legal defense can be devastating, especially for small companies. Many don't have the finances to survive a major lawsuit, even if they win.

Doctors are particularly vulnerable. If their services are poor, lives can be lost; malpractice suits often follow. Many of these suits are settled for millions of dollars. That is why malpractice insurance rates are so high.

Database companies are also vulnerable. That is why they try to ensure their information is correct. As an example, some databases provide statistical information for stock market investors. If an investor loses millions of dollars because the database was faulty, a suit can follow. Medical databases have even more to lose; lives are at stake.

Insider trading is a form of poor quality service. During 1986–87 several noted financiers were put out of business for misusing information obtained from company insiders. Quality flaws of this nature may also put participants in jail.

Even lawyers can be sued for malpractice, and they're the ones who started it all.

SUMMARY

A manager who doesn't have a firm understanding of what is going on is apt to be blind-sided as often as a rookie quarterback with a weak offensive line playing his first game in the National Football League. Devastating body-slams can come from a wide variety of unprotected places.

Tools of value for keeping on top of things include:

- Tours of duty with the troops
- Management By Wandering Around (MBWA)
- Scheduled informal meetings
- Audits
- Quality cost analyses

FOOD FOR THOUGHT

1. Develop a list of five areas where you believe the cost of poor quality is highest in your organization. Rank them with the most expensive on top.
2. Get similar lists from associates in the quality, production and accounting departments.
3. Discuss the results with one another.

REFERENCES
1. Kaoru Ishikawa, *What is Total Quality Control? The Japanese Way* (Englewood Cliffs, NJ: Prentice-Hall, 1985), pp. 193–195.
2. Thomas J. Peters and Robert H. Waterman, Jr., *In Search of Excellence* (New York: Warner Books, 1984), p. 167.
3. Earl M. Welty and Frank J. Taylor, *The Black Bonanza* (New York: McGraw-Hill, 1956), p. 65.
4. Thomas J. Peters and Nancy Austin, *A Passion for Excellence* (New York: Random House, 1985), p. 378.
5. William B. Martin, *Quality Customer Service* (Los Altos, CA: Crisp Publications, 1987), p. 38.
6. Peters and Austin, *A Passion for Excellence*, pp. 389–390.
7. William J. Latzko, *Quality and Productivity for Bankers and Financial Managers* (Milwaukee, WI: ASQC Quality Press, 1986), p. 159.
8. William J. Latzko, "Quality Will Determine Winners in Competitive Banking Market," *Bank System & Equipment,* March 1984, p. 204.
9. Frank Caplan, *The Quality System* (Radnor, PA: Chilton Book Company, 1980), pp. 48–49.
10. Caplan, *The Quality System,* pp. 72–73.
11. Ishikawa, *What is Total Quality Control? The Japanese Way,* p. 127.

54   QUALITY SERVICE PAYS: SIX KEYS TO SUCCESS!

12. H. James Harrington, *Poor-Quality Cost* (Milwaukee, WI: ASQC Quality Press, 1987), p. 121.
13. Frank Scanlon, "Cost Reduction Through Quality Measurement," *ASQC Technical Conference Transactions,* May 20–22, 1980, p. 271.
14. William J. Latzko, *Quality and Productivity for Bankers and Financial Managers,* p. 83.
15. John Ryan, "1987 ASQC/Gallup Survey," *Quality Progress,* December 1987, pp. 12–17.
16. Caplan, *The Quality System,* pp. 19–27.
17. Harrington, *Poor-Quality Cost,* pp. 17–20.
18. Martin, *Quality Customer Service,* pp. 9, 24.
19. Harrington, *Poor-Quality Cost,* p. 126.

Chapter 5

Steps to Quality Excellence

Companies on the path to quality excellence are like teenagers headed toward the adult world. Both have an uphill climb ahead; both go through many stages of development. With teenagers, if they don't do it right, they can remain teenagers at heart for the rest of their lives. With companies, if they don't do it right, they are doomed to mediocrity or failure.

Steps on the path toward quality excellence include

1. Evaluation
2. Control
3. Prevention
4. Improvement

EVALUATION

Evaluating quality is like monitoring the price of stocks in your brokerage account. You can look at their closing prices every day; you can even study their trends after plotting them on a chart. You can't improve their quality, however, unless you make a change. With the stock market, this usually involves selling shares you own, buying some you don't, or both. With service companies, the problem is similar; you are evaluating, not controlling, until you have a *system* for reacting to unfavorable trends—and start using it.

Evaluation involves measuring how good or bad the quality is; it can also include determining whether the service is getting better or worse (trend analysis). During the 1973 ASQC Technical Conference, Thomas C. Staab[1] of the Internal Revenue Service emphasized the need for evaluation and feedback in the service sector: "No quality program, or any system for that matter, can function efficiently without a good feedback system to inform management of the effectiveness of their system and the quality of their operations." Without a program that evaluates quality, you can't give meaningful feedback to management; you can't show them the quality of service their organization provides.

When to Evaluate Quality and Analyze Trends

Here are some good uses for evaluation and trend analysis:

When starting a new quality control program

In the service sector, many companies have never used objective methods of evaluating or controlling quality. These organizations should start with evaluation and trend analysis. As they grow to understand the techniques and concepts, they can add control systems.

When control is not practical

With the insurance industry, for example, Huls[2] does trend analyses on backlogs, work produced, sales and other variables that are not readily controllable.

When projections are important

The Air Force Accounting and Finance Center used to study trends and do time-series analyses to predict the monthly disbursements and reimbursements of the entire Air Force.[3] The projections were used to ensure that the government had adequate funds available without carrying a surplus; they had to pay interest on standby funds whether they were needed or not. How important is this problem? According to *Investor's Daily:*[4] "The 18 agencies which account for about 95% of federal expenditures, pay 25% of their bills late, incurring millions of dollars in interest penalties annually. Another 25% of the government's bills are paid too early. That, too, cost the government lost interest, more than $350 million in 1986 alone."

When keeping corporate offices informed

This is particularly true when a corporation or government agency has field offices in other cities. The Air Force Accounting and Finance Center, for example, monitors the work of base accounting offices all over the world. One of their functions is to keep top management up-to-date on whether their quality assurance systems are working. They make exception reports when problems arise; they also offer technical assistance. The people in the field, however, are in the best position to actually control their quality.

When briefing plant managers and other executives

Briefings provide information; they are not used to control. Executives don't have time to run subordinate operations; they do, however, need to know what's happening. They have to be assured that their control systems are working.

CONTROL

Evaluation of quality is a good start; normally the control of quality should follow. Controlling quality involves measuring it against a standard or specification and then taking corrective action when unacceptable conditions develop. "Unacceptable conditions" can involve failure to meet the standard or the detection of conditions that are statistically "out of control."

Control systems used in the service sector include:

- *Military Standard 105D.* It specifies rejection of work or materials when "excessive" defects are found. 105D is discussed in Chapters 8 and 9.

- *Control charts.* They specify corrective action when "out of control" conditions are detected. Control charts are discussed in Chapters 15 and 16.
- *Continuous sampling.* Continuous sampling under CSP-1 specifies corrective action when "excessive" discrepancies are found. It is discussed in Chapter 11.
- *Local systems.* Latzko[5] refers to one local system for controlling keypunch error where qualified operators are given 10 points when they start keypunching. Their work is sampled and verified. If a batch of their work is accepted, they are given an additional point up to a maximum of 20 points. If a lot is rejected, they lose a point. Operators who lose all of their points are taken off the job.

When to Control Quality

Once you have developed a system for evaluating quality, it's time to consider controlling it at the worker level. Latzko[6] supports the worker-level concept when he observes that many papers on quality control for clerical processes limit their interest to departmental performance. Although he admits this information can be useful, he notes that it fails to give satisfactory data for improving the quality of the department. He favors developing standards of quality "which each clerk can achieve."

Programs for controlling quality should be initiated as soon as management has developed the ability to evaluate it at the employee level. Bosses who have no procedures for controlling worker quality are implying that the individual's performance is not important; subordinates pick up that implication very quickly. That is why many government employees, if not subject to quality control, refer to their output as being "good enough for government work."

Elements in the Evaluation and Control of Quality

Important elements in the evaluation and control of quality include

- Measurement
- Procedures
- Standards
- Sampling

Measurement

In the service sector, most measurement systems concentrate on attributes. These attribute measurements usually involve comparing work or performance with the standard. Latzko,[6] for example, emphasizes the need for clerical operations to distinguish between correct and incorrect—a form of attribute measurement.

There are times, however, when variables are also monitored; this includes costs, backlogs and sales. It is also possible to convert attributes to variables by developing your own scales. As an example, you can evaluate the behavior of a five-year-old boy as good or bad; this is an attribute measurement. You can also evaluate him using a scale of 1 through 10; this is a variables measurement. A rating of 10 would mean he was an angel; you didn't have to prompt him once. He made his own bed and asked to help with the dinner dishes. His halo sparkled in the sun. This level of exemplary conduct, however, might have a seasonal bias; level 10 behavior is most common around Christmas. An evaluation of 1 would mean he was belligerent, uncooperative and got into everything. He spent most of the day in the corner and sassed you when he was there. An evaluation of 5 would apply to average behavior. At times, he was an angel; at times, he was a mischievous five-year-old boy striving for independence.

Once the scale is established, it is easier to describe your day. On meeting your spouse at the door, you could say: "Today *your* son was a solid 2. He would have been a one except for his nap." Armed with this information, your spouse might suggest getting a baby-sitter and going out for dinner.

If you want to identify trends, you can plot the boy's ratings day by day. Eventually you should see an improvement. If the boy's behavior doesn't get better with age and maturity, you may have to develop a better control system—assuming you had one in the first place.

Another example of making subjective evaluations more objective involves grading the quality of directions for finding a farm. Instructions like "It's a hoot and a holler down the gravel road" deserve a 2. A 1 would be more proper if the road had not been described; it was gravel.

Grade 9 directions can be: "It's on the south side of country road 33, exactly 4.3 miles west of here." These directions can be rated a 10 if they include: "The farm you are looking for has a white, two-story house 20 yards off the road. You will also find the tenant's name on the mail box located at the entrance to the farm."

The first statement gives you a vague, subjective approximation; the last gives you clear directions.

Providing directions is a service. If you get poor directions from a farmer, you are apt to get lost. If you give poor directions to subordinates, their quality will probably slip. If you give poor information to customers, you may lose their business.

We just measured the quality of directions given by a farmer. We also evaluated the behavior of a child. If you can make variables measurements of these, you can make variables measurements of almost anything. Even the effectiveness of a supervisor can be graded on a scale of 1 to 10. A 1 would represent the worst supervisor you have ever had. A 10 would represent the best.

In many service organizations, supervisors are quick to point out their high and low quality workers without ever making a measurement. It is better to measure, evaluate and control. Once measurements are initiated, the entire picture can change. In one government agency, for example, a supervisor thought the quality of work coming from one of his employees was very poor—worse than the output of anyone else in his organization. Once each technician's quality was measured, however, the worker with the poor reputation showed up in the middle of the pack. Either the supervisor's perception was wrong or the technician put forth additional effort when his work was audited.

Making measurements helps evaluate the quality of individuals and organizations. Numbers, however, are no substitute for good supervision. When people know they are being measured, some develop ways of beating the system. For example, one technician had a friend check all of his calculations. This worked well for the technician but it hurt his friend's production. Although the buddy never complained, the ruse was eventually detected.

Procedures

The instructions that specify how work is done are called procedures. An elementary form of procedure is verbal instruction given during on-the-job training. Verbal instructions, however, tend to be inconsistent; trying to keep them from changing is like trying to keep drunken drivers from shifting lanes. Each trainer has a little to add and a little to subtract; as students become trainers, additional modifications occur. Written instructions, however, minimize unintentional change.

Standards

According to Webster, a standard is "something that is set up and established by authority as a rule for the measure of quantity, weight, extent, value or quality."[7] When measuring quality, standards are often used to judge service as acceptable or unacceptable, good or bad, right or wrong. Standards formalize procedures, definitions and in some instances quality requirements. It is difficult to separate the three because changes in procedures or definitions often change the values of measurements.

In the service sector, quality standards usually specify what is acceptable service or performance; they identify the target and acceptable limits surrounding it (the target zone). Questions asked by many managers include: "How large should I make the target zone? How should I define it? Should it be easy to hit so that the workers are encouraged or should it be difficult so that workers are challenged?" There are no simple answers, but tools for setting standards are available:

- Use subjective evaluation (pick a number).
- Let the government set them for you.
- Have them set by trade organizations.
- Base them on capability studies.
- Negotiate with the customer.

Subjective evaluations are risky; they can do more harm than good. If the standards and specifications are too tight, the workers won't even try to meet them; if they are too loose, quality can suffer.

Government standards can be set by decree or consensus. In the United States, the federal government may open hearings or conduct studies to determine limits that can and should be met. Then, states, organizations or individuals are required to comply. As an example, the Health Care Financing Administration (HCFA) sets standards for acceptable levels of error in Medicaid cases and claims. States that fail to meet these standards can get reduced Medicaid payments.[8] Many standards of this type are imposed when people or organizations fail to police themselves.

Trade organizations, like the Japanese Union of Scientists and Engineers (JUSE), have helped develop a series of national standards for their countries. Many Japanese industries use JUSE-generated standards for guidance; they are called Japanese Industrial Standards (JIS). According to Ishikawa, "JIS also became the basis of standards established for the International Standards Organization (ISO)."[9] In the United States, trade organizations like the American Society for Quality Control (ASQC) have also developed national standards.[10] Most of these, however, involve definitions and procedures, not quality levels.

Capability studies can be used for setting most quality standards. Latzko[6] and Aubrey[11] use them to identify the standards of quality each clerk should achieve. In the process of setting these standards, Latzko recommends looking for outliers or atypical performance data. When outliers are found, they are rejected and the process capability is recalculated without them. Ott[12] defines inherent process capability as the process mean plus or minus three standard deviations. More on standard deviations is contained in Chapter 14; more on capability studies is found in Chapter 17.

Negotiated standards, involving the customer, are favored by Barbara J. Young[13] and Julie MacLean.[14] If "Quality Is in the Eye of the Customer,"[14] this approach makes sense. On one side of the negotiations lie the needs, desires and demands of the customer; in most instances, the customer is right. On the other side lies the capability of the provider; as a supplier, it is not practical to agree to quality standards that can't be met. Rather than lose the business, however, providers can make management-controllable improvements to the process capability. These changes can involve better training, equipment, facilities or procedures.

Sampling

Sampling, which is covered in the next two chapters, is a critical element of most quality assurance systems.

Of course, sampling can range from looking at zero percent of the output (abdication) to looking at everything two or more times (redundancy). Scientific or statistical sampling, however, enables you to look at a portion of the total population, draw valid conclusions and calculate the probability that your conclusions are right.

PREVENTION

Discrepancy prevention is a prime part of any good quality assurance program. Although placed third in this chapter, its priority is often first. When properly developed, parts of the prevention program start during conception of the product or service and continue until the operation shuts down.

What goes into discrepancy prevention? According to the fourth edition of *Juran's Quality Control Handbook,*[15] it includes

- Quality planning
- New-product review
- Process planning
- Process control

- Quality audits
- Supplier quality evaluation
- Training

Many of these elements should precede quality evaluation and prevention; they are also needed after the evaluation and prevention systems are in place and working. More detail is contained in the following paragraphs.

Quality planning should be one of the first elements considered. It should start at the beginning of the quality program and continue until the end. Without planning, you are like a ship without a rudder; you drift indefinitely.

New-product review should also precede the actual work. Does the new product or service make sense? Can a quality service be produced with the available resources? How should you define the service's quality? What is the competition's quality?

Process planning includes capability studies; it is difficult to set objective standards without them. Capability studies are covered in Chapter 17.

Process control involves setting up procedures for in-process inspection and tests for determining the status of the process. Procedures for the work, and for inspection of the work, should be written before the process starts up, whether it involves data entry, statistical calculations or making a pizza. The procedures should also be reviewed at regular intervals. Few services can be both static and competitive for long.

Quality audits help ensure that existing systems are followed and are achieving the level of quality that is required. Audits were covered in Chapter 4.

Supplier quality evaluation helps keep companies out of trouble. Selecting vendors by cost alone can create quality problems that are beyond the company's control—even in the service sector.

Training should precede production and continue throughout the life of the program. Without good training, new workers don't learn the right procedures, and experienced workers drift into bad habits.

IMPROVEMENT

Quality is seldom stagnant; it is either getting better or worse. When discussing quality improvement, J. M. Juran wrote:[16] "Making improvements is one of the processes of the quality trilogy. . . . Every chronic quality problem shows up as a symptom—the outward evidence of some deficiency. The improvement process analyzes the symptoms, theorizes as to causes, and tests the theories to find the real cause. Having found the real cause, the improvement process provides a remedy to eliminate the cause."

Procedures for identifying quality problems are discussed in Chapters 3, 4, 13, 15 and 16. Procedures for identifying the most important problems and comparing potential solutions are contained in Chapters 18 and 19. More advanced approaches are contained in references (17) through (20).

SUMMARY

Steps on the path toward quality excellence in the service sector include the following:

- *Evaluation.* If you don't know how good your services are, you're in trouble.
- *Control.* Without controls, companies drift into oblivion; no service runs by itself.
- *Prevention.* An ounce of prevention is worth 1000 apologies.
- *Improvement.* If you're not getting better, you're falling behind.

Food for Thought

1. Make a list of the service functions in your organization that are covered by quality standards.
2. Find out how the standards were determined.
3. Make a list of the service functions not covered by quality standards.
4. List techniques that could be used to develop meaningful standards for those functions listed under item 3.

REFERENCES

1. Thomas C. Staab, "Quality Applicable to Paperwork? Probably!" *ASQC Technical Conference Transactions,* May 21–23, 1973, pp. 393–397.
2. Rebecca L. Huls, "Dedication to Quality Spans All Industries," *ASQC Quality Congress Transactions,* May 4–6, 1987, pp. 90–95.
3. Henry L. Lefevre, "Time-Series Forecasting for Non-mathematicians," *ASQC Quality Congress Transactions,* May 27–29, 1981, pp. 1029–1034.
4. "Poor Accounting, Weak Controls Cost Gov't Heavily, Report Says," *Investor's Daily,* December 31, 1987, p. 7.

5. William J. Latzko, *Quality and Productivity for Bankers and Financial Managers* (Milwaukee, WI: ASQC Quality Press, 1986), p. 20.
6. Latzko, *Quality and Productivity for Bankers and Financial Managers*, pp. 60–62.
7. *Webster's Third International Dictionary* (Springfield, MA: G&C Merriam, 1976).
8. A. C. Rosander, *Applications of Quality Control in the Service Industries* (Milwaukee, WI: ASQC Quality Press, 1985), p. 78.
9. Kaoru Ishikawa, *What is Total Quality Control? The Japanese Way* (Englewood Cliffs, NJ: Prentice-Hall, 1985), p. 7.
10. ANSI/ASQC A3-1987, *Quality Systems Terminology* (Milwaukee, WI: American Society for Quality Control, 1987).
11. Charles A. Aubrey, II, *Quality Management in Financial Services* (Wheaton, IL: Hitchcock Publishing, 1985), p. 16.
12. Ellis R. Ott, *Process Quality Control* (New York: McGraw-Hill, 1985), p. 63.
13. "Keeping the Subcontractors Away From Your Door," *Quality Control Supervisor's Bulletin,* May 10, 1987, pp. 1–3.
14. "Quality Is in the Eye of the Customer," *Quality Control Supervisor's Bulletin,* November 25, 1987, pp. 3–4.
15. J. M. Juran and Frank M. Gryna, *Juran's Quality Control Handbook,* 4th ed. (New York: McGraw-Hill, 1988), p. 4.6.
16. J. M. Juran, *Juran on Planning for Quality* (New York: Free Press, 1988), p. 289.
17. George E. P. Box, William G. Hunter and J. Stuart Hunter, *Statistics for Experimenters* (New York: Wiley, 1978).
18. Thomas B. Baker, "Quality Engineering by Design: Taguchi's Philosophy," *Quality Progress,* December 1986, pp. 32–42.
19. Raghu N. Kackar, "Taguchi's Quality Philosophy: Analysis and Commentary," *Quality Progress,* December 1986, pp. 21–29.
20. Roy E. Wheeler, "Quality Starts With Design," *Quality,* May 1986, pp. 22–23.

Chapter 6

Key 2: Understanding Sampling

As an art, sampling is practiced by almost everyone. In many cases, experience has taught us how to avoid problems, even though our sampling techniques seldom meet the standards of an experienced statistician. A few typical cases of everyday sampling are listed below. Some of their advantages and disadvantages will be explained before we enter into a formal discussion of sampling processes.

1. Sampling food
2. Sampling cars
3. Sampling clerical records

Sampling Food

In the kitchen, cooks develop a knack for sampling although few have formal training in the proper procedures. Good cooks become masters of the art, if not the science. Take the sampling of stew, for example. Most cooks taste a small sample to see if it's ready to eat. Tasters assume the sample represents the entire contents of the pot; they don't need to eat the whole stew before deciding it's ready. Consuming the contents of the pot would involve oversampling; no one but the cook would get to eat. Oversampling is undesirable in both the kitchen and the workplace. A second option would be to serve the stew without tasting it. This would be zero percent sampling or leaving quality to chance. Experience has shown this procedure (undersampling) is also impractical for most kitchens and work stations.

Good cooks not only know how much to sample; they also know how to take their samples. When checking the stew's temperature, for example, those that take their sample from the side of a heating pot, without thorough stirring, get temperature readings that are almost as hot as the container. The center of the pot, however, may be lukewarm. If they sample stew that has been off the stove for some time, the sampling error may be in the other direction. By sampling from the side of a cooling pot, they normally observe temperatures lower than the average content. Pots cool faster than the stews they contain.

When cooks don't stir the pot enough after adding salt, they can get another faulty sample. Then their stew can have too much or too little seasoning. Without formal training in statistics, good cooks learn to take representative samples, checking the quality of their products before serving. Quality control people also try to take representative samples.

Sampling Cars

The process of looking at cars before buying them is another illustration of sampling. Buying a car takes a different kind of sampling than tasting a stew, and the price of mistakes is higher. Sampling, however, is still involved.

When people travel a lot and use rented cars, they get to sample a variety of brands. This experience helps them make better decisions when they buy. I was afraid of foreign cars until 1973. Then, however, I had a chance to travel on business and was able to rent a variety of cars. The Japanese models I rented performed well; the domestic cars started to fall apart before I left the parking lot. My next car was a Toyota and I liked it very much.

When buying a car, there are advantages in test-driving the specific vehicle you want before making a deal. The further you drive and the more conditions you encounter, the more you get out of the sample. As an example, some cars tend to heat up during hot weather. You won't spot this weakness if all of your testing is in the middle of winter and you live in the frozen North. Quality professionals must be aware of this type of problem when they take samples as part of a designed experiment. In most cases, results of the experiment are applicable to the conditions of the test. If their samples don't represent conditions encountered during real life, their test results can be misleading.

Buyers who order their cars from the factory instead of the showroom are more apt to be surprised by what they get. The cars they use during test drives can be much better than the ones they eventually receive from the factory. Test-driving cars and trying out new products involve performance sampling. The better the samples, the more assurance that the products will meet the sampler's expectations.

Sampling Clerical Records

Sampling clerical records is similar to sampling stews and cars. The primary differences are in the materials being tested, not in sampling fundamentals. As an example, it's not practical to verify the quality of a stew by eating it all; you would end up getting fat and everyone else would go hungry. Nor should you try to sample every piece of data in a data bank or every calculation a technician makes or every travel voucher that is handled by the travel desk or every transaction processed by a bank teller. Additional information on sampling in the service sector has been published by Latzko,[1] Dodge and Romig,[2] Rosander[3] and Deming.[4]

WHAT DOES SAMPLING INVOLVE?

Test-driving a car, tasting a stew and checking records involve taking samples. So does an audit of IRS returns,[5] Medicaid payments[6] or the work of insurance technicians.[7] In each case, you want your sample to be representative.

There are many ways to sample; some are much better than others. Typical sampling techniques used in service operations include

- 300-percent sampling[8]
- 100-percent sampling[3, 8–10]
- Subjective sampling[11,12]
- Grab sampling
- Judgment sampling[12,13]
- Interval sampling
- Interval sampling with a random start[7]

- Random sampling[3, 13–15]
- Stratified sampling[3,13,14,16]

300-Percent Sampling

Although sampling each item three times (300-percent sampling) is redundant and expensive, it is occasionally needed when the cost of external defects is high. Latzko[8] documents instances where it has been used in the banking industry for transactions worth more than $50,000. High risks were accompanied by marginal inspection; individual checkers were locating approximately 75 percent of the defects. Calculations on the effectiveness of various levels of inspection are documented in Latzko's book.[10] Multiple reviews, however, are generally uneconomical; recognizing this, Latzko's organization subsequently implemented a computerized method of handling transactions. Redundant inspection may be justified on a short-term basis; system improvements, however, usually provide a better long-term solution.

100-Percent Sampling

Technically, 100-percent sampling, like 300-percent sampling, is still sampling; in both instances, you check the entire population. Both are expensive. There are, however, instances where they are justified.

As an example, a supervisor reviewing expense accounts will seldom inspect every account crossing the desk. 100-percent sampling, however, may be justified for large accounts. On November 20, 1980, the Comptroller General of the United States issued authorization for statistical sampling during the prepayment examination of disbursement vouchers not in excess of $750.[17] Larger vouchers, however, required 100-percent inspection. The government didn't want to spend more money looking for errors than could be saved by finding them. Incidentally, the $750 lid is periodically reviewed; by now it may have been raised due to increases in the cost of auditing vouchers.

There are problems associated with 100-percent sampling:

- When there are many items or individuals to review, 100-percent sampling becomes time consuming and expensive. As an example, 100-percent visual inspection of all of the entries in a large computer database is economically impractical. On the other hand, computerized audits have limited accuracy. A good alternative is to randomly

select records from the database and check them against the source documents.[18]
- 100-percent sampling seldom identifies all of the errors. After looking at records, computer screens or numbers for a long time, you tend to see what you expect instead of what is actually there. During my work in the service area, I have found that an accuracy around 95 percent is rather good for most reviewers. My experience, however, appears to be better than the observations of many. Frank Squires[19] places the reported effectiveness of inspection between 80 and 95 percent. Richard Laford[9] claims that 85 percent is typical and William Latzko,[8] when working in the banking industry, found that checkers detected approximately 75 percent of the defects actually present. This number is not constant. Variables influencing inspection effectiveness include the complexity of the operation, the number of problems, the inspector, the time of day and the reviewer's experience.

Production personnel often become dependent on their inspectors. The quality analysis branch of a large government facility ran into this problem. The auditors reviewed the work of a group of statistical technicians. When excessive errors were found, up to 20 cases were returned to those doing the work. Production people were supposed to rework all calculations in the rejected documents before returning them. A few workers, however, tried to take shortcuts; they did their best to get the quality personnel to identify which of the samples had errors. In some cases, they also wanted to know the right numbers. In these instances, those being audited wanted to use the checkers as crutches; they didn't want to be responsible for their own work.

Subjective Sampling

Subjective sampling is like shopping; you inspect the units that you like. Some workers often try to sample the cases or units that are easiest to review. With reports, cases, expense accounts, retirement calculations and the like, this usually means the thinnest pile of paper. In many operations, the thinner units have a single page; the thicker units have up to a dozen. The concept is the same as letting a typist choose between two sets of documents—one with lots of numbers and one without. In most cases, the typist will avoid the ones with numbers because they are harder to type and take longer.

If size is not the sampling criterion, some inspectors choose the samples on top; they are the most readily available. When production personnel are aware of this tendency, they make sure the most difficult work is on the bottom of the pile.

Conscientious inspectors, with no training in sampling, can go to the other extreme by choosing the fattest and the most complex files to review. Others go for files in the middle or on the bottom of the pile. These choices can be based on the desire to be needed. By reviewing the toughest and most inaccessible cases, they usually find more errors. The more errors they find, the more they feel needed.

Neither the search for easy work nor the quest for difficult cases produce representative samples. As a consequence, both approaches to sampling mislead anyone trying to evaluate the quality of work coming out of the office.

Rosander[11,13] speaks of **accessibility sampling** where samples are selected from the most accessible units or elements. This can include selecting the most cooperative person when doing an interview or drawing conclusions from a mail survey where the response rate is low. Both approaches are subject to unknown amounts of bias or error; both tend to result in questionable conclusions.

Deming[12] speaks of **chunk sampling**, which is similar to accessibility sampling. He cites the following examples:

- Surveying a specific city because the surveying organization has a field-force there
- Surveying any group that is handy
- Interviewing "average people" on street-corners

Grab Sampling

Grab sampling is a special case of subjective sampling. Here, the inspector grabs a bunch of records or files for review. Since they are grouped together, they tend to be produced over a short period of time. Those doing the work may have finished the files before their first cup of coffee when they were half-asleep or around lunchtime when they were hungry or at the end of the shift when they were tired. Thus, their observed error rates might not be representative.

Judgment Sampling

According to Deming,[12] a judgment sample is planned with expert judgment whereas a chunk sample is dictated by convenience. Having an "expert" involved in the design may be comforting to the user. Deming,[12] however, observes that "judgment-samples, so far as I know, are not amenable to statistical analysis." He also adds, "The usefulness of data from judgment-samples is judged by expert knowledge of the subject-matter and comparisons with the results of previous surveys, not from knowledge of probability."

Rosander[13] also objects to judgment sampling. He says: "In judgment sampling, personal judgment, including the judgment of experts, is used to select the sampling units. This leads to all kinds of sampling such as selecting 'typical' units, selecting 'average' units, selecting 'bell-wether' units, selecting 100 percent of the frame for two days, or selecting all units for 'typical' days in each of several months. This too can be very biased."

Intentional bias is another type of subjective sampling. One inspector in a government records operation used to go out of his way to inspect the work of a production worker he liked. As long as he did the inspection, she was never charged with an error. Once this was discovered by supervision, however, corrective action was initiated.

Interval Sampling

Of the sampling techniques mentioned so far, interval sampling involves the least bias. Interval sampling with a random start, however, is generally preferred.

With plain interval sampling, inspectors select files that are a constant interval apart. In many cases, the interval is 10. This ensures that 10 percent of the files are reviewed. If the interval were 20, 5 percent of the files would be reviewed. The interval times the percent of files being reviewed always equals 100 percent.

Interval sampling is acceptable as long as the data to be inspected is not cyclic and the workers are not able to anticipate which files will be inspected. Problems could occur, however, if the inspector consistently started with the first file and reviewed every tenth one after that. If the people to be audited were aware of this tendency, they could arrange their work to ensure that difficult records were not selected for review.

Interval Sampling With a Random Start

Interval sampling with a random start eliminates some of the risk associated with straight interval sampling. This procedure was used extensively within nonstatistical areas of the Air Force Accounting and Finance Center. The

United States Fidelity & Guaranty Company also found it beneficial.[7] Some statisticians, like Rosander,[3] use the term "systematic sampling" instead of "interval sampling." The two terms, however, have similar meanings.

In interval sampling with a random start, you still have a constant number of units between those that are reviewed. The first sample number, however, can't be predicted; therefore, neither can subsequent sample numbers.

The following sequence would be typical if you had 50 records to sample and you used an interval of 10.

The first sample would be chosen at random from the first ten records. Random selection means that any record in the first interval has an equal chance of being selected. Methods of choosing random sample numbers include using a table of random numbers, drawing numbers out of a hat, spinning a "Wheel of Fortune" and having a computer do the selection.

Assume you selected the number "3" as your random start. Under these conditions, the files you would review are

Sample Sequence	Sample Number	Calculation Used
1	3	The random start = 3
2	13	3 + interval = 3 + 10 = 13
3	23	13 + interval = 13 + 10 = 23
4	33	23 + interval = 23 + 10 = 33
5	43	33 + interval = 33 + 10 = 43

If, on the other hand, you had a sample size of 30 and wanted to sample 1 out of 5 (20 percent), the procedure would be as follows.

Randomly select a number within the first interval; in this instance, the number would have to fall between 1 and 5. For illustration, assume the number you select is 2. Then, the files you would review would be

Sample Sequence	Sample Number	Calculation Used
1	2	The random start = 2
2	7	2 + interval = 2 + 5 = 7
3	12	7 + interval = 7 + 5 = 12
4	17	12 + interval = 12 + 5 = 17
5	22	17 + interval = 17 + 5 = 22
6	27	22 + interval = 22 + 5 = 27

If interval sampling with a random start is new to you, repeat the above calculations without looking at the book. Then check your results. Once you master the concept, the rest is easy.

Random Sampling

Random sampling is similar to interval sampling with a random start. The difference is that all samples are selected randomly—not just the first one. The advantage of this approach is that each record in the population has an equal chance of being reviewed.

The following example shows how to take a sample of 5 travel vouchers from a population using random numbers from Table 6-1.

When using a random number table, enter it at a random point. This usually involves dropping a pencil and selecting the point where the pencil hits. In this example, the pencil I dropped was near the 0 in the seventh number from the top in the second column of Table 6-1 (0479). Since there are only 50 vouchers, the number must fall between 1 and 50; therefore only the first two digits in the chosen column will be used. If the population were between 100 and 999, three digits would be used. If the population were between 1000 and 9999, all four digits would be used.

The next number down the column is 55 (using the first two digits). Because 55 is greater than 50, it is ignored. Going down the column, you come to a 10; it is between 1 and 50, so it will be used. The next number is 34; it is also between 1 and 50 and will be used. The 98 will be discarded because it is too large; so will the 51. The next eligible number is 44; it will be used. The following 65 will be discarded but the 02 will be used. Now,

Sample Sequence	Numbers From Table	Portion Used	Remarks
1.	0479	04	Select voucher number 4
—	5591	55	Number 55 is too large
2.	1087	10	Select voucher number 10
3.	3414	34	Select voucher number 34
—	9862	98	Number 98 is too large
—	5126	51	Number 51 is too large
4.	4478	44	Select voucher number 44
—	6580	65	Number 65 is too large
5.	0271	02	Select voucher number 2

Table 6-1. **Random Number Table**

3501	8609	8611	7624	8530
6980	3127	5189	2495	5103
8702	8640	1614	9328	1278
5151	9367	4214	2188	5722
7751	8768	9405	1432	8530
2702	8795	9690	4481	2681
5361	0479	0648	8573	4500
2614	5591	9701	3247	9986
2636	1087	1529	7815	1122
9710	3414	8898	7657	0750
8360	9862	7362	3842	2465
7411	5126	9321	9718	4577
6850	4478	3249	6970	0706
9807	6580	9029	8376	5253
4871	0271	6311	6466	6173
1540	6978	1049	2680	1258
0107	4806	1973	1678	3946
7998	8278	5128	6506	1585
3707	0265	6818	3483	9517
8325	6173	4810	7352	9371
9383	6138	0498	8544	6022
3740	5133	2315	1681	5844
1574	4732	9217	8882	5528
3670	0002	3736	9345	7083
5172	1993	3263	9254	6882
2195	6663	7043	9551	6083
9315	6138	1113	4854	2630
7306	4268	5408	0910	2642
7733	6597	2597	1819	7488
5477	1524	8337	8030	3556
8166	5777	3623	3046	0885
4043	9545	3113	7188	5624
3339	6125	4969	1831	6066
3903	3765	9056	3549	3971
6002	5020	7632	5807	8249
5019	7418	7092	2462	8181
0532	9958	7241	3708	4359
7244	9074	7134	7305	8740
3592	6568	0037	7437	6815
8949	6741	5784	6405	6295

we have the numbers of the 5 vouchers to be sampled (4, 10, 34, 44, 2). The table on page 75 reviews the selections.

This example shows how to use random number tables when taking a random sample. In practice, however, computers are normally used to make the selections.

For a more technical review of this subject, refer to Deming[15] or Rosander.[3, 13]

Stratified Sampling

Sampling a large storage tank filled with gasoline is similar to sampling stew on the stove. In order to get a representative sample, you have to make sure that the material is thoroughly mixed. The technique normally used in petroleum refineries is to take one sample from the top, one from the center and one from the bottom of the tank. If tests show that all three are the same, you can be reasonably sure the tank is adequately mixed and the samples represent the tank as a whole. This is called stratified sampling; the sample comes from different strata of the tank.

Measuring the performance of a group of workers is another case where stratified sampling is helpful. The production of each individual can be considered a stratum. Therefore, the production of each worker should be measured.

The best way to select units within strata is via random sampling; another common way is interval sampling with a random start.

Stratified sampling is most important when you expect significant variability between different parts of the population. With a storage tank, you expect significant differences if the contents are not thoroughly mixed. With individual workers, you expect differences because people are people; no two have identical skills, motivation or experience.

With stratified sampling by individual, you may be able to evaluate each worker but have difficulty drawing conclusions about the group. One procedure for obtaining group information from individual statistics is as follows:

1. Multiply average error rates of each individual by the volume of work produced by that individual.
2. Add results from step 1 for all individuals in the group.
3. Divide the results from step 2 by the total volume of work produced by the group.

The results shown in step three should approximate those obtained from random samples of the entire population.

The following example illustrates this approach.

GIVEN:

Individual	Volume	Error Rate
Gerry	100	5 percent
Terry	50	6 percent
Lynn	200	7 percent

PROBLEM:

Using the above data, determine the average error rate for the group.

Step 1: Gerry   100 × 5 = 500
Terry   50 × 6 = 300
Lynn   200 × 7 = 1400

Step 2:   500 + 300 + 1400 = 2200

Step 3: 2200/(100 + 50 + 200) =
2200 / 350 = 6.3 percent

In other words, the calculated error rate of the group is 6.3 percent. More information on calculating error rates as well as an introduction to confidence limits will be given in the following chapters.

Those interested in a more theoretical study of stratified sampling should read the works of Deming and Rosander listed under References.

SUMMARY

Redundant sampling and 100-percent sampling are generally inefficient and expensive; they should be limited to operations where the cost of undetected errors is high. Subjective sampling and grab sampling are generally inaccurate and subject to error or bias; these procedures should be avoided. Interval sampling, interval sampling with a random start, random sampling and stratified sampling are the preferred procedures; their results are less apt to produce inaccurate conclusions. Of the last four, however, interval sampling without a random start is the most likely to provide a sample that is not representative.

Food for Thought

Isolate 100 records, files, letters, transactions or other units of work. Then sample them using each of the above sampling procedures. With the exception of 100-percent and 300-percent sampling, use a sample size of 10.

1. Use 300-percent sampling to determine the accuracy of your checkers; each of the three 100-percent checks should be made by a different individual.
2. Compare the error rates detected by each sampling technique with those identified through 300-percent sampling.

REFERENCES
1. William J. Latzko, *Quality and Productivity for Bankers and Financial Managers* (Milwaukee, WI: ASQC Quality Press, 1986), pp. 40–45.
2. Harold F. Dodge and Harry G. Romig, *Sampling Inspection Tables* (New York: Wiley, 1944).
3. A. C. Rosander, *Applications of Quality Control in the Service Industries* (Milwaukee, WI: ASQC Quality Press, 1985), pp. 180–199.
4. William Edwards Deming, *Some Theory of Sampling* (New York: Dover Publications, 1950).
5. A. C. Rosander, *Washington Story* (Greeley, CO: National Directions, 1985), pp. 168–169.
6. Rosander, *Applications of Quality Control in the Service Industries,* pp. 78–79.
7. R. L. Rohrbaugh, "One Company's Approach to Data Sampling and Audits," *ASQC Technical Conference Transactions,* May 14–16, 1979, pp. 297–299.
8. Latzko, *Quality and Productivity for Bankers and Financial Managers,* pp. 89–90.
9. Richard J. Laford, "Don't Settle for More Inspectors," *Quality,* January 1986, p. 46.
10. Latzko, *Quality and Productivity for Bankers and Financial Managers,* pp. 171–174.
11. Rosander, *Washington Story,* pp. 14, 57.
12. Deming, *Some Theory of Sampling,* pp. 9–14.
13. Rosander, *Applications of Quality Control in the Service Industries,* pp. 137–142.
14. American National Standard ANSI/ASQC A2-1987, *Terms, Symbols, and Definitions for Acceptance Sampling,* (Milwaukee, WI: American Society for Quality Control, 1987).

15. Deming, *Some Theory of Sampling,* pp. 76–134.
16. Deming, *Some Theory of Sampling,* pp. 213–246.
17. Rosander, *Applications of Quality Control in the Service Industries,* p. 55.
18. Henry L. Lefevre, "Quality Control and Database Management Systems," *ASQC Technical Conference Transactions,* May 8–10, 1978, pp. 371–374.
19. Frank H. Squires, "To Sample or Not to Sample," *Quality Management & Engineering,* April 1974, pp. 20–23.

Chapter 7

Sample Plans and the Service Sector

Sample plans help you evaluate quality without spending excessive money on inspection. They are like road markers, giving you guidance for selecting the proper sample size and criteria for determining whether to accept or reject the population you sampled. When substituted for 100-percent sampling, they help reduce inspection costs. When introduced to an area with no sampling, they help evaluate services or products previously ignored. Sample plans, however, have one major drawback; they don't tell you *what* to sample.

Examples of sample plans in action have been included in this chapter to stimulate your thinking. In some cases, the examples should give you ideas for applications of your own. This chapter, however, is just an introduction. More information on specific sample plans and proven applications is contained in Chapters 8 through 10.

Two common areas for sampling are procurement and production. Both receive extensive attention in the manufacturing sector; both receive inadequate attention in the service sector.

PROCUREMENT SAMPLING

Latzko[1] refers to a bank's purchasing department that found a bargain on ribbons for the company's encoding machines. "In actual practice," he says, "bargain encoding ribbons caused a sudden decrease in encoding productivity. Luckily, the quality control department was vigilant and the cause of the sudden decrease in productivity was found before too much damage occurred." If the bank had been using a sample plan to inspect ribbons before accepting them, this problem of defective, low-quality merchandise could have been avoided.

When banks buy blank checks, should they have quality requirements in their purchase orders? Should they sample and inspect incoming materials? Most checks are processed through Magnetic Ink Character Recognition (MICR) equipment. MICR enables banks to process billions of drafts annually. If the MICR imprint is poor, however, checks get rejected and have to be processed manually. According to Rosander,[2] the added cost of reconciliation and manual entry of a check into the computer ranges from 10¢ to 30¢. Poor MICR printing by the check suppliers can increase the number of hand-processed checks significantly. To some, the savings of 10¢ to 30¢ per check seems as unimportant as counting paper clips. Volume, however, changes the picture. Deluxe Check Printers, Inc., have around a billion dollars in annual sales and a large part of it comes from their line of checks. Printing and processing checks is big business; small unit savings can net huge benefits when the volume is large.

Unless banks work with their vendors, as they would with Ship-To-Stock and Just-In-Time procurement systems, the inspection of purchased products (receiving inspection) is important. Following the Ship-To-Stock and Just-In-Time concepts, some banks protect themselves from poor-quality checks by getting control charts of the printer's process prior to acceptance of shipments.[1] In the absence of close vendor liaison, however, receiving inspection or pre-production testing is important to smooth operations.

Ship-To-Stock and Just-In-Time inventory control programs are beyond the scope of this book. Both, however, involve screening vendors and ensuring they have effective quality control systems; vendors are becoming part of the company team. Outstanding communications and exceptional quality control programs are needed to make the Just-In-Time and Ship-To-Stock programs work.[3–6]

One government organization had no receiving inspection or pre-production testing for floppy disks used in the agency's personal computers. In fact, they had no reliable method of vendor control. As a consequence, low quality disks were accepted and users lost large quantities of data. Subsequent requisitions from user organizations insisted that the offending vendor be excluded from consideration, but the damage had already been done. Floppy disks, used with personal computers, sound like nickel-and-dime items. Loss of data, however, can be very expensive. It's a lot like the ancient fable about a missing nail in a horse's shoe that led to the loss of a kingdom. The cost of one unit doesn't seem important until the consequences of failure escalate or volume gets large.

Defective materials, like those above, can be screened out before the products are accepted. Had they failed to meet the requirements of a sample plan like Military Standard 105D,[7] discussed further in Chapters 8 and 9, the unacceptable materials could have been rejected and returned to the vendor. This acceptance function is normally called receiving inspection; it is standard procedure for the procurement of raw materials in many manufacturing plants. In some cases, it is also used by service industries. Many nonusers in the service sector could benefit by introducing it to their operations. The cheapest product is not always the most cost-effective; failure of inexpensive units can have a pronounced effect on profits.

A common alternative to receiving inspection is the squeaky wheel system. Purchasing agents may continue to buy the cheapest product on the market until the users start to squeak, holler and revolt. Then, they blacklist the offending source and go to the next cheapest vendor. Without feedback from the users, however, the purchasing departments of many service companies continue buying defective, low-cost products. The fact that some people consider this practice acceptable, even when the costs of failure are high, is unfortunate.

SAMPLE PLANS AND SERVICE SECTOR PRODUCTION

Sample plans can be used in a production environment, even when the "product" is a stack of travel vouchers, a pile of hospital admission reports, a batch of case studies or a day's worth of statistical calculations. Production is production. It doesn't have to be a manufactured product that will be sold to the general public. Sample plans can be used in most areas where supervisors and management want to control quality.

When I was with the Air Reserve Personnel Center, we used the Dodge & Romig sample plans[8] to help control the quality of technician production. One objective was to ensure that reservists received retirement credit for the work they performed. To the reservists, this work was important. One small error could result in an individual not getting retirement credit for a full year of reserve activity. Additional information on the Dodge & Romig sample plans is presented in Chapter 10.

Rosander[9] documents the use of Military Standard 105D as a sample plan for controlling quality in the data-entry section of a computer installation. Additional tools that Rosander used with this clerical project included control charts, continuous sampling and learning-curve analyses. At another installation, Rosander records the use of sampling to verify the accuracy of a store inventory. Sampling can be used in diverse places.

Sample plans like Military Standard 105D, Dodge & Romig Tables and Continuous Sample Plan CSP-1[10] can help control quality; unacceptable work is rejected and done over. In addition, trend analyses or control charts can be used to identify trends and create early alerts so that problems can be anticipated and prevented. Details on the actual use of trend analyses, control charts and Continuous Sample Plan (CSP-1) are covered in subsequent chapters.

OTHER SAMPLE PLANS

Sample plans covered in this book are a small fraction of those available. Additional plans are listed in references at the end of this chapter. They include

- Military Standard 414, which is used for sampling variables[11,12]
- Skip-lot sampling[12,13]
- Chain sampling[12,14]
- PPM sampling for very low error rates[15–17]

Most of the sample plans found in literature involve attribute or go/no-go type sampling. The prime exception is Military Standard 414; it is the most prominent plan used for sampling variables (where the number of possible measurements is large if not infinite).

EXTERNAL VS INTERNAL SAMPLES AND AUDITS

Worker quality in the service sector can be sampled, monitored and reviewed internally by supervision or externally by an independent quality organization. Each approach has its advantages.

When a worker's quality is controlled by supervision, the worker normally gets prompt feedback from someone who has a direct impact on that person's career. Supervisors who don't have an objective evaluation of the work coming out of their departments are not doing their jobs. By sampling and performing internal quality audits, supervision can identify who needs additional training, who needs motivation and who needs clearer instructions. Then, supervision can initiate corrective action as required. More information on quality audits is found in Chapter 4.

Sampling often shows that the need for additional training is not limited to the new clerk on the block. When an administrative job is complex, old-timers occasionally start taking shortcuts and forget how the job was supposed to be done. Once the problem is identified, supervision can initiate corrective action. Sampling the work of subordinates helps identify realities; it enables supervision to make objective performance evaluations.

When sampling identifies a performance problem and motivation is at the bottom of it, supervision has a chance at a different type of corrective action; many attitude problems are management controllable. With motivation, however, the solution is seldom simple. Poor supervision can discourage employees a lot faster than good supervisors can motivate them. Improved communications, better standards, retraining and other management-controllable factors are usually involved.

Although sampling and auditing by supervision is important, review by independent inspectors should not be ignored. If nothing else, external monitoring can be used to ensure that the quality control system is working. People within an organization have a vested interest in making their department look good. As a consequence, they often overlook problems that make them look bad. One service organization reported that its quality was better than 99 percent error-free. An independent audit, however, showed it was closer to 95 percent.

One problem with many independent, external audits is that the feedback can be slow. This is particularly true when the sampling and audits are performed at corporate level or the auditors are housed in separate facilities. A second problem often arises when criticism comes from outsiders; it is seldom accepted with enthusiasm. Us-vs-them confrontations develop.

For maximum benefits, it is best to have both internal and external sampling, auditing and review. That way, feedback can be both quick and free of bias.

SUMMARY

Many sample plans developed for use in manufacturing are also applicable to the service sector. In order to find appropriate applications, it is necessary to have some idea of the sample plans available. Then, it is necessary to know the work area well enough to figure out where sampling will help.

FOOD FOR THOUGHT

Review your own work area. Then answer the following questions:

1. Which jobs, functions, records, letters or data are not reviewed? What are the risks of leaving their quality to chance?
2. Which jobs, functions, records, letters or data receive a minimum of 100-percent inspection? Do the costs of review exceed the benefits obtained from the reviews?

REFERENCES
1. William J. Latzko, *Quality and Productivity for Bankers and Financial Managers* (Milwaukee, WI: ASQC Quality Press, 1986), pp. 41–42.
2. A. C. Rosander, *Applications of Quality Control in the Service Industries* (Milwaukee, WI: ASQC Quality Press, 1985), p. 11.
3. Richard J. Laford, "Tools for Effective Communications Between Suppliers, Purchasing and Quality," *BOSCON '87*, Boston Section of ASQC, 1-Day Conference, March 19, 1987.
4. Henry L. Lefevre's interview of Richard J. Laford, "Cut Inspection Costs and Improve Vendor Quality With Ship-To-Stock," *Productivity Improvement Bulletin*, March 25, 1986, pp. 1–3.
5. Roger Brooks, "MRP: The Right Stuff For Just-In-Time," *Quality* May 1985, p. 20.
6. Richard J. Schonberger, "Just-In-Time Production—the Quality Dividend," *Quality Progress*, October 1984, pp. 22–24.
7. Military Standard 105D, *Sampling Procedures and Tables for Inspection by Attributes* (Washington, D.C.: U.S. Government Printing Office, April 29, 1963).
8. Harold F. Dodge and Harry G. Romig, *Sampling Inspection Tables* (New York: Wiley, 1944).
9. Rosander, *Applications of Quality Control in the Service Industries*, pp. 109–118.
10. Kenneth S. Stephens, *How to Perform Continuous Sampling* (Milwaukee, WI: ASQC Quality Press, 1979).
11. Military Standard 414, *Sampling Procedures and Tables for Inspection by Variables for Percent Defective* (Washington, D.C.: U.S. Government Printing Office, 1957).
12. J. M. Juran, Frank M. Gryna, Jr. and R. S. Bingham, Jr., *Quality Control Handbook*, 3d ed. (New York: McGraw-Hill, 1974), Chapters 24–25.
13. Harold F. Dodge, "Skip-Lot Sampling Plans," *Industrial Quality Control*, February 1955.

14. Harold F. Dodge, "Chain Sampling," *Industrial Quality Control,* January 1955.
15. Gerald Hurayt, "Sample Size for PPM," *Quality,* March 1986, p. 75.
16. D. K. Murphy, "Sample Size for PPM," *Quality,* June 1986, p. 10.
17. Murakami, Kishii and Inamura, "PPM Control for Electronic Parts," *Quality Progress,* November 1984, pp. 24–34.

Chapter 8

Military Standard 105D— The Basics

Do you want a sample plan that is popular, generally recognized and included in many government contracts? Then consider Military Standard 105D.[1] According to Ellis Ott,[2] "The most frequently used government plans are the Military Standards Acceptance Plans by Attributes (MIL-STD-105D)."

The Military Standard 105 series provides a system for controlling quality. In its original form, it was one of the first product acceptance systems based on statistics and sampling. In its present form, it is one of the most popular. The latest version, Military Standard 105D, was officially introduced on 29 April 1963; although given a military designation, it is used by quality control departments across the country. It is specified by many purchasing agents and is quoted in most government contracts.

Although known for its applications in high volume manufacturing operations, Military Standard 105D can also be used in the service sector.

WHAT IS MILITARY STANDARD 105D?

Military Standard 105D is an acceptance system for attributes (defect-vs-no-defect evaluations). It can be used to accept or reject materials, documents or just plain work like statistical calculations and typing. It also helps determine the sample size you need with little hassle and limited risk of being challenged.

As a system for controlling quality, Military Standard 105D will help you accept or reject batches of work or materials. It appears relatively simple, but it has a lot of fine print; the standard is more complex than it seems.

Finally, Military Standard 105D has rules for increasing or relaxing the sampling requirements. When everything is going well, the risks are less and you can take smaller samples. When problems arise, the risks are higher and you should sample more. The idea is to have the most inspection when the risks are greatest.

HOW DOES MILITARY STANDARD 105D WORK?

Before using the standard you need to determine the level of quality you will accept. This is a management decision and involves picking the appropriate AQL (Acceptable Quality Level). Then each batch of material, documents or work is measured against that AQL using variables set by the sample plan.

Another management decision involves selecting the right sample plan. You can choose one that does a good job of ensuring that poor work is not released (one with a low consumer risk). On the other hand, you can choose one that protects the worker from having good work rejected (one with a low producer risk). Or you can choose one that is somewhere in between. Additional material on producer and consumer risks is included in the definitions section of this chapter.

ADVANTAGES OF MILITARY STANDARD 105D

105D is not the only sampling system available; Chapter 7 has references to a few alternatives. Therefore, the question arises, "Why use Military Standard 105D?"

First, it is a well-recognized system. Most established quality control organizations have copies. Most of them also have quality engineers with some experience in using the standard. Choosing sampling systems is a little like choosing computers; people tend to prefer systems they understand. As an example, managers who have Apple computers at home are likely to recommend similar computers for their place of business; few would recommend the IBM brand. Those with IBMs at home would reverse the process. Following similar logic, quality engineers familiar with Military Standard 105D and no other plan will probably recommend it. Those having experience with CSP-1[3] and no other plan will probably have different preferences.

Second, 105D *seems* to be easy to use. In its simplest form, it can be implemented in a couple of days. Mastery, however, takes much longer.

Third, it is specified in many government contracts. This advantage, however, seldom applies to service industries; few service companies have government contracts that require it. It may, however, show up in purchase documents for *materials* used by the service sector. This could apply to floppy disks, bank checks, printer ribbons and many other office items that are purchased in volume.

Fourth, it is economical. As an example, sample sizes specified by Military Standard 105D are much smaller than those found in many comparable parts of CSP-1.

Fifth, it helps you control quality. Its rules tell you when to accept work and when to reject it. They also tell you to increase sample sizes or reduce acceptance numbers when things get bad.[4]

Sixth, it can handle a wide range of batch sizes from very small to very large.

DISADVANTAGES OF MILITARY STANDARD 105D

With all of these advantages, how can you go wrong with 105D?
Easy! Here are some of the disadvantages of this standard:

1. The concept of Acceptable Quality Level (AQL) can be misleading. The AQL identifies the average level of quality you are willing to live with over a period of years. It doesn't, however, identify whether garbage can slip through the screen process; in some instances, low-quality batches do slip through. You have to understand the fine print to know why.
2. Military Standard 105D is designed to evaluate completed batches of material or work. You may have to accumulate a sizeable amount of production before taking your sample; the accumulation process slows production.
3. If the batch from a technician doesn't meet the acceptance criteria, it

is rejected and returned to its source. This process is also time consuming and slows down production.
4. Sections of the standard imply that errors are inevitable and therefore acceptable. In many cases, batches will be accepted under the plan even though some errors are found in the sample. This philosophy is challenged by those who expect perfection. In the service sector, however, perfection is only needed when the cost of errors is high. In routine operations, perfection is seldom found and its cost is hard to justify.
5. The standard contains complex terms and acronyms that should be understood before the system is implemented. Those people using the terms are easier to find than those understanding them.

DEFINITIONS

In order to use sample plans effectively, it is necessary to master some definitions. All of the terms defined in this chapter are applicable to Military Standard 105D. Some, however, are not universal and may not apply to all of the other sample plans.

Ac. The abbreviation "Ac" represents the acceptance number; it is shown near the top of the sampling tables. If the number of defectives in the sample doesn't exceed the Ac number for the sample plan, the batch is accepted.

AQL. The abbreviation "AQL" stands for the Acceptable Quality Level. It represents the average percent defectives the customer is willing to tolerate over an extended period. A data-entry supervisor might impose an inspection plan having an AQL of 4 percent. The plan, however, would not work efficiently if the clerks had average error rates much larger than 4 percent (the AQL) because too many batches would be rejected.

Batch. The term "batch" refers to the collection of units from which a sample is drawn. For a keypunch operator, a batch can be one hour's production. For a bank teller, a batch can be all of the transactions handled by that teller over a two-hour period. For a technician working on retirement cases, a batch can be a day's worth of records. In this book, the terms "batch" and "lot" are used interchangeably.

Consumer's Risk. Consumer's risk identifies the level of risk of accepting a "bad" batch where the percent defective matches the Rejectable Quality Level (RQL) or Lot Tolerance Percent Defective (LTPD). When the consumer's risk is 10 percent (which is customary) the consumer (inspector) will unknowingly accept a "bad" lot approximately 10 percent of the time. The quality level used to identify a "bad" lot is the same as the RQL or LTPD; it is set when you select the sample plan. Batches with a lower percent defectives than the RQL should be accepted more than 10 percent of the time.

Defect. A defect is a characteristic that doesn't meet the requirements, standards or specifications. A unit that has one or more defects is called a defective. For example, a letter with three spelling errors has at least three defects (it could have defects in addition to the three spelling errors). Each error is a defect. The letter is a defective.

Defective. The term "defective" represents a unit that doesn't comply with the requirements. For a data-entry clerk, that could involve a file entered into the computer and having at least one error. For a bank teller, that could involve making an erroneous transaction at the window. For a motel maid, it could involve a room that was not prepared properly. For a loan officer, it could involve a loan that was made but shouldn't have been; it could also involve a loan that wasn't made but should have been. ANSI/ASQC Standard A2-1987, an American National Standard that defines terms, symbols and definitions for acceptance sampling, refers to a defective as "a unit of product or service containing at least one defect."[5]

Lot. The term "lot" refers to the collection of units from which a sample is drawn. This book uses the terms "lot" and "batch" interchangeably.

LTPD. The abbreviation "LTPD" stands for Lot Tolerance Percent Defective. It represents the average percent defectives the user is willing to accept 10 percent of the time (assuming the consumer's risk is 10 percent). LTPD has the same meaning as the abbreviation "RQL."

Multiple Sample Plans. Although Military Standard 105D has numerous multiple level sample plans, they are not given much coverage in this text. Most of the people I have worked with do not like them because of the amount of record keeping these plans require. Although I do not recommend them for use in the service sector, some experienced engineers have found instances where they reduce the cost of sampling. Average sample size curves for double and multiple sampling are found in reference (6).

Normal Sample Plan. The standard has four types of sampling levels. In most cases, normal sample plans are the first to be used. Other sample plans include reduced, tightened and special.

OC Curve. An OC Curve or Operating Characteristic Curve is a curve that plots the "percent of lots expected to be accepted" against "the quality of the submitted lots." Each sample plan has a different OC curve. Military Standard 105D shows OC Curves for its single sample plans toward the end of the Document.[7] Figure 8-1 shows the OC Curve for normal, single sample plan J of Military Standard 105D when the AQL is 1.0 percent. Note that the probability of accepting a lot with 1.0 percent defectives is approximately 95 percent. Conversely, the probability of rejecting that lot is approximately 5 percent (the producer's risk rate is 5 percent). The producer's risk is found directly to the left of the point where the OC Curve crosses the AQL value. It may, however, have to be converted from probability of acceptance to probability of rejection by subtracting it from 100. The sample plan shown in Figure 8-1 has its consumer's risk set at the customary 10-percent level. Therefore, the RQL is found directly below the point where the 10 percent probability of acceptance line intersects the curve; for this plan, the RQL is approximately 6.5 percent. In other words, a lot with 6.5 percent defectives will be accepted 10 percent of the time. It is important that these risks be known by anyone using a sample plan. Otherwise, they may take unacceptable risks without knowing it. If these risks are too large, the user should take a larger sample size.

Producer's Risk. Producer's risk identifies the probability of rejecting a "good" batch where the percent defective matches the AQL. When the producer's risk is 5 percent (which is customary) the producer, worker or vendor will unknowingly have a "good" lot rejected, by chance, 5 percent of the time. The quality level used to identify a "good" lot is the same as the AQL; therefore, it is set by the individuals selecting the sample plan. Batches with a lower percent defectives than the AQL will be rejected less than 5 percent of the time.

Re. This abbreviation represents the rejection number. It is located to the right of the acceptance number in the tables. If the number of defectives in a batch equals or exceeds the rejection number, the batch should be rejected.

Reduced Inspection Level. This level can be used when everything is going well. As an example, a clerk working on retirement records may have worked three months without making an error. That individual might qualify for the reduced inspection level. The standard has very explicit rules for switching between the reduced, normal and tightened levels. Many engineers avoid reduced sampling because the risk of accepting "bad" product is high and the rules for switching to reduced sampling are stringent.

RQL. The abbreviation "RQL" stands for the Rejectable Quality Level. It is also called the Lot Tolerance Percent Defective (LTPD). The RQL represents the worst average percent defectives the user is willing to accept 10 percent of the time (assuming the consumer risk is set at the customary 10 percent).

Special Inspection Levels. Military Standard 105D has four special inspection levels. Sample sizes for these plans are lower than even the reduced-inspection-level sample plans. As a consequence, their use should be limited to quality control situations where the cost of testing is very high or superficial controls are acceptable; some control is better than none. Special-inspection-level sample plans generally have very high RQLs. Because of this, they are not given detailed coverage in this book. They have limited application and create excessive risks for those with limited experience in sampling.

Tightened Inspection Level. This is also called tightened sampling or tightened sample plans. Of all the sample plans in the standard, the tightened sample plans are the toughest to meet. For a given set of conditions, the tightened sample plans have the largest sample sizes. They are normally used when the worker or process is in trouble or when new processes are being developed. Supervisors, for instance, might want to use a tightened sample plan on employees who have just qualified for sampling. It isn't practical to apply too loose a sample plan to an inexperienced worker.

SUMMARY

Military Standard 105D is the most frequently used set of governmental sample plans in the United States.[2] It helps you select the proper sample size and tells you when to accept the batch being tested. The function of 105D is to help control quality. Work that meets the requirements of the standard is accepted. Work that doesn't meet the requirements is returned to its source for rework or correction.

FOOD FOR THOUGHT

Assume you were using single sample plan J with an AQL of 1.0 percent and the OC Curve in Figure 8-1.

1. What percent of the lots that are 5 percent defective would you expect to accept?
2. What percent of the lots that are 6.5 percent defective would you expect to accept?
3. What percent of the lots that are 1 percent defective would you expect to reject?

(The solutions follow the References for this chapter.)

Figure 8-1. **Operating Characteristics Curve: Normal Sample Plan**

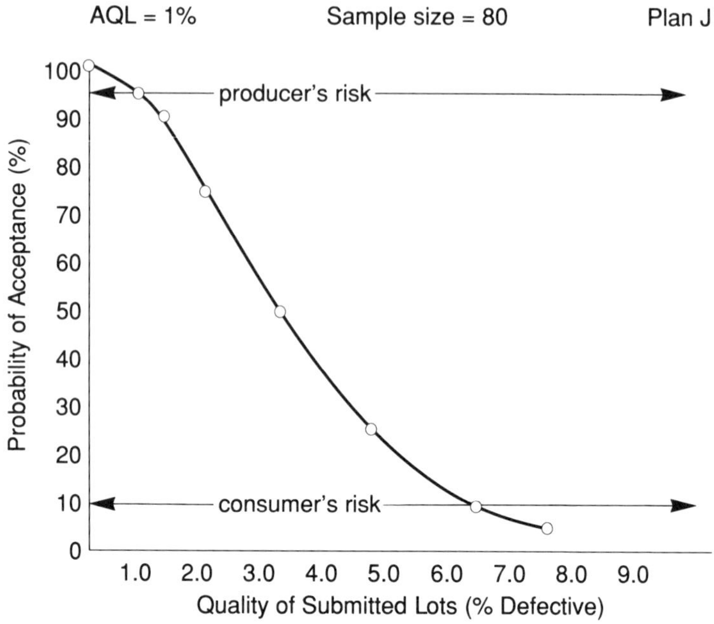

AQL = 1%   Sample size = 80   Plan J

[Graph: Probability of Acceptance (%) vs. Quality of Submitted Lots (% Defective), showing OC curve with producer's risk indicated near top and consumer's risk near bottom.]

NORMAL SAMPLING

Population	=	1000
Sample size	=	80
Acceptance number	=	2
Rejection number	=	3
AQL	=	1.0%
RQL	=	6.5%

REFERENCES

1. Military Standard 105D, *Sampling Procedures and Tables for Inspection by Attributes* (Washington D.C.: U.S. Government Printing Office, April 29, 1963).
2. Ellis R. Ott, *Process Quality Control* (New York: McGraw-Hill, 1975), p. 172.
3. Kenneth S. Stephens, *How to Perform Continuous Sampling* (Milwaukee, WI: ASQC Quality Press, 1979).
4. Military Standard 105D, *Sampling Procedures and Tables for Inspection by Attributes*, p. 5.

5. American National Standard, ANSI/ASQC A2-1987, *Terms, Symbols, and Definitions for Acceptance Sampling* (Milwaukee, WI: American Society for Quality Control, 1987).
6. Military Standard 105D, *Sampling Procedures and Tables for Inspection by Attributes*, p. 29.
7. Military Standard 105D, *Sampling Procedures and Tables for Inspection by Attributes*, pp. 30–61.

SOLUTIONS

1. Approximately 23 percent
2. Approximately 10 percent
3. Approximately 5 percent

Chapter 9

Military Standard 105D In Action

Military Standard 105D[1] is a 64-page document designed to guide those involved in controlling quality. This includes the purchasing departments of service companies; they use it to help define acceptable performance. It's not enough to measure the production of workers. The quality of their efforts should also be reviewed.

In the service sector, Military Standard 105D is not used as much as it should be. In addition, many who use it don't use it properly.

Why? The length and complexity of the document make it difficult to understand; beginners need something less complex. Simplified portions of the standard (Figures 9-1 through 9-3) were developed to fill this need—to give newcomers an exposure to the standard without giving them an overdose.

This chapter includes discussions on three portions of the standard most applicable to the service industry. Once you have mastered these, you might develop the will to tackle an unabridged version of the document.

NORMAL INSPECTION

In the service sector, normal inspection levels identify the tables most frequently used. In this book, they are referred to as normal inspection, normal levels, normal tables and normal sample plans. In Military Standard 105D, they are referred to as "type II general inspection levels" or "normal inspection."

Figure 9-1 represents an abbreviated version of the Military Standard 105D normal inspection plan. It shows batch sizes ranging from 2 to 1200. Tables for a batch size of 1 would have no value; you would either do 100-percent inspection or none. Batch sizes larger than 1200 are uncommon. They were dropped from the tables in this book to keep from overwhelming beginners.

Acceptable Quality Levels (AQLs) shown in Figure 9-1 are for 2.5, 4.0, and 10.0 percent. In service areas where I have helped, an AQL of 2.5 is considered demanding. An AQL of 4.0 is fairly common. An AQL of 10.0 is loose.

Management might use an AQL of 2.5 for entry of sensitive information into a mainframe computer. Financial data at a bank or insurance company would qualify. This implies that error rates over 2.5 percent would not be acceptable; corrective action might be initiated whenever a sample didn't comply with the requirements of the sample plan.

An AQL of 4.0 would be typical for a clerk checking the retirement points of an Air Force Reservist. Audits of the work of quality control inspectors might also qualify. So would the work of admission clerks at a hospital. For these groups, a 2.5 AQL might be too tight and a 10.0 AQL might be too loose.

With secretaries, where a unit represents an entire letter, an AQL of 10.0 might be appropriate. This means that, on the average, only one document out of ten could have a misspelled word or typographical error. Even this quality level would be difficult to attain, however, without a word processor, plus software that could check the spelling.

Selection of the proper AQL is a management decision. Before making it, however, the manager should be briefed on the ramifications of AQL, RQL, consumer risk, producer risk and OC curves. Otherwise the risks they take may exceed the risks they think they are taking.

Each table has a column for batch sizes. Each AQL level is divided into columns for sample size (n), acceptance number (Ac) and rejection number (Re). The sample size identifies the number of units to take from a batch for review or audit. The acceptance number provides a basis for acceptance. If the volume of defectives in a sample doesn't exceed that number, the batch is considered acceptable. The rejection number provides a basis for rejection. If the defectives spotted in a sample equal or exceed that number, the batch is considered unacceptable.

Problems 9-1 through 9-3 show how Figure 9-1 works.

PROBLEM 9-1

You are auditing a batch of 400 time cards for a subcontractor involved with defense work. It is important that all charges be assessed to contracts that haven't been closed. As a consequence, management set the AQL at 2.5. You are on a normal level of sampling.

How many time cards would you review?

What is the maximum number of time cards with bad charges you could find and still accept the batch?

SOLUTION 9-1

There are 400 time cards. Go down the batch-size column for the normal inspection plan (Figure 9-1) until you reach a range that includes 400. The next to the last entry (281–500) meets this requirement.

Figure 9-1. **Military Standard 105D in a Simplified Form: Single Sampling Plans for Normal Inspection**

Batch Size	2.5% n	2.5% Ac	2.5% Re	4.0% n	4.0% Ac	4.0% Re	10.0% n	10.0% Ac	10.0% Re
2 – 25	5	0	1	3	0	1	5	1	2
26 – 50	5	0	1	13	1	2	8	2	3
51 – 90	20	1	2	13	1	2	13	3	4
91 – 150	20	1	2	20	2	3	20	5	6
151 – 280	32	2	3	32	3	4	32	7	8
281 – 500	50	3	4	50	5	6	50	10	11
501 – 1200	80	5	6	80	7	8	80	14	15

Ac= Acceptance number
AQL= Acceptable Quality Level
n= Sample size
Re= Rejection number

NOTE: If sample size exceeds batch size, sample 100%.

Now, move to the right until you are under the 2.5% AQL column. For batch sizes between 281 and 500, the sample size (n) is 50 and the acceptance number (Ac) is 3. Therefore, accept the batch as long as there are 3 or less discrepant time cards in the sample.

Procedures for selecting samples were covered in Chapter 6. In this example, a random sample is recommended. The entire sample plan is based on the assumption that each of the 400 time cards has an equal chance of being selected as part of the sample.

Another rule is that no known defects will be allowed to proceed with the batch. When defects are detected, they should be returned to their source. This concept is not always clear to those being inspected. Many believe that it is OK to send known defects to the customer. After all, many sample plans allow acceptance of batches after defects have been found—as long as the acceptance number is not exceeded. To remove this source of confusion, many supervisors try to stick to sample plans where the acceptance number is zero.

PROBLEM 9-2

You are starting to sample and have 15 travel vouchers from one of your technicians. Management wants to keep the average error rate below 4 percent.

How many vouchers should you have in your sample?
What are the acceptance criteria?

SOLUTION 9-2

Since you are just starting to sample, and don't have directions to the contrary, you should use a normal sample plan (Figure 9-1).

Management wants to keep the average error rate at 4 percent or less so you would pick an AQL of 4.0.

Go down the left column in Figure 9-1 until you get to a range of batch sizes that includes 15. The first row, with a batch size of 2–25, meets this requirement. Then move to the right until you are under the 4.0% AQL column. The numbers under the 4.0% column are:

$n = 3$ sample size
Ac = 0 acceptance number
Re = 1 rejection number

$n = 3$ means the sample size should be 3.

$Ac = 0$ means you should accept the batch if there are no improperly prepared vouchers.

$Re = 1$ means you should reject the batch if there are any defectives. A defective is a unit that has at least one error.

PROBLEM 9-3

Quality requirements vary with the importance of the item being audited. In Problem 9-1, an AQL of 2.5% was applied to time cards because the organization was having difficulty with employees charging against accounts that were out of funds. In this problem we return to the typical time card situation where there isn't as much at risk.

The normal sample plan is still being used. In this case, there are 1000 time cards and management will accept a long-term average error rate of 10 percent.

How many time cards should be in the sample?

What are the acceptance criteria?

SOLUTION 9-3

Since you are on a normal sample plan, you should continue to use Figure 9-1. Management will accept a long-term average error rate of 10 percent, so the AQL is 10.0. Go down the left column in the Figure until you get to a batch size that includes 1000. In this case it is the last row. Now go to the right until you are under the 10.0% AQL column. The numbers under the AQL = 10.0% column are:

$n = 80$ sample size
$Ac = 14$ acceptance number
$Re = 15$ rejection number

$n = 80$ means you should audit 80 time cards.

$Ac = 14$ means you should accept the batch if there are no more than 14 discrepant cards.

$Re = 15$ means you should reject the batch if there are 15 or more discrepant cards.

What should you do if rejection of batches becomes too common? Typical steps include the following:

- Return all the cards to the Division they came from with a note requesting corrective action.
- Set up a training program for the supervisors who signed the time cards.
- Review the regulations on time cards to see if the problem stems from unclear instructions.

TIGHTENED INSPECTION

When problems develop and rejections become frequent, tougher sample plans are required. They may also be used where the cost of accepting bad work is high or the people being inspected have not proven themselves.

Figure 9-2. Military Standard 105D in a Simplified Form: Single Sampling Plans for Tightened Inspection

Batch Size	\multicolumn{9}{c}{Acceptable Quality Level (AQL)}
	2.5%			4.0%			10.0%		
	n	Ac	Re	n	Ac	Re	n	Ac	Re
2 – 15	8	0	1	5	0	1	8	1	2
16 – 25	8	0	1	20	1	2	8	1	2
26 – 50	32	1	2	20	1	2	13	2	3
51 – 90	32	1	2	20	1	2	20	3	4
91 – 150	32	1	2	32	2	3	32	5	6
151 – 280	50	2	3	50	3	4	50	8	9
281 – 500	80	3	4	80	5	6	80	12	13
501 – 1200	125	5	6	125	8	9	125	18	19

Ac= Acceptance number
AQL= Acceptable Quality Level
n= Sample size
Re= Rejection number

NOTE: If sample size exceeds batch size, sample 100%.

Military Standard 105D in Action 105

During their training period, employees usually get 100-percent inspection. Once they have proven themselves, normal or reduced sampling may be appropriate. Between training and proven competence, however, something between normal inspection and 100-percent review might be appropriate. Tightened sample plans provide this alternative. An abbreviated version of the Military Standard 105D single tightened sample plan is shown in Figure 9-2. Military Standard 105D has the following rules for switching to and from tightened sampling:

- When two out of five consecutive batches have been rejected, you should switch from normal to tightened sampling.
- You should not switch back until five consecutive batches have been accepted under the tightened plan.
- If ten consecutive batches are inspected on a tightened plan, consider shutting down the operation and analyzing the problem. There's no need to keep going if everything's coming out wrong.

The next two problems illustrate this process in action.

PROBLEM 9-4

You are reviewing a batch of 15 retirement cases processed by Sam Jones. The last two batches he submitted under the normal sample plan failed to meet the acceptance criteria. Supervision wants to keep the average error rate at 4 percent or less.
How many cases should you have in your sample?
What are the acceptance criteria?

SOLUTION 9-4

Since Sam Jones failed to meet the acceptance criteria for two of the last five batches, you should use a single tightened sample plan. Figure 9-2 provides a condensed version of the tables.
Management wants to keep the average error rate at 4 percent or less so the AQL is 4.0.
Go down the left column in Figure 9-2 until you get to a range of batch sizes that includes 15. Then, move to the right until you are under the 4.0% AQL column. The numbers under AQL = 4.0% are:

> $n = 5$ sample size
> $Ac = 0$ acceptance number
> $Re = 1$ rejection number

$n = 5$ means the sample size should be 5.
$Ac = 0$ means you should accept the batch if there are no improperly prepared vouchers.
$Re = 1$ means you should reject the batch if there are 1 or more improperly prepared cases.

PROBLEM 9-5

Sam Jones was mortified when he was placed on the single tightened inspection plan. His response was to ask for additional training; up until now, he had depended on his high production to get him by. When in doubt about the proper procedures, he guessed.

After undergoing additional training, Sam's work improved. His next five batches passed the tightened sample plan. The sixth batch contained another 15 retirement records.

How many cases should the sample have?
What are the acceptance criteria?

SOLUTION 9-5

Now that Sam has had five successive batches pass the criteria for the tightened sample plan, he is eligible for the normal sample plan again. The population is still 15 records. The AQL is still 4.0.

Using Figure 9-1 this time, go down the left column until you get to a range of batch sizes that includes 15. In this case, it is the first set of batch sizes (2–25). Now, move to the right until you are under the 4.0% AQL column.

The numbers under AQL = 4.0% are:

> $n = 3$ sample size
> $Ac = 0$ acceptance number
> $Re = 1$ rejection number

n = 3 means the sample size should be 3.
Ac = 0 means you should accept the batch if there are no improperly prepared vouchers.
Re = 1 means you should reject the batch if there are 1 or more improperly prepared cases.

The only real difference between the two plans turns out to be the sample size. The inspector or auditor requires only three samples under the normal plan where five were required under the tightened plan. The normal plan is more risky than the tightened plan.

REDUCED INSPECTION

When everything is going well, reduced inspection is more economical than normal inspection; the sample sizes are smaller. Figure 9-3 represents an abbreviated version of the Military Standard for reduced inspection.

When everything is falling apart, reduced sampling is too risky; poor quality batches are likely to slip through the inspection screen. In view of the risks of reduced sampling, Military Standard 105D has strict rules for going from the normal to the reduced level. Rules for staying with reduced sampling are also hard to meet.

In order to go from normal to reduced inspection, you need to meet all of the following requirements:

1. The preceding 10 batches must have been on normal inspection with no rejections.
2. The total number of defectives in the preceding 10 batches must have met the requirements specified by Figure 9-4 (Added Criteria for Reduced Sampling). If an asterisk is shown, the number of consecutive acceptable batches must exceed 10; you continue normal sampling until you get out of asterisk territory. In other words, normal sampling continues until the requirements of Figure 9-4 are met.
3. Production is at a steady state.
4. Reduced inspection is considered desirable by the responsible authority.

Requirement 1 ensures that the person or product going on reduced sampling has a good record. Reduced sampling should be avoided until a reputation for good quality has been established.

Figure 9-3. **Military Standard 105D In a Simplified Form: Single Sampling Plans for Reduced Inspection**

Batch Size			Acceptable Quality Level (AQL)							
			2.5%			4.0%			10.0%		
			n	Ac	Re	n	Ac	Re	n	Ac	Re
2	–	25	2	0	1	2	0	1	2	0	2
26	–	50	2	0	1	2	0	1	2	0	2
51	–	90	2	0	1	2	0	1	2	0	2
91	–	150	2	0	1	5	0	2	3	1	3
151	–	280	8	0	2	5	0	2	5	1	4
281	–	500	8	0	2	8	1	3	8	2	5
501	–	1200	13	1	3	13	1	4	13	3	6

Ac= Acceptance number
AQL= Acceptable Quality Level
n= Sample size
Re= Rejection number

NOTE: If sample size exceeds batch size, sample 100%

Figure 9-4. **Added Criteria for Reduced Sampling**

Number of sample units taken from the last 10 batches	Maximum number of defectives found among samples from the first 10 batches		
	AQL = 2.5	AQL = 4.0	AQL = 10.0
20 – 49	*	*	0
50 – 79	*	0	2
80 – 129	0	0	4
130 – 199	0	2	7
200 – 319	2	4	14
320 – 499	4	8	24
500 – 799	7	14	40

Total number of sample units is not large enough. More than 10 successive acceptable lots are needed to qualify.

Requirement 2 gives added emphasis to a history of good quality.

Compliance with the criteria set forth in Figure 9-4 ensures that the switch to reduced sampling is not based on 10 small samples; with small samples, the risk of questionable quality slipping through is fairly high. If the total number of units taken under normal sampling is under 80 and the AQL is 2.5, additional batches have to qualify. When the AQL is 4.0, the magic number is 50. The table does not show any asterisks for an AQL of 10.0. This means, for AQL = 10.0, the number of batches required for switching to reduced sampling should never exceed 10.

Requirement 3 is designed to ensure that foreseeable problems don't disrupt production. As an example, a change of supervisors might signal potential problems.

Requirement 4 gives emphasis to the risks involved. If the cost of poor quality is high, many supervisors would avoid going to reduced sampling; the risks are too great. An example might be where medication dispensed by nurses is being audited. Here, an error could be fatal.

Rules for going from reduced sampling to normal are also stringent. The plan requires going off reduced sampling the moment a suspicion of trouble develops. The switch is made if any of the following events occur:

1. A batch is rejected.
2. The number of defectives is between the acceptance number (Ac) and the rejection number (Re); this can only happen with reduced sampling. The normal and tightened plans do not have gaps between the acceptance and rejection numbers. When the number of defectives falls in the gap, the batch just sampled is still accepted. The next batch, however, goes under the rules for normal sampling.
3. Production becomes irregular or delayed.
4. Other conditions warrant a return to normal inspection.

PROBLEM 9-6

Sam Jones did so well after being retrained that he breezed through the next 10 batches without an error being detected. Each of the 10 batches had less than 25 cases. During this period, Sam's production was steady. In addition, the organization was short on auditors and management wanted to go to reduced sampling to solve the inspection bottleneck.

This time, Sam's batch size increased to 30; the AQL stayed at 4.0.

How many cases should the sample have?

What are the acceptance criteria?

SOLUTION 9-6

The big question now centers around whether Sam is ready for reduced sampling.

Requirements 1, 3, and 4 have been met. Sam completed 10 acceptable batches, production was steady and reduced sampling was considered desirable by supervision. To this point, however only 10 batches were inspected and a sample size of 3 was taken in each instance. Figure 9-4 shows that at least 50 sample units have to be taken before reduced sampling can be initiated. Therefore, Sam stays on normal sampling.

In this case, the sample criteria come from the normal sampling tables in Figure 9-1 again. A batch size of 30 falls in the second row from the top. Here, the sampling criteria are:

$$n = 13 \text{ sample size}$$
$$Ac = 1 \text{ acceptance number}$$
$$Re = 2 \text{ rejection number}$$

The sample size is 13. The batch will be accepted if less than two errors are detected.

PROBLEM 9-7

The batch in Problem 9-6 passed with no errors. So did the next batch, which had 50 records. Now, Sam has started his work and submits a 100-case batch. Conditions shown in Problem 9-6 still prevail.

What are the sampling criteria now?
What happens if one defective is found in the sample?

SOLUTION 9-7

The only thing that kept Sam off reduced sampling was the shortage of samples. Now the number of samples taken without any defectives being found is:

Samples taken before Problem 9-6	30	(3 × 10)
Samples taken during Problem 9-6	13	(30 records)
Samples taken from the next batch	13	(50 records)
Total number of units taken	56	

Since 56 cases were inspected and no defectives were found, Sam met the requirements of Figure 9-4; more than 50 records had been submitted for inspection. If any of Sam's batches had been rejected during the period he was having 56 units inspected, he would not qualify.

All requirements for reduced sampling have been met; Sam has finally qualified. Now, the sampling criteria will be taken from Figure 9-3. For a 100-unit batch and a 4.0 AQL, the criteria are:

$$n = 5 \quad \text{sample size}$$
$$Ac = 0 \quad \text{acceptance number}$$
$$Re = 2 \quad \text{rejection number}$$

If one error was found, the number of defectives would be in the gap between the acceptance and the rejection numbers. Under these conditions, the batch would be accepted but Sam would have to return to normal sampling.

PROCESS STABILITY

Military Standard 105D was designed to control quality through acceptance sampling. Its rules for switching from one level of sampling to another, however, give users an indication of process stability and changing error rates. Rules for shifting from reduced to normal sampling are quite sensitive; they are triggered by minor increases in error rates. Rules for shifting from normal to tightened sampling are more tolerant; they involve rejecting two out of five successive batches. Rules for shutting down production are not triggered unless something serious has happened; having to remain on tightened inspection for ten successive batches won't occur unless major problems have developed.

Although Military Standard 105D gives some indication of shifts in error rates or other elements of a service sector process, control charts are more effective. Control charts help anticipate problems; they are not limited to spotting past mistakes. Details on the preparation and interpretation of control charts are contained in Chapters 15 and 16.

SUMMARY

The basics for Military Standard 105D are relatively simple. They get much more complicated, however, when you start working with reduced sampling. As a consequence, many organizations stick to the normal and tightened sample plans. This approach has less risk of misinterpretation; it also cuts the record keeping. Many people ignore the reduced sampling tables rather than put up with the hassle.

Additional information on sampling with Military Standard 105D is contained in references (2) through (6).

FOOD FOR THOUGHT

Review your own department:

1. Determine whether Military Standard 105D sampling is applicable to any of your work areas such as time cards, typing, personnel reviews, statistical calculations, data entry, database quality or inventory levels. This is only a partial list. Having an in-depth knowledge of your own functions, you should be able to add many more.
2. Ask your boss and your top subordinate to prepare similar lists.
3. Compare.

REFERENCES
1. Military Standard 105D, *Sampling Procedures and Tables for Inspection by Attributes* (Washington, D.C.: U.S. Government Printing Office, April 29, 1963).
2. *Quality Control Training Manual* (State University of Iowa Section, American Society for Quality Control, 1965), Chapter XVI.
3. J. M. Juran, Frank M. Gryna, Jr. and R. S. Bingham, Jr., *Quality Control Handbook,* 3d ed. (New York: McGraw-Hill, 1974), Chapter 24.
4. Ellis R. Ott, *Process Quality Control* (New York: McGraw-Hill, 1975), Chapter 8.
5. Thomas Pyzdek, "Some Tips On the Use of . . . Mil-Std-105D," *Quality,* November 1984, pp. 31–32.
6. Thomas Pyzdek, "Small Lot Sampling Can Comply With Mil-Std-105D," *Quality,* March 1986, pp. 30–31.

Chapter 10

Dodge & Romig Sample Plans

Military Standard 105D[1] provides the user with systematic procedures for controlling quality through sampling. Despite its popularity, however, 105D is not perfect. Its greatest weakness is a tendency to stress producer rather than consumer protection. A sample plan with an AQL of 4.0 percent is designed to accept batches with 4.0 percent defectives 95 percent of the time. A plan with an AQL of 2.5 percent is designed to accept batches with 2.5 percent defectives 95 percent of the time. In both cases, the level of quality that will be accepted 10 percent of the time is not readily identified without referring to the OC Curves in the back of the standard. In the service sector, these defectives can be records, cases, admission forms, motel rooms, memorandums, IRS forms, data entries, letters, etc.; they are flawed, have errors, are not done properly or don't meet the standard.

Dodge & Romig sampling tables[2] stress Lot Tolerance Percent Defective (LTPD) and Average Outgoing Quality Limit (AOQL); they help identify consumer risks. You might call them tools of the consumer advocate.

LTPD, also called RQL, is used by Dodge & Romig tables to identify the percent defectives a sample plan will accept 10 percent of the time. A plan with an LTPD of 5 percent, for example, will accept a lot with 5 percent defectives 10 percent of the time. A plan with an LTPD of 7 percent will accept a lot with 7 percent defectives 10 percent of the time. With Dodge & Romig tables, the stress is on protecting those being audited including clerks, technicians, secretaries, nurses and managers.

The reason for stressing the 10-percent risk of accepting a bad lot is that the Dodge & Romig LTPD tables are based on a 10 percent consumer's risk; they don't specify the producer's risk. If you want to protect the producer (or the worker being audited), you concentrate on the AQL as Military Standard 105D does. If you want to protect the consumer, you concentrate on the LTPD as the Dodge & Romig tables do.

DEFINITIONS

Ac (Acceptance number). Dodge & Romig tables have the same definition for acceptance number as Military Standard 105D. The acceptance number is the maximum number of defectives that can be found in the sample of an acceptable lot or batch.

AOQL (Average Outgoing Quality Limit). The AOQL is the maximum average percent defectives going to the consumer after inspection is complete. According to the Dodge & Romig plans, batches that do not pass the sample plan are subjected to 100-percent inspection; defectives that are identified are replaced. The plan also assumes that 100-percent inspection is 100 percent effective. The fallacy of this assumption was discussed in Chapter 6. Frank Squires[3] places the effectiveness of 100-percent inspection between 80 and 95 percent. Richard Laford[4] sets it around 85 percent and William Latzko[5] sets it around 75. The average effectiveness I observed at the Air Reserve Personnel Center was around 95 percent. The assumption of 100-percent inspection being 100 percent effective is not limited to the Dodge & Romig tables. It is also hidden in Military Standard 105D and many other sampling systems. As a consequence, the limitations of this assumption should not be used as a basis for favoring one of these plans.

Defect. A defect is a characteristic that doesn't meet the standard. With a typewritten letter, for example, one spelling error is a defect. Two spelling errors are two defects. The letter with the two spelling errors, however, is one defective.

Defective. A defective is anything that has one or more defects. In fast foods, a hamburger that is cold, greasy and squashed is a defective; the cold temperature, the greasiness and the squashed appearance are three defects. In the hotel business, a room with no towels, a dirty sink and an unmade bed is a defective. The missing towels, dirty sink and unmade bed are three separate defects.

Figure 10-1. **Dodge & Romig — LTPD Sampling Tables (Modified)**

LTPD = 10.0% Consumer's Risk = .10

Batch Size	Process Average (%) 2.01 – 3.00			3.01 – 4.00			4.01 – 5.00		
	n	Ac	AOQL (%)	*n*	Ac	AOQL (%)	*n*	Ac	AOQL (%)
1 – 20	ALL	0	0	ALL	0	0	ALL	0	0
21 – 50	17	0	1.3	17	0	1.3	17	0	1.3
51 – 100	33	1	1.7	33	1	1.7	33	1	1.7
101 – 200	48	2	2.2	48	2	2.2	60	3	2.4
201 – 300	65	3	2.4	75	4	2.6	85	5	2.7
301 – 400	65	3	2.5	90	5	2.7	100	6	2.9
401 – 500	75	4	2.8	90	5	2.9	110	7	3.2
501 – 600	80	4	3.0	100	6	3.2	125	8	3.3
601 – 800	90	5	3.1	100	6	3.3	140	9	3.4
801 – 1000	90	5	3.2	115	7	3.4	150	10	3.7

Ac = Acceptance number
AOQL = Average Outgoing Quality Limit
LTPD = Lot Tolerance Percent Defective
n = Sample size

Based on: H. F. Dodge and H. G. Romig, *Sampling Inspection Tables,* New York: Wiley, 1944, Table SL-10.

LTPD (Lot Tolerance Percent Defective). In these sample plans, LTPD represents the percent of defectives that will be accepted by the sample plan 10 percent of the time. It shows how much protection is given the consumer. Dodge & Romig sampling tables emphasize this feature. Although not mentioned by Dodge and Romig, the Rejectable Quality Level (RQL) has the same meaning as the LTPD.

Process Average. The process average is the average percent defectives in a series of lots or batches. With the Dodge & Romig sampling plans, the process average must be estimated before you can determine the sampling criteria. Figure 10-1 shows three ranges of process averages. One is for 2.01 to 3.00 percent defectives, one is for 3.01 to 4.00 and one is for 4.01 to 5.00. The unabridged tables located in reference (2) have a wider selection.

Sample Size (*n*). The sample size represents the number of units you remove from the batch and inspect. A similar definition is given in Military Standard 105D.

LTPD SAMPLE PLANS

Harold F. Dodge and Harry G. Romig were pioneers in quality control through sampling. Their sample plans stressed protection of the consumer rather than the producer. A condensed version of one of their LTPD sample plans is shown in Figure 10-1.

The following problem emphasizes differences between the AQL-oriented sample plans of Military Standard 105D and the LTPD-oriented sample plans of Dodge & Romig.

PROBLEM 10-1

In Problem 9-1, we audited a batch of 400 time cards for a subcontractor involved with defense work. It was important that all charges be assigned to contracts that were still open. As a consequence, we set the AQL at 2.5. Using Military Standard 105D, we came up with a sample size of 50 and an acceptance number of 3. Although the LTPD was not calculated in Problem 9-1, the OC Curves in Military Standard 105D show that it was 12.9 percent.

What would the comparable acceptance criteria be using the Dodge & Romig LTPD sample tables?

SOLUTION 10-1

Since we are using LTPD tables, we will refer to Figure 10-1. We selected the sample plan for LTPD = 10.0, which is as close to the 12.9 as we could get with readily available tables. The batch size of 400 falls in the range of 301–400 units. Find this range in the column to the left. Then move to the right until you reach the range of process averages that include 2.5 percent defectives; the process average normally approximates the AQL. Here, 2.5 falls in the range of the first set of process averages (2.01–3.00). The numbers in the block are:

$$n = 65$$
$$Ac = 3$$
$$AOQL = 2.5 \text{ percent}$$

Notice that the sample size of 65 obtained from Figure 10-1 is larger than the sample size of 50 obtained in Problem 9-1. This larger sample requirement is due in part to the lower LTPD we chose; Problem 9-1 had an

LTPD of 12.9 and we now have an LTPD of 10.0. The lower LTPD should give the supervisor more confidence that bad batches of the time cards will be caught; fewer will slip through.

The acceptance number (Ac) is still 3. With a larger sample size and the same acceptance number, the sample plan will be tougher on the people signing the time cards because more of their marginal batches will be rejected.

An AOQL of 2.5 indicates that, over the long term, the average quality of time cards coming out of the inspection operation will not exceed 2.5 percent defectives. If the quality of the time cards gets worse than 2.5 percent defectives, more of them will be subjected to 100-percent inspection. If the quality of the time cards improves, fewer batches will be caught by the sample plan; fewer batches will get 100-percent inspection.

WHY USE LTPD TABLES?

Advantages of the Dodge & Romig LTPD sampling tables include the following:

- LTPD tables clearly identify the risk of accepting bad batches. When using tables with an LTPD of 7 percent, there is a 10-percent chance that a lot with 7 percent defectives will pass as acceptable. When using tables with an LTPD of 5 percent, there is a 10-percent chance that a lot with 5 percent defectives will pass as acceptable. When using the Dodge & Romig tables, the LTPD and the 10-percent consumer risk go together. Although consumer risks above or below 10 percent can be chosen, they seldom are.
- Dodge & Romig LTPD tables identify the Average Outgoing Quality Limit (AOQL). The AOQL provides a worst-case scenario. Chances of the average quality being that poor, after inspection and screening, are low.

Disadvantages of the Dodge & Romig LTPD sampling tables include the following:

- LTPD tables often require more sampling than Military Standard 105D. At least part of this difference occurs because users who are forced to acknowledge the LTPD tend to require reasonably low LTPD numbers; those unaware of its value take what they get. With everything but LTPD and sample size held constant, lower LTPD values result in larger sample sizes.

118 QUALITY SERVICE PAYS: SIX KEYS TO SUCCESS!

- LTPD tables require the user to estimate the process average. At times, this is difficult, especially when a new operation or process is being inspected.
- The Dodge & Romig LTPD tables are not as well known as Military Standard 105D. Many quality engineers I have worked with didn't know that Dodge & Romig tables existed. Of those who had heard of the tables, many were unaware of their advantages and disadvantages. They were, however, familiar with Military Standard 105D; it was specified on their purchase orders.

AOQL SAMPLE PLANS

A second contribution Dodge and Romig made to the art of sampling was their AOQL-type sample plans. These plans help consumers negotiate the level of quality they require. They were used extensively at the Air Reserve Personnel Center when I was there.

Figure 10-2 presents a condensed and modified version of the Dodge & Romig AOQL-oriented sample plans.[2] An illustration of their use is found in the following problem. This segment of the original charts was chosen because it involves an AOQL of 4.0—one of the more common sampling levels used in service industries.

PROBLEM 10-2

In Problem 9-2, 15 travel vouchers were sampled using normal sampling tables from Military Standard 105D. The AQL was 4.0, the sample size was 3 and the acceptance number was 0. How would these acceptance criteria change if you switched to a Dodge & Romig AOQL-type sample plan?

SOLUTION 10-2

The AQL, the AOQL and the process average should come pretty close to each other. Therefore, it is reasonable to use tables for an AOQL of 4.0 and an estimated process average of the same value. Figure 10-2 covers both of these variables.

The batch size of 15 falls within the set of numbers showing a range of 11–50. The process average falls in the 3.21 to 4.00 column on the right. Based on this data, the sampling criteria are:

Sample size = 8
Acceptance number = 0
LTPD = 23
AOQL = 4.0 (given)

Here, the sample size is more than twice as large as the one in Problem 9-2. The acceptance number is the same.

Figure 10-2 also shows that the LTPD is 23; a batch that is 23 percent defective will be accepted 10 percent of the time. Although backup data is not shown in this book, the LTPD is 54 when you use the Military Standard 105D plan found in Problem 9-2. Then, a batch containing 54 percent defectives would be accepted 10 percent of the time. When the acceptance number is held constant, larger sample sizes give the consumer more protection.

Figure 10-2. **Dodge & Romig — AOQL Sampling Tables (Modified)**

LTPD = 4.0% Consumer's Risk = 10%

Batch Size	\multicolumn{3}{c}{Process Average (%)}						
	\multicolumn{3}{c}{1.61 – 2.40}	\multicolumn{3}{c}{2.41 – 3.20}	\multicolumn{3}{c}{3.21 – 4.00}
	n	Ac	LTPD (%)	n	Ac	LTPD (%)	n	Ac	LTPD (%)
1 – 10	ALL	0	—	ALL	0	—	ALL	0	—
11 – 50	8	0	23	8	0	23	8	0	23
51 – 100	8	0	24	17	1	21	17	1	21
101 – 200	19	1	20	19	1	20	19	1	20
201 – 300	20	1	19	31	2	17	31	2	17
301 – 400	32	2	16	32	2	16	43	3	15
401 – 500	32	2	16	32	2	16	44	3	15
501 – 600	32	2	16	45	3	15	60	4	13
601 – 800	33	2	16	46	3	14	60	4	13
801 – 1000	46	3	14	60	4	13	75	5	12

Ac = Acceptance number
AOQL = Average Outgoing Quality Limit
LTPD = Lot Tolerance Percent Defective
n = Sample size

Based on: H. F. Dodge and H. G. Romig, *Sampling Inspection Tables,* New York: Wiley, 1944, Table SA-4.0.

WHY USE AOQL TABLES?

Advantages of the Dodge & Romig AOQL sampling tables include the following:

- AOQL tables identify the Average Outgoing Quality Limit (AOQL). It is handy to know the worst average quality the system will allow. In addition, the AOQL provides a worst-case scenario. Chances of the average quality being as poor as the AOQL, after inspection and "perfect" screening, are low.
- LTPD information is shown as part of the AOQL tables. As a consequence, you know the highest percentage of defectives that will be accepted 10 percent of the time. When the sampling criteria show that the LTPD is 23 percent, you know that a batch with 23 percent defectives will be accepted approximately 10 percent of the time.

Dodge & Romig AOQL sampling tables and Dodge & Romig LTPD sampling tables have similar disadvantages when compared to Military Standard 105D:

- Dodge & Romig AOQL sampling tables often require larger samples than Military Standard 105D; this was illustrated by Problem 10-2.
- They require some knowledge of the process average; an estimate of the process average is needed before the tables can be used.
- The Dodge & Romig tables are not as widely available as Military Standard 105D.

Additional information on the Dodge & Romig approach to sampling is contained in references (6) through (9).

SUMMARY

The Dodge & Romig sampling tables are effective at catching poor work (LTPD) and identifying the worst average level of quality that will reach the customer after screening (AOQL). The customer may be the supervisor, the department next door, people who use the typing pool or a patient being admitted to the hospital.

The main weakness of the Dodge & Romig sampling systems is their tendency to disrupt production. When defective batches are identified by the plan, they have to undergo 100-percent screening. In addition, defective work must be replaced; this adds to the record keeping. This problem also applies to Military Standard 105D but is less applicable to Continuous Sample Plan CSP-1. More information on CSP-1 will be given in the next chapter.

FOOD FOR THOUGHT

Explain LTPD, AOQL and AQL to two of your customers and two of your suppliers. Then ask if they would like to use sample plans based on the LTPD, the AOQL or the AQL.

1. Which type of plan did the customers prefer?
2. Which type of plan did the suppliers prefer?

Customers can be people you work for or people you supply. Suppliers can be people who work for you or people who provide you with services—including information.

REFERENCES
1. Military Standard 105D, *Sampling Procedures and Tables for Inspection by Variables* (Washington D.C.: U.S. Government Printing Office, April 29, 1963).
2. Harold F. Dodge and Harry G. Romig, *Sampling Inspection Tables* (New York: Wiley, 1944).
3. Frank H. Squires, "To Sample or Not to Sample," *Quality Management & Engineering,* April 1974, pp. 20–23.
4. Richard J. Laford, "Don't Settle for More Inspectors," *Quality,* January 1986, p. 46.
5. William J. Latzko, *Quality and Productivity for Bankers and Financial Managers* (Milwaukee, WI: ASQC Quality Press, 1986), p. 89.
6. Western Electric Company, *Statistical Quality Control Handbook,* 11th ed. (Charlotte, NC: Delmar Printing, 1985), pp. 237–265.
7. J. M. Juran, Frank M. Gryna, Jr. and R. S. Bingham, Jr., *Quality Control Handbook*, 3d ed. (New York: McGraw-Hill, 1974), Chapter 24.
8. A. C. Rosander, *Applications of Quality Control in the Service Industries* (Milwaukee, WI: ASQC Quality Press, 1985), Chapter 21.
9. Eugene L. Grant and Richard S. Leavenworth, *Statistical Quality Control* (New York: McGraw-Hill, 1988), pp. 433–444.

Chapter 11

Continuous Sampling

Military Standard 105D and the Dodge & Romig sample plans are excellent tools for controlling processes and materials. They are also useful for controlling the output of administrative personnel such as secretaries, data-entry clerks, bank tellers and even supervisors. Their main shortcoming, in the area of administrative quality control, is that they slow down production.

Continuous sampling, on the other hand, is designed to control continuous processes, not batches. We introduced it to the Air Reserve Personnel Center in Denver, Colorado, as part of a record cleanup project. Later, we introduced it to the Air Force Accounting and Finance Center to help improve records, calculations and databases. It has also been used by manufacturing companies like MiniScribe[1] for controlling manufacturing processes.

Continuous Sampling Plan CSP-1[2] is not as well known as Military Standard 105D or the Dodge & Romig sampling tables. It is, however, effective for helping service companies control the quality of their production, including personnel records, filing, typing, performance reviews, customer contacts, interviews, motel housekeeping and customer service.

WHAT IS CONTINUOUS SAMPLING?

Continuous sampling is a technique for inspecting vouchers, records, transactions, cases and materials as they are produced. As an example, continuous sampling can be used for auditing a technician who is working on expense accounts, statistical calculations, data-entry work, hospital records, bank transactions, travel vouchers or insurance claims.

When using continuous sampling, the audit process starts with 100-percent inspection. After a predetermined number of consecutive, error-free cases passes inspection, the auditor goes to reduced sampling. The operation stays on reduced sampling until an error is detected. Then the reviewer reverts to 100-percent inspection, which is continued until another predetermined number of consecutive cases passes inspection.

DEFINITIONS

Like any statistical system, continuous sampling has its own set of definitions. Some are common to other sampling systems; many are not. A few of the critical definitions follow.

AOQL (Average Outgoing Quality Limit). With continuous sampling, AOQL has the same definition it did with the Dodge & Romig tables. The AOQL is the highest average percent defectives that can be expected to reach your customers when you follow the plan—assuming error-free inspection.

Clearance Number. The clearance number is the number of consecutive, error-free items that must be reviewed before reduced sampling can be initiated. Most charts and tables identify the clearance number with the symbol i.

Continuous Sampling. Continuous sampling involves sampling a continuous operation without having clearly defined lots. The system starts with 100-percent inspection. Workers qualify for reduced sampling by producing the quantity of error-free units that equals the clearance number.

Fraction of Production. The fraction of production is the fraction of work reviewed under reduced inspection. It is identified by the symbol f. If $f = 1/4$, 25 percent of the work is sampled. If $f = 1/10$, 10 percent of the work is sampled.

Reduced Sampling. When all units are audited, you have 100-percent inspection. When a fraction of the units are reviewed, you have reduced inspection. With reduced inspection, the fraction of production (f) determines how often you take a sample.

Examples illustrating the use of these variables are shown near the end of this chapter.

ADVANTAGES OF CONTINUOUS SAMPLING

Advantages of continuous sampling include the following:

- Causes less disruption
- Facilitates quick response to problems
- Helps users understand sampling
- Recognizes quality performance
- Identifies special needs
- Provides goals
- Places inspection money where the problems are

Causes less disruption

Many batch-oriented sample plans disrupt production. They are most effective with receiving inspection; they also work well with large batches that may accumulate over a period of many hours or even days. Both Military Standard 105D and Dodge & Romig systems slow down production when large batches are rejected; these batches are supposed to get 100-percent review or sorting. With continuous sampling, a single random sample is used to determine whether to continue on reduced sampling. As a consequence, batches are usually small; large accumulations are not necessary. Disruption of production is minimized.

Facilitates quick response to problems

Another advantage of continuous sampling is that the small batches help expedite the identification and correction of problems. When samples are taken every hour or less, feedback is much more prompt and workers are much more likely to remember what they did wrong. With regular batch sampling, it often takes days to go from doing the work to seeing the results. By then, the workers forget the logic behind their actions and can't explain their mistakes.

Helps users to understand sampling

Once it is implemented, continuous sampling is fairly easy to understand. There are only two items to remember: the clearing interval and the lot size for reduced sampling. Workers and auditors can use the system without understanding technical terms like the Average Outgoing Quality Limit.

Recognizes quality performance

With continuous sampling, it is easy to identify quality-oriented workers; those who make no errors will stay on reduced sampling. Supervisors can use this information during performance reviews; it is politically hazardous to chide a subordinate for low quality production without having the numbers to back you up. Supervisors can also use the results from continuous sampling when selecting quality-oriented people for more responsible assignments. Intuitive judgments about whose quality is best can result in supervisors being challenged and subordinates being disillusioned.

Identifies special needs

When individuals are unable to qualify for reduced inspection, the need for corrective action surfaces. With some, this involves a need for additional training. With others, motivation is required. Still others need medical assistance. (For instance, assignments requiring good eyesight are not appropriate for workers with eye problems.) Either the problems have to be resolved or the workers reassigned. Continuous sampling helps identify these situations.

Provides goals

As quality-oriented workers are recognized for their performance, others will strive to gain similar recognition. Workers can set their own goals; those unable to attain them can ask for additional training. In addition, supervisors can have goal-setting sessions with workers who stay on 100-percent inspection too long.

Places inspection money where the problems are

One of the biggest advantages of continuous sampling is that it puts inspection dollars where the problems are. Workers who do quality work don't require intensive monitoring. Time saved when workers qualify for reduced sampling can be used to help their less capable associates. The savings can also be used to fund preventive measures like improving training, procedures and systems.

DISADVANTAGES OF CONTINUOUS SAMPLING

Disadvantages of continuous sampling include the following:

- It is different.
- Inspection work load varies.
- Paperwork is necessary.
- Reasonable quality is required.
- Management support is critical.

It is different

Being different has its advantages and disadvantages. Some people are always looking for something new. Others resist change. In the workplace, it is common for people to prefer doing something wrong over trying something new. If they don't understand it, they don't like it. Since continuous sampling is different, it can be misunderstood.

Inspection work load varies

The work load for inspectors and auditors is high during qualification when 100-percent inspection is required. It drops off once everyone qualifies for reduced sampling. In addition, surges in the inspection requirement occur when errors are found and workers have to requalify for reduced inspection. Similar problems exist, however, when batches are rejected and 100-percent screening is required under the Dodge & Romig and Military Standard 105D sample plans.

Paperwork is necessary

Many people hate paperwork; they would rather get on with the job. There are times when this is a legitimate complaint; you don't want a system that eats up the profits through excessive record keeping. At the Air Force Accounting and Finance Center, our rule of thumb was: "Continuous sampling is usually economical where the time spent inspecting each unit exceeds two minutes." At MiniScribe, the rule of thumb was one minute.[1]

Both organizations wanted to ensure that the ratio of "time spent on paperwork" to "time spent on inspection" didn't get out of hand.

Reasonable quality is required

The need for reasonable quality can be considered an advantage or a disadvantage. If the quality of a worker is not equal to or better than the AOQL, that individual will have a difficult time getting off 100-percent inspection. The advantage is that problems become obvious. The disadvantage is that 100-percent inspection is expensive; in addition, it is often inefficient.

Management support is critical

Continuous sampling was installed in one directorate of a large government agency. The colonel in charge liked the system; he was particularly impressed by the way it helped identify his best and worst producers. When his tenure was up, however, his replacement let it die a painful death. Few quality control systems work well without management support.

CHOOSING A CONTINUOUS SAMPLE PLAN

Continuous sampling plan CSP-1 uses three variables: AOQL, clearance number and fraction to be inspected. If one is changed, one of the others has to be adjusted. Since each can be changed over a wide range, however, the variety of possible plans is endless. For simplicity's sake, this text covers only three sets of sampling criteria. Once you have mastered these, and want to explore others, refer to references (2) through (9) and (11).

Variables for continuous sampling that can be used for most service area applications are shown in Table 11-1.

The following problems will help you understand Table 11-1 and show you how to use it.

PROBLEM 11-1

An insurance technician is calculating the costs of small policies received from the field. The quality control department is in the process of implementing a continuous sample plan in this area. The error rate for the

Table 11-1. Variables for Continuous Sampling

Plan	AOQL (%)	Clearance Number (i)	Fraction to be Inspected (f)
1. For low risk production	10.0	10	1/10
2. For medium risk production	5.0	14	1/5
3. For high risk production	2.0	30	1/4

work is not known, but management will be satisfied if no more than 10 percent of the policies leaving the office have errors.

How would you set up a continuous sampling plan for this inspection operation?

SOLUTION 11-1

In this case, the low risk sample plan should be acceptable. It provides an Average Outgoing Quality Limit (AOQL) of 10.0 because management said they would be satisfied if the policies with errors were kept under 10 percent. Here, the key variables are:

$$\text{AOQL (\%)} = 10.0$$
$$\text{Clearance number } (i) = 10$$
$$\text{Fraction of production } (f) = 1/10$$

It is necessary to audit every policy until the technician qualifies for reduced sampling. This requires producing 10 consecutive error-free policies.

Once the technician qualifies for reduced sampling, it is necessary to audit 1 out of every 10 policies. The sample to be audited, however, must be selected at random. When selecting this random sample, it is necessary that each of the 10 policies has an equal chance of being inspected. Picking the first or the tenth sample from the batch each time can cause questionable results; the sample is too predictable. Procedures for selecting random samples are covered in Chapter 6. Additional material on random sampling is contained in reference (6).

Table 11-2. Simulated Sampling Sequence (Problem 11-1)

Sample Sequence	Results (OK or not OK)	Action Required
1 – 9	OK	10 consecutive OK samples are needed before you can qualify for reduced sampling. This requirement hasn't been met. Continue with 100-percent review of the work.
10	not OK	The policy had an error; it is necessary to restart the counting.
11	not OK	The policy had an error; it is necessary to restart the counting.
12 – 21	OK	10 consecutive samples were OK. The technician qualifies for reduced sampling.
22 – 31	—	10 consecutive samples are accumulated. Take a random sample. In this case, assume policy #25 was chosen.
25	OK	Continue sampling 1 out of 10 of the policies.
32 – 41	—	10 consecutive samples are accumulated. Take a random sample. In this case, assume policy #40 was chosen.
40	not OK	This sample had an error and didn't pass inspection. Now, it is necessary to return to 100-percent sampling, starting with sample #32. The new count starts after the last bad sample, which was #40.
32 – 39	OK	This is part of the screening process. It is similar to screening a batch that failed under the Dodge & Romig sample plan. Start the review with the first unit in the batch and end it with the unit in front of the one that had the error.
41 – 50	OK	Policy #41 follows right behind the unit that had the error. 10 consecutive samples are good. This requalifies the technician for reduced sampling.

If the random sample has no errors, release the 10 policies and wait for the next 10 to accumulate. If the random sample is defective, return to 100-percent sampling until the technician requalifies for reduced sampling; the 100-percent sampling includes inspecting the other 9 policies from the batch that failed.

Table 11-2 simulates a sampling sequence. It shows what happens with each sample and the action taken by the reviewers.

PROBLEM 11-2

You are auditing the work of a technician who calculates the relocation pay given military personnel when they are moved by the government. Your organization has been getting a lot of heat in this area. Budgets are tight and the organization can't afford overpayments. On the other hand, fairness is important. Because of these considerations, the commander wants to ensure that less than 2 percent of the payments are off by more than a dollar. Errors of less than a dollar are not considered defects.

SOLUTION 11-2

The key variables are:

$$AOQL\ (\%) = 2.0$$
$$\text{Clearance number } (i) = 30 \text{ (from Table 11-1)}$$
$$\text{Fraction of production } (f) = 1/4 \text{ (from Table 11-1)}$$

It is necessary to audit every payment voucher until the technician qualifies for reduced sampling. This requires producing 30 consecutive error-free vouchers. Once the technician qualifies for reduced sampling, it is necessary to audit 1 out of every 4 vouchers. The sample to be audited, however, must be selected at random.

After the technician qualifies for reduced sampling, accumulate the next 4 vouchers the technician completes. Then audit 1 at random. (Procedures for selecting a random sample are covered in Chapter 6.) Notice that the sample numbers selected in these problems vary in an unpredictable manner; they are random.

If the random sample has no errors, release the 4 vouchers and wait for the next 4 to accumulate. If the random sample is defective, return to 100-percent sampling until the technician requalifies for reduced sampling.

Table 11-3. **Simulated Sampling Sequence (Problem 11-2)**

Sample Sequence	Results (OK or not OK)	Action Required
1 – 12	OK	30 consecutive OK samples are needed before you can qualify for reduced sampling. Continue at 100 percent.
13	not OK	Voucher #13 had an error. It is necessary to start counting again.
14 – 41	OK	Not enough continuous OKs to qualify for reduced sampling. Continue 100-percent sampling.
42	not OK	Another error was detected. Continue 100-percent sampling. Resume counting the clearing sequence with #43.
43 – 72	OK	30 consecutive samples are OK. Reduced sampling can begin.
73 – 76	—	Four consecutive samples are ready for review. In this case assume #74 randomly selected.
74	OK	Random sample was OK. Resume sampling 1 out of 4.
77 – 80	—	The 4 vouchers are ready for sample selection. In this case, assume #77 was selected.
77	not OK	This sample had an error and didn't pass inspection; it is necessary to return to 100-percent sampling, starting with sample #78.
78 – 107	OK	There are 30 error-free vouchers in a row. Resume reduced sampling with voucher #108.

Table 11-3 simulates the sampling sequence. It shows what happens with each sample and the action taken by the reviewers.

HOW DO DIFFERENT PLANS STACK UP?

Table 11-4 was developed to give readers an idea of the advantages and disadvantages of sample plans discussed thus far. Some of the ratings are subjective, some are an educated guess and some will be challenged by other statisticians. Don't accept these ratings blindly; learn enough about the sample plans to make up your own mind. Meanwhile, the ratings will give you guidance on which plans to try out first.

Table 11-4. Comparing Sample Plans

Characteristic	MIL-STD-105D	Dodge-Romig	CSP-1
Evaluating batches	GOOD	GOOD	FAIR
Evaluating continuous processes	FAIR	FAIR	GOOD
Evaluating an individual's work	FAIR	FAIR	GOOD
Responding to problems	SLOW	SLOW	FASTER
Receiving inspection	GOOD	GOOD	POOR
Protecting consumers	POOR	GOOD	GOOD
Protecting workers	GOOD	FAIR	GOOD
Minimizing interference with production	FAIR	FAIR	GOOD
Increasing sampling when problems arise	FAIR-GOOD	POOR	GOOD
Short-run evaluations	GOOD	GOOD	POOR
Long-run evaluations	GOOD	GOOD	GOOD
Broad-based usage	GREAT	FAIR-GOOD	FAIR
Consistent inspection work load	FAIR	FAIR	FAIR

SUMMARY

Continuous sampling under the rules of CSP-1 helps supervisors keep track of the quality of work produced by their subordinates. It can also reduce the cost of sampling. The system is most effective for AOQLs between 4 and 10. With AOQLs much lower than 4 percent, the clearing sequence tends to be large; workers can get discouraged before they qualify for reduced sampling. In addition, the percentage inspected tends to be large, even when you are on reduced sampling. With AOQLs greater than 10, you show a willingness to accept a relatively large percentage of defectives.

The greatest advantage of continuous sampling is that it helps you put your inspection dollars where your problems are. Why use the same level of sampling on all employees? Those doing quality work require less auditing.

Additional information on continuous sampling is found in references (1) through (11).

FOOD FOR THOUGHT

Review the moderate and high volume functions of your department where the quality is important. This could include correspondence, data entry, filing, personnel evaluations or any other administrative activity. If you can find an area where continuous sampling looks feasible, try it out for one month.

1. If you are currently inspecting that area, use the plan with an AOQL comparable to the average quality you currently have.
2. If you are not sampling the area, use the 10-percent AOQL just to get a feel for the system.
3. After using the plan for one month, compare your results with those you were getting previously.

REFERENCES
1. "Continuous Sampling: Spending Inspection Dollars Where They're Most Needed," *Quality Control Supervisor's Bulletin,* July 25, 1985, pp. 1–2.
2. Kenneth S. Stephens, *How to Perform Continuous Production* (Milwaukee, WI: ASQC Quality Press, 1979).
3. Harold F. Dodge, "Sampling Plans for Continuous Production," *Industrial Quality Control,* November 1947.
4. Western Electric Company, *Statistical Quality Control Handbook,"* 11th ed. (Charlotte, NC: Delmar Printing, 1985).
5. Eugene L. Grant and Richard S. Leavenworth, *Statistical Quality Control* (New York: McGraw-Hill, 1988), pp. 520–534.
6. J. M. Juran, Frank M. Gryna, Jr. and R. S. Bingham, Jr., *Quality Control Handbook,* 3d ed. (New York: McGraw-Hill, 1974), Chapter 24.
7. Acheson J. Duncan, *Quality Control and Industrial Statistics* (Homewood, IL: Richard D. Irwin, 1959), pp. 299–312.

8. Harold F. Dodge and M. N. Torrey, "Continuous Sampling Inspection Plans," *Annals of Mathematical Statistics,* 1943.
9. H107, Single-level Continuous Sampling Procedures and Tables for Inspection by Attributes (Washington, D.C.: U.S. Government Printing Office, 1959).
10. H106, Multi-level Continuous Sampling Procedures and Tables for Inspection by Attributes (Washington, D.C.: U.S. Government Printing Office, 1958).
11. *Military Standard 1235B, Single- and Multi-Level Continuous Sampling Procedures and Tables for Inspection by Attributes* (Washington, D.C.: U.S. Government Printing Office, 1981).
12. Harold D. Dodge and M. N. Torrey, "Additional Continuous Sampling Inspection Plans," *Industrial Quality Control*, March 1951, pp. 7–12.

Chapter 12

Key 3: Mastering the Basic Tools

Once you understand the fundamentals of quality service, it's time to study other basic quality assurance tools. Many of them come from the manufacturing sector. Most, however, are applicable to service industries and the service sector of manufacturing plants. It doesn't matter where the tools come from; knowing how to use them is what counts. Those unfamiliar with the proper tools are like clerks with mechanical calculators trying to compete with those using personal computers. The first group may do a creditable job, but they have a hard time keeping up, and they usually make more errors.

Chapters 13 through 19 show you some of the tools that are available and how they can be used. An understanding of these chapters will help you answer the following questions:

- How can you identify trends?
- How does variation affect you?
- Where can you use variables control charts?
- Where can you use attributes control charts?
- How can you make your standards objective?
- Are you using the right processes and products?
- How efficient are your service operations?

How can you identify trends?

The most common approach involves trend charts. They are easier to understand than control charts and require less math. As a consequence, they are more popular, especially in the service sector. Techniques for preparing and interpreting trend charts are shown in Chapter 13.

How does variation affect you?

Almost everything varies. No two people, snowflakes or fingerprints are alike. Types of variation that influence quality in the service sector include person-to-person, project-to-project and time-to-time. Variation is also affected by equipment changes, procedure adjustments and environmental shifts. Two tools that will help you spot the presence of change are histograms and Multi-Vari analyses; they are discussed in Chapter 14.

Where can you use variables control charts?

Have you thought of evaluating how fast your people respond to customer requests? Or employee suggestions? Or field inquiries? Would you like to control task completion times? Or absenteeism? Or productivity? Variables control charts can be used for all of these—and more. Procedures for setting up and interpreting them are discussed in Chapter 15.

Where can you use attributes control charts?

Would you like to get better control of the percentage of defects, late deliveries, erroneous billings, designs needing change, faulty paperwork, time your computer is down, erroneous money transfers, incorrect teller transactions or technician calculations that have to be redone? Attributes control charts can be used for these operations—and many more. Procedures for setting up and interpreting attributes control charts are discussed in Chapter 16.

How can you make your standards objective?

How good are your employees? Capability studies will help you answer this question. Managers who haven't investigated capability studies are like amateur aviators plowing through visibility-zero fog with no knowledge of instrument flying. First, they are not using the best available training. Second, their ignorance can be costly.

Most organizations have production requirements; fewer have quality standards. Both are needed. Without them, many employees have no idea of what you expect of them; capability studies help resolve this problem. Procedures for running and evaluating them are contained in Chapter 17.

Are you using the right processes and products?

There is never one ultimate process or one perfect product. As you progress in the field of quality assurance, you will find there are many ways of doing things. Are your high-quality workers using different procedures than your marginal employees? Find out. Then compare the two procedures using techniques explained in Chapter 18. This exercise, by itself, is apt to show you that quality pays—and can be measured—even in the service sector.

How efficient are your service operations?

During the 1980s, there has been rapid progress in the development of tools and procedures for the service sector. Has your company benefited from the change? Flow charts and Ishikawa diagrams will help you take a new look at old processes. There may be better ways of doing things—and Chapter 19 will help you find them.

SERVICE INDUSTRY VS MANUFACTURING TOOLS

Key 3 will expose many people to procedures and techniques they considered foreign to the service sector. If they are foreign, it is because few people have taken the time to discover how tools of the manufacturing plant can be applied to service areas.

Similar problems arise when people are exposed to new tools and procedures coming from other industries. As an example, techniques developed in banks often have a place in the insurance, hotel, data processing and transportation industries—and also in the government. It is easy to sit back and say, "Those tools don't apply to my type of work. We are different." In reality, this resistance to new ideas screens out many opportunities. Those who can take the tools that others have developed and adapt them to their own unique situation have an edge on their less adventurous competition; they are the ones who prove that quality service pays.

Food for Thought

Look at the major operations within your department and see if you can answer the following questions:

1. What is the level of quality your workers are capable of achieving for each operation?
2. Which operations are getting better and which are getting worse?
3. Which operations or tasks would you like to control better?
4. Can you determine whether proposed changes will be for the better or for the worse?
5. Which tasks have you flow-charted during the last five years?

Chapter 13

Trend Charts

Trend charts are widely used in the service sector. They help management evaluate whether critical variables are getting better or worse without wading through confusing tables and voluminous reports. To paraphrase an old Chinese proverb, "A trend chart may be worth 1000 words."

Typical applications for trend charts include the following:

- At the Air Force Accounting and Finance Center, we used trend charts to monitor the quality of services provided by satellite accounting offices.
- In the insurance sector, Rebecca L. Huls[1] used trend charts to monitor "work produced" and "sales."
- At IBM, Joseph P. King[2] used trend charts to monitor "cost of quality."
- At General Dynamics, H. C. Hays[3] used trend charts to monitor service reports (percent answered on time).
- At the Continental Illinois National Bank of Chicago, Charles A. Aubrey, II,[4] used trend charts to monitor "defect rate" and "average investigation turnaround time."

WHAT ARE TREND CHARTS?

Trend charts are what you get when you plot key variables against time; they are generally used to identify trends. Although they are popular and show up in many management briefings, they may be called by different names. At the Air Force Accounting and Finance Center, we called them trend charts because of their function. The Basic Training Review section of *Quality* magazine has given them the same name.[5] D. A. Guyton and J. Tang of Bell Laboratories[6] use the term "quality trend charts" but expand them to include additional statistical data like interval estimates. A. C. Rosander[7] calls them "time plots," but includes "Shewhartian" control charts in the same category. W. Edwards Deming[8] calls them "run charts," but doesn't include a goal or standard for the variable being plotted.

HOW ARE TREND CHARTS USED?

Management and staff personnel often use trend charts to monitor key variables to see whether their systems are working. The higher up you go is the organization, the more systems you have to monitor and the more you must depend on visual aids. Trend charts are excellent visual aids. Experienced observers can glance at them and tell whether an operation is running smoothly, headed for trouble or swamped by customer complaints. Common patterns to look for when reviewing a trend chart include the following:

- The "Happy Days" pattern (Figure 13-1)
- The "Yo-Yo" pattern (Figure 13-2)
- The "Early Warning" pattern (Figure 13-3)
- The "Get Well" pattern (Figure 13-4)
- The "Sad Sack" pattern (Figure 13-5)
- The "Why Plot?" pattern (Figure 13-6)
- The "Jump-Shift" pattern (Figure 13-7)
- The "Freak" or "Oddball" pattern (Figure 13-8)
- The "Déjà Vu" pattern (Figure 13-9)
- The "Total Chaos" pattern (Figure 13-10)

These patterns are found at many boardroom presentations; they are also found in technical literature. Although the patterns are covered in this chapter on trend charts, most of them are also found in control charts. (Control charts are covered in Chapters 15 and 16.) The main difference between the two types of charts is that trend charts generally show standards, specifications or goals; control charts generally show control limits.

The patterns shown here are only a few of those that are possible; you may think of others. Each of the patterns discussed in this chapter, however, has unique characteristics; each has its own story to tell.

The "Happy Days" Pattern

There are times when everything looks great. That's when the "Happy Days" pattern appears.

Characteristics of the "Happy Days" pattern are: all entries are comfortably above the standard, no unfavorable trends are visible and data points are scattered randomly (there is no clearly defined pattern). Figure 13-1 is a typical example. This pattern is common for operations that are "in control" or running smoothly. As a consequence, the "Happy Days" pattern is found in many trend charts, as well as control charts like the one on absenteeism (region E) found in reference (9).

When your operation has trend charts or control charts like the one in Figure 13-1, you can sleep easy. The biggest problem with "Happy Days"

Figure 13-1. **Trend Chart for an Operation That Is In Control ("Happy Days" Pattern)**

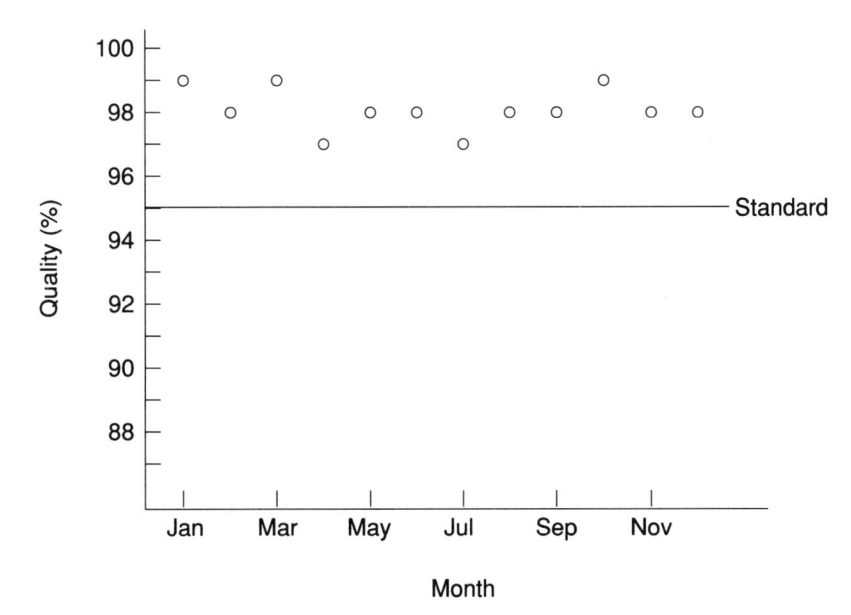

charts is they promote complacency; in many cases, complacency leads to deterioration.

Most processes can be improved. If you have a "Happy Days" pattern, and all data is much better than the standard, determine whether a tougher standard is justified; if so, make it tighter. You might also look at the production numbers. True productivity is a combination of volume and quality. Neither should be stressed at the exclusion of the other; neither should be ignored.

The "Yo-Yo" Pattern

When a chart has excessive ups and downs, with many of the points falling below the standard, it has a "Yo-Yo" pattern like the one in Figure 13-2.

This type of chart is seen when standards are too tight, operations are too loose or both. When a "Yo-Yo" chart is observed by management and the standards are not being met, capability studies can be used to help identify the problem.

Capability studies help determine whether the goal, standard or specification is reasonable. They can also be used to find out whether high variability is due to a few poor workers or the group as a whole. In either

Figure 13-2. **Trend Chart for an Operation That Is Out of Control ("Yo-Yo" Pattern)**

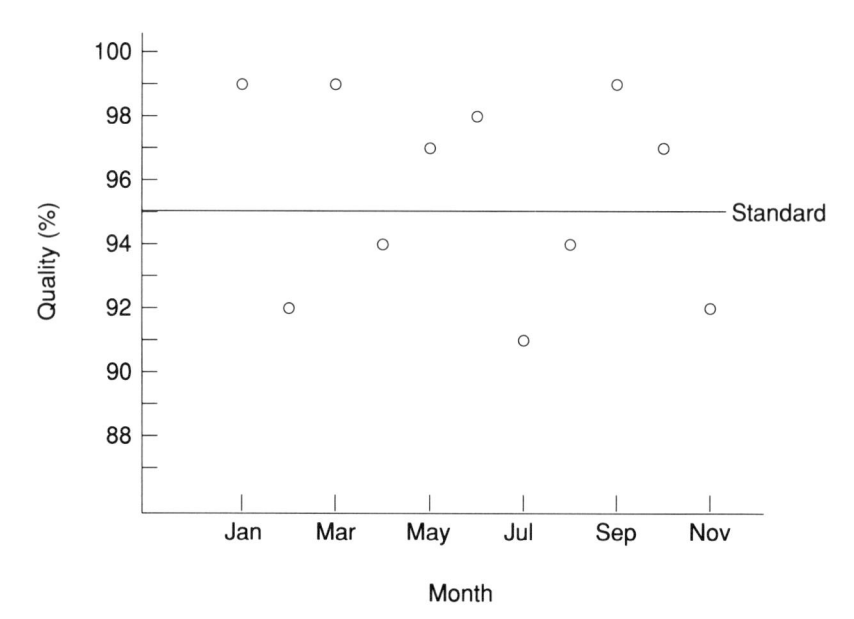

Trend Charts 145

case, corrective action is necessary. Information on capability studies and techniques for raising the capability of the system are discussed in Chapter 17.

Aubrey's chart on productivity in a banking environment appears to have a typical "Yo-Yo" pattern.[10] Variability of this magnitude makes it difficult to interpret the data. With "Yo-Yo" data, *trends* are easier to identify when 12-month averages are plotted instead of individual points.[11]

The "Early Warning" Pattern

The "Early Warning" pattern, shown in Figure 13-3, alerts management to the probability of impending problems.

Quality problems often develop slowly. "Early Warning" trend charts help management spot unfavorable trends before disaster strikes. The points in Figure 13-3 are not random; they have a distinct pattern. Successive lows are lower than previous lows; successive highs are lower than previous highs. These are the elements of a falling trend.

In this illustration, the trend should have been clear by August; by then, a stepwise downward trend was identifiable. Armed with this information,

Figure 13-3. **Trend Chart for an Operation That Drifts ("Early Warning" Pattern)**

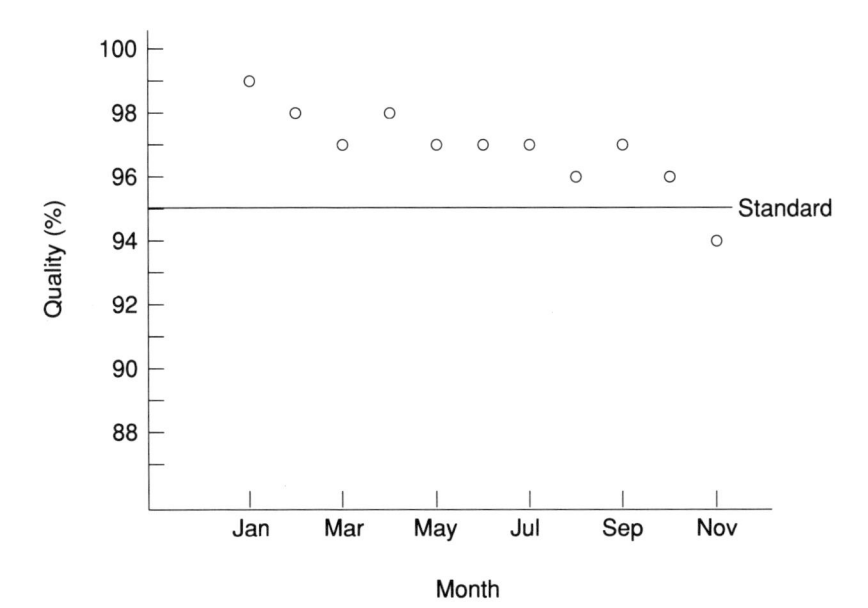

management could have initiated corrective action before the quality level dropped below the standard.

The "Get Well" Pattern

"Early Warning" charts, like the one in Figure 13-3, are bad news. Bosses need to be aware of impending problems, however, so that corrective action can be initiated in a timely manner. "Get Well" charts, like the one in Figure 13-4, are good news; they make bosses aware of impending successes. Armed with this information, supervision can anticipate accomplishments and acknowledge them promptly.

Why would management be happy about a chart where all but one of the points fall below the standard? Because the trend is upward—the problem is being resolved. Corrective action, however, seldom clears up problems overnight. This is particularly true where training is involved; training takes time.

Patterns like the ones in Figures 13-3 and 13-4 were fairly common at the Air Force Accounting and Finance Center. The center was monitoring the quality of outlying Air Force finance offices. When the "Early Warning"

Figure 13-4. **Trend Chart for an Operation That Is Improving ("Get Well" Pattern)**

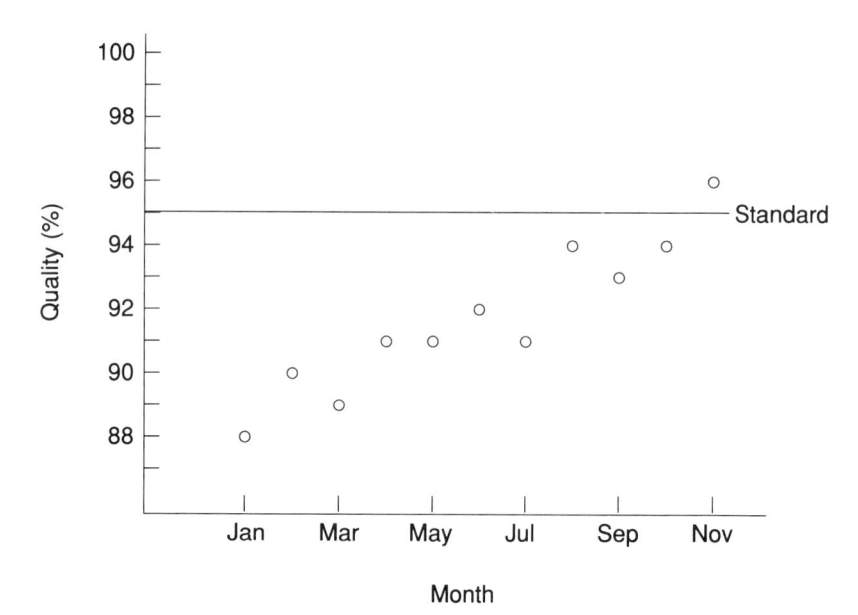

pattern was noted, the bases were alerted and corrective action was requested. Monthly comments were made until it appeared that the situation was in control.

Bases showing "Get Well" patterns, even though performance was below standard, caused less concern than bases with "Early Warning" patterns. The Finance Center let them solve their own problems as long as the trend was upward.

The "Sad Sack" Pattern

The "Sad Sack" chart pattern (Figure 13-5) gives management many sleepless nights.

With the "Sad Sack" pattern, quality is bad and isn't getting better. Extensive training may be required to get out of this totally unacceptable situation. Corrective action, however, is not always as difficult as the chart implies. In some cases, the standard is too demanding. In some cases, the inspectors are too severe. In other cases, the organization is actually having problems.

The use of capability studies for setting standards keeps most "Sad Sack" situations from occurring. There is no value in having unattainable

Figure 13-5. **Trend Chart for an Operation That Is In Trouble ("Sad Sack" Pattern)**

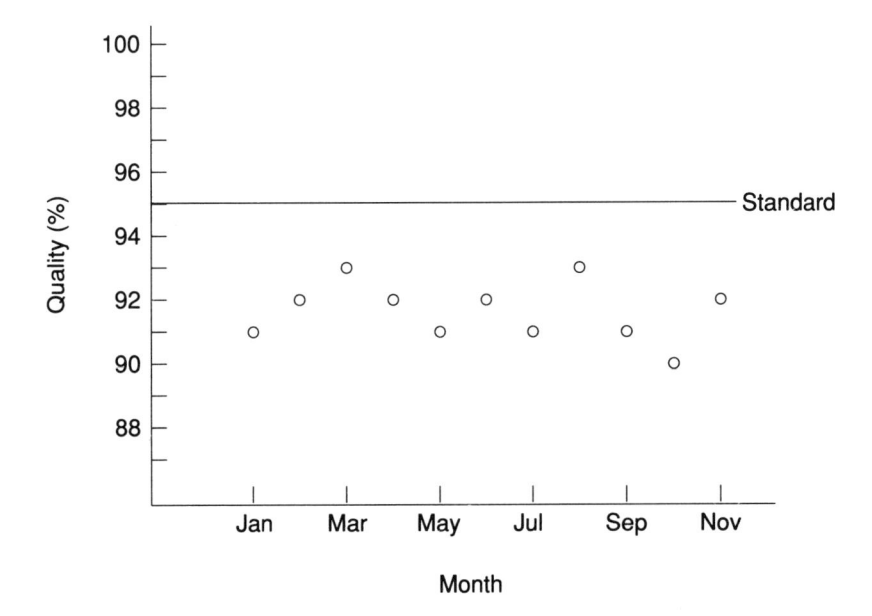

standards. If management requires quality better than the group's capability, management must also supply the tools. This could involve a better environment, additional training, a more realistic work load or even automation.

Environment affects quality. Corrective action could include better lighting, better temperature-and-humidity controls, or quieter surroundings.

Training is a traditional tool for attaining better quality. In most cases it pays for itself.

Work loads also affect quality. Excessive backlogs often encourage workers to take shortcuts. Insufficient backlogs often result in people slowing down to make the work last. Unfortunately, slowing down doesn't always lead to better quality.

Automation often helps. Where calculations are involved, computers generally do the work faster and more accurately than statisticians and accountants. Where typing is involved, computers with word processing software generally catch most of the spelling errors. Computerized spelling checkers, however, should be supplemented by grammar-checking software. Otherwise, the computer won't differentiate between similar words like "to," "too" and "two"; all three are found in the dictionary.

The "Why Plot?" Pattern

Trend charts occasionally look too good to be true. Sometimes they are.

Trend charts like the one in Figure 13-6 raise the question, "If the quality is that good, why plot the data on a chart?" Although the question seems valid, the quality may not be as good as it appears. These areas should be checked before abandoning the chart:

- Is the data accurate?
- Is the standard realistic?
- Are the inspectors doing a good job?
- Is the variable critical?

Is the data accurate?

If the data isn't accurate, the chart does more harm than good; management can be led to believe the quality is exceptional when it may be poor.

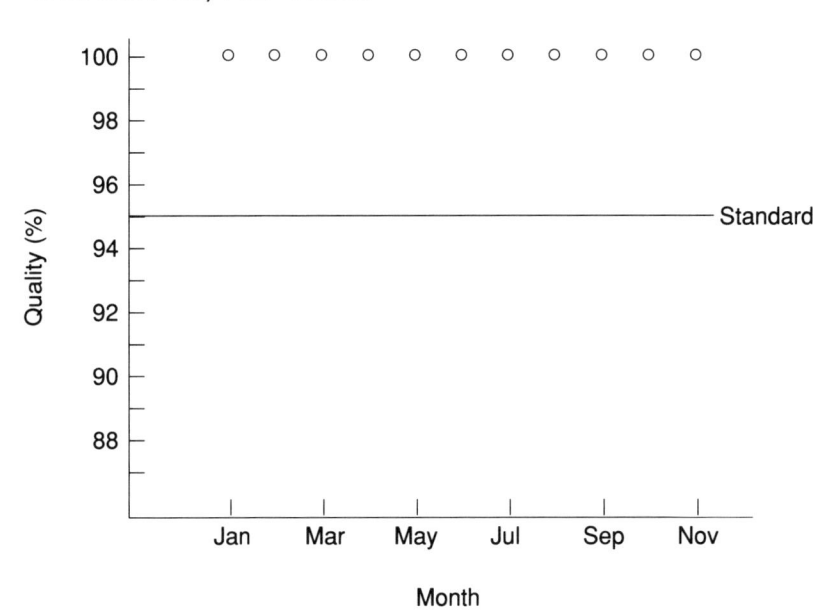

Figure 13-6. Trend Chart for an Operation That Is Too Good to Be True ("Why Plot?" Pattern)

Is the standard realistic?

If a tighter standard is warranted, it should be made tighter. Standards that are too loose are often found after the process is changed, training is improved, environmental problems are overcome or management introduces better equipment. They can also occur when the original standards were based on faulty capability studies or subjective reasoning. When standards don't reflect capability, workers may adjust their work habits to the requirements; this invites sloppiness. If management is satisfied with the standard, the need for the chart should be reevaluated. In many cases, the plots can be reduced or even eliminated. Circumstances change. The needs of a year ago are not necessarily the needs of today, and no dynamic organization has time to do all the things on its wish list. In some cases, personnel used to develop and plot the data can be used more effectively elsewhere. More information on standards is contained in subsequent chapters.

Are the inspectors doing a good job?

The problem occasionally lies with the inspectors and auditors. Inspection quality should be verified. Inspectors with too much to do often reduce their personal standards. Those with too little to do often nitpick. Those with inadequate training or poor equipment may be flying blind; they can't be expected to do well.

Is the variable critical?

When a variable is critical, plotting should continue even though a "Why Plot?" pattern exists. With critical variables, however, control charts are usually better than trend charts.

The "Jump-Shift" Pattern

At times, problems seem to come from nowhere. When this happens, trend charts are apt to show a "Jump-Shift" pattern like the one in Figure 13-7. The "Jump-Shift" pattern provides troubleshooters with a lot of assistance. This pattern gives clear evidence that something changed. It also identifies when the problem occurred. With this information, troubleshooters can usually identify the reason for the change and initiate corrective action. Typical problems causing this pattern in the service sector include

- A change of supervisors
- A change of workers
- A change in the work
- Revised procedures
- New equipment

A change of supervisors

A new supervisor can have an adverse impact on quality, contributing to chart patterns like the one in Figure 13-7. This can occur even when the incoming supervisor is good; many people resist change. The reverse, however, can also occur. A new supervisor can contribute to a favorable shift—if the new is better than the old.

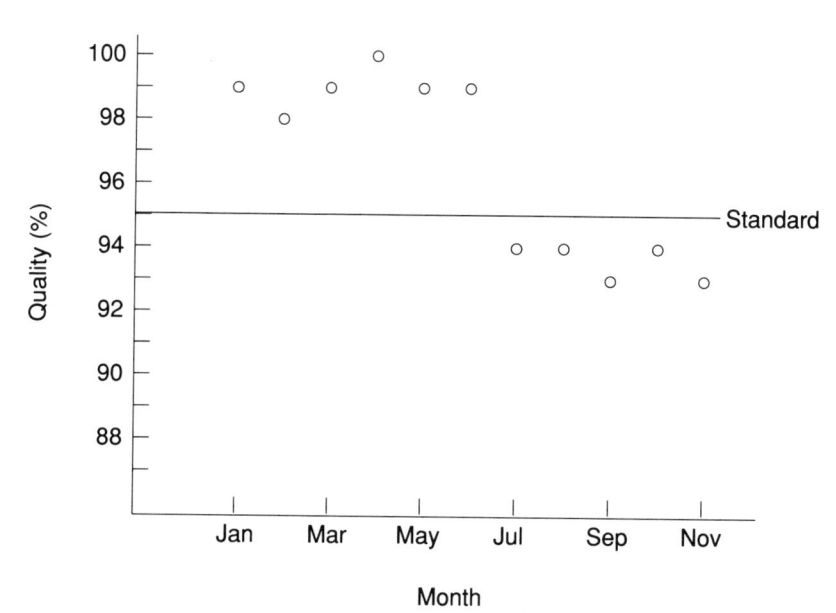

Figure 13-7. **Trend Chart for an Operation With Sudden Changes In Quality ("Jump-Shift" Pattern)**

A change of workers

Reorganizations, promotions and rapid growth can result in inexperienced or incapable workers taking over the work load. Formal and on-the-job training usually corrects problems associated with inexperience. When workers are incapable of handling the job, however, the problem is more difficult. I worked in a lab where one of the chemists was color-blind; it was quite difficult for him to do colorimetric analyses. Although he compensated by looking for slight differences in the shade of the indicator, his work was slow, laborious and occasionally inaccurate. It was judicious to give him assignments that did not require detection of colors. In another case, it was found that the eyesight of an inspector was not sharp enough for the work at hand; here again, reassignment was the logical solution.

A change in the work

In the Air Force Accounting and Finance Center, the types of travel vouchers often change during the summer when a larger number of reservists and reserve units go on active duty. Technicians who haven't handled this type of paperwork for nine months may take longer and make more errors than they do with their routine assignments. When this occurs, trend charts on error rates or productivity can show a jump-shift pattern.

Revised procedures

When procedures are changed, quality often drops until the workers become accustomed to the new way of doing things. This is particularly true when supervision makes the change without consulting with people doing the work.

New equipment

In the long run, new equipment should improve quality and productivity. At first, however, the workers need to get used to the change. New computers are a good example. Each computer or computer program has its own personality; each computer or computer program requires a little adjustment in the worker's routine.

Jump-Shift patterns are common in technical literature. One was noted in the trend chart for Air Force funds requirements when the Mideast oil cartel increased fuel prices.[11] Another was noted by Latzko in a trend chart for "total cost of quality" after changes were made in the inspection procedures.[12] Jump-shift patterns are present in the trend charts of most successful quality improvement projects.

The "Freak" or "Oddball" Pattern

The "Freak" or "Oddball" pattern occurs when an isolated anomaly occurs; one point drops below the standard, specification or goal, as shown in Figure 13-8.

Since the "Freak" pattern identifies an isolated point, there is a tendency to ignore it. Don't. An investigation of a "freak" point often gives you added insight into your process. Occasionally, "freak" points are a normal part of the operation[13] or a clue to undetected weaknesses in the system. As an example, a "freak" point could occur in an error-rate chart the week the guru of the technicians went on vacation. Without the sage being present in the work area, less experienced workers might guess at the proper procedures rather than show their ignorance to the supervisor. Information of this nature can highlight the need for additional training, and the guru or sage may be the ideal candidate for the assignment of trainer.

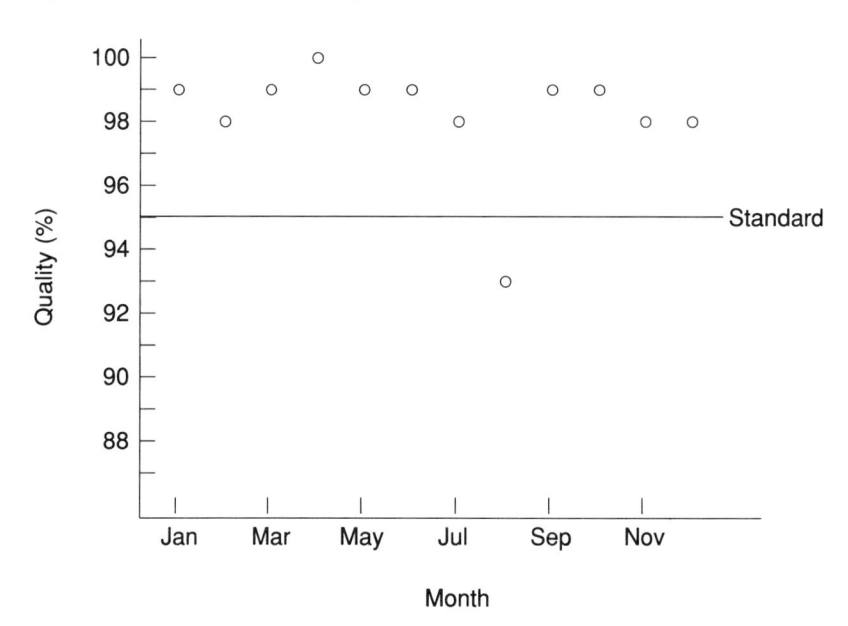

Figure 13-8. **Trend Chart for an Operation With an Isolated Anomaly ("Freak" or "Oddball" Pattern)**

The "Déjà Vu" Pattern

Have you ever seen a chart that looked familiar? The "Déjà Vu" pattern fits that mold.

Some trends are seasonal. As an example, the trend chart in Figure 13-9 shows a dip in quality during the summer months. One year's data, however, doesn't verify a seasonal trend; two or three years of data may.

Trends like the one shown in Figure 13-9 can occur in organizations that tie vacation selection to departmental seniority. In most cases, summer is favored and senior employees stake claims to it. This leaves the less experienced personnel to carry on. Then, the effects of time-on-the-job become obvious; most junior employees I have worked with have more to learn and have higher error rates than old-timers.

A seasonal pattern was identified in the "funds requirement" trend charts at the Air Force Accounting and Finance Center.[11] Using historical data, the magnitude of the seasonal trend was determined and seasonal corrections were made to the data; this resulted in improved trend forecasts. Another technique we used to compensate for seasonal trends involved plotting 12-month averages. That way, every point had one December and one July; seasonal variations were balanced out.

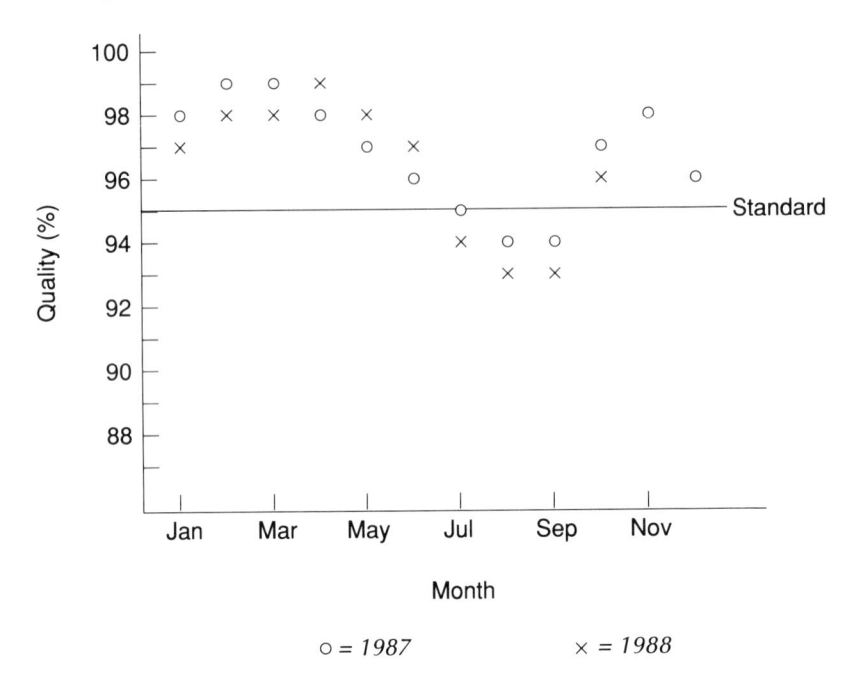

Figure 13-9. Trend Chart for an Operation That Has Seasonal Changes ("Déjà Vu" Pattern)

○ = 1987   × = 1988

The "Total Chaos" Pattern

One of the basic rules of trend charting is to avoid the "Total Chaos" pattern.

With the "Déjà Vu" illustration in Figure 13-9, two years were overlaid on the same chart. This technique is good when a seasonal trend is anticipated. Plotting more than two sets of data on the same chart, however, leads to confusion. The "Total Chaos" presentation in Figure 13-10 is a good example; it mixes data from five different years. If year-to-year comparisons are needed, it may help to have separate charts for each year plotted on a single page.

Transparencies also help. When separate transparencies are made for each year, trend charts for different years can be overlaid on top of each other. Then, individual years can be shown as well as comparative data for two. Three sets of curves get confusing, even when overlays are used.

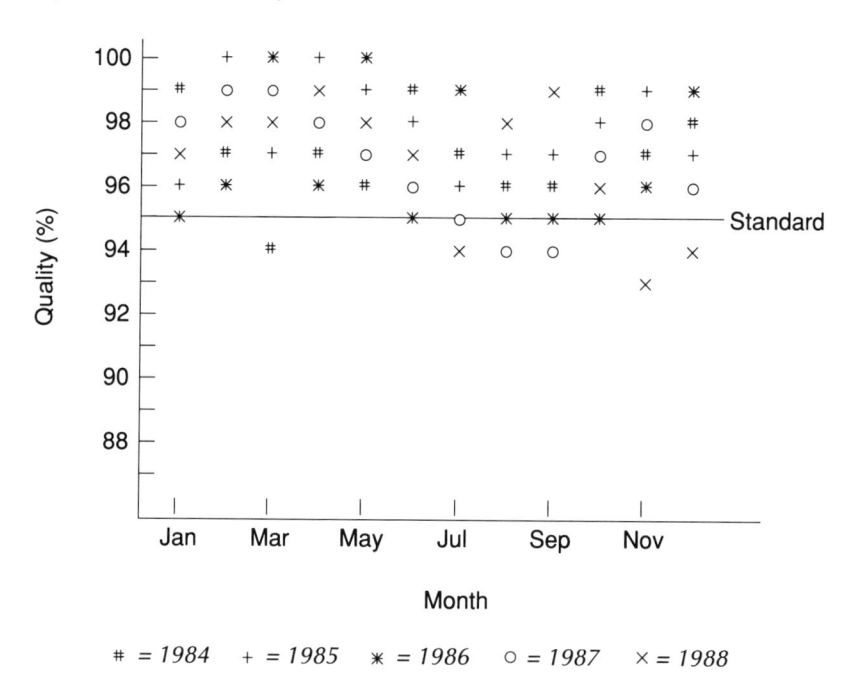

Figure 13-10. **Trend Chart That Talks Too Much ("Total Chaos" Pattern)**

= 1984   + = 1985   ✶ = 1986   ○ = 1987   × = 1988

SUMMARY

The trend chart is an excellent tool for monitoring variables that change with time. It is used extensively by management and staff personnel interested in verifying that the system is working.

Ten trend chart patterns were discussed in this chapter. Learn to recognize them; they can help you understand what is going on and why. They are not, however, the only patterns that exist; in time, you may find a few favorites of your own.

FOOD FOR THOUGHT

1. Ask the quality, production and accounting managers in your

company for copies of the charts they use to brief upper management. Then review them.
   a. How many use trend charts?
   b. How many of the charts have one of the above patterns?
   c. Using information supplied in this chapter, list ways their presentations can be improved.
2. If you can't get access to charts from within your own company, obtain annual reports from several major companies and conduct the same exercise.

REFERENCES
1. Rebecca L. Huls, "Dedication to Quality Spans all Industries," *ASQC Quality Congress Transactions,* May 4–6, 1987, pp. 90–95.
2. Joseph P. King, "Executive Survival Guide to Meeting Requirements," *ASQC Quality Congress Transactions,* May 4–6, 1987, pp. 827–832.
3. H. C. Hays, "Quality Improvement—Specific Measures," *ASQC Quality Congress Transactions,* May 19–21, 1986, pp. 530–535.
4. Charles A. Aubrey, II, *Quality Management in Financial Services* (Wheaton, IL: Hitchcock Publishing, 1985), p. 21.
5. Henry L. Lefevre, "Interpreting Trend Charts," *Quality,* October 1982, p. 67.
6. Deborah A. Guyton and Jen Tang, "Reporting Current Quality and Trends: 'I' Plots," *ASQC Quality Congress Transactions,* May 19–21, 1986, pp. 591–599.
7. A. C. Rosander, *Applications of Quality Control in the Service Industries* (Milwaukee, WI: ASQC Quality Press, 1985), p. 242.
8. W. Edwards Deming, *Out of the Crisis* (Cambridge, MA: Massachusetts Institute of Technology, 1986), p. 6.
9. B. B. Affourtit, "Statistical Process Control (SPC) Implementation—Common Misconceptions," *ASQC Quality Congress Transactions,* May 19–21, 1986, pp. 440–445.
10. Aubrey, *Quality Management in Financial Services,* p. 39.
11. Henry L. Lefevre, "Time Series Forecasting for Non-mathematicians," *ASQC Quality Congress Transactions,* May 26–29, 1981, pp. 1029–1034.
12. William J. Latzko, *Quality and Productivity for Bankers and Financial Managers* (Milwaukee, WI: ASQC Quality Press, 1986), p. 91.
13. Western Electric Company, *Statistical Quality Control Handbook,* 11th ed. (Charlotte, NC: Delmar Printing, 1985), p. 162.

Chapter 14

Variation in the Service Sector

Control charts are *similar* to trend charts, but they have control limits added. In addition, some control charts include ranges, others don't. On the surface, the shift from trend to control appears simple. Some knowledge of variation, however, is helpful if you want to control your operations effectively.

Variation can be good or bad. With no variation, the world would be dull and monotonous. With too much variation, the world would be a celestial madhouse with nothing in control.

SOURCES OF VARIATION

Almost everything varies. No two eyes, flowers or palmprints are alike. Types of variation that influence quality in the service sector include:

- Person-to-person variation
- Project-to-project variation (the type of work)
- Time-to-time variation
- Equipment variation

- Process variation
- Environmental variation

Additional ideas on variation are covered by Grant and Leavenworth,[1] Traver,[2] and Rosander.[3]

Person-to-person variation is based on people being different; no two technicians, secretaries, clerks, engineers or managers are identical. Therefore, no two will have identical daily error rates over a long period of time. The individual with the best training, motivation, skill and physical abilities will probably make the least errors, everything else being equal. A similar variability in inspectors, auditors and checkers adds to the total variation; at times they accept work that is incorrect or reject work that is good.

Project-to-project variation reflects differences in the work we do. A secretary can get a clearly written, one-paragraph memo to type or a complex, technical report with many Greek symbols and difficult-to-decipher handwriting. A technician calculating retirement points can get the record of a new recruit with one month of active duty or the record of a colonel with 29 years' service, eight overseas assignments, three breaks in service and 15 organization changes. A data-entry clerk can be assigned 30 short, simple records where all data is similar or 30 complex records with widely diverse data. In each case, the length and complexity of the work will probably have an impact on the error rate and apparent productivity of the worker.

Time-to-time variation also affects quality. W. Edwards Deming[4] observes, "The performance of anybody on any one day is useless as a basis for prediction of his performance on any other day." Although this statement sounds a little extreme, individuals do show time-to-time variation in their quality and productivity. As an example, repetitious work is often tiring. Some workers produce large volumes of error-free work in the morning but slow down and get error-prone by quitting time. Others can start out slow but improve as the day progresses. Few, however, work with the same speed and quality throughout the entire day. Similar patterns can also occur over longer periods. Some sages suggest that you should never buy a car that was made on Monday; they assume that Mondays are "poor-quality" days and Wednesdays are "good-quality" days. Similar patterns can be detected among some workers in the service sector; their error rates on Monday can exceed those noted later in the week. At times they do; at times they don't.

Equipment variation in the service sector includes different typewriters, word processors, computers, data-entry keyboards, calculators and many other items. Any time you change a worker's typewriter, for example, you will probably change the individual's productivity and error rate; in some cases the change is for the worse and in others it is for the better. Changes from a typewriter to a word processor or computer can have an even greater effect. In many cases, the impact of an equipment change can be anticipated using the Ends Test or Tukey-Duckworth Test discussed in Chapter 18.

Process variation is similar to equipment variation; it can be evaluated using the Ends Test or the Tukey-Duckworth Test prior to implementation. The tests are more likely to be valid when the users are equally familiar with the alternate processes. If one process is new, try to estimate the impact of the learning curve. Users unfamiliar with the new process may do worse at first. As a consequence, tests favoring the new process are more likely to be valid than those favoring the old—unless you are able to accurately estimate the performance that should be achieved once the users become accustomed to the new way. Case histories showing the importance of learning curves in the service sector are documented by Rosander.[5]

Environmental variation can also influence service quality. In some cases, quality and productivity are hampered by abnormal temperatures, excessive humidity, noise or smoke. If the environmental variations are influenced by time, however, they will normally show up in the time-to-time studies. As an example, World War II weather observers in hot, humid states had difficulty keeping sweat off their weather maps during the summer. During the winter, they didn't have that problem.[6] Today, however, few weather observers worry about sweat on their maps; they usually work in air-conditioned rooms.

MEASURES OF VARIATION

Three common measures of variation are range, variance and standard deviation. These statistics are used extensively in many process control calculations; anyone trying to control a process should be familiar with all three of them.

Range

The range is the difference between the smallest and the largest measurement in a sample. If you have the following sample of error rates:

the range is 5%, 6%, 7%

(7% − 5%) or 2%

Range is normally identified by the symbol R and is used extensively with $\bar{X}$ (average) and R (range) charts.

Variance for Variables

Variables are measurements such as backlog, cost, time-to-run-a-computer-program and time-to-do-a-job. In contrast, attributes are right vs wrong, good vs bad or defect vs no-defect evaluations.

The formula that is often used for variance calculations with variables is

$$\text{Variance} = \frac{\text{Sum (Average} - \text{Measurement)}}{(\text{Sample size} - 1)}$$

or

$$\text{Variance (or } S^2) = \frac{\Sigma(\bar{X} - X)^2}{(n-1)}$$

where

S^2 = the variance
n = the sample size
X = an individual measurement
$\bar{X}$ = the average of n values of X
$\Sigma(\bar{X} - X)^2$ = sum of n values of $(\bar{X} - X)^2$

The average (or $\bar{X}$) is the sum of the individual values of X divided by the sample size (n) or

$$\bar{X} = \frac{\Sigma(X)}{n}$$

PROBLEM 14-1

You are concerned about how long your customers have to wait in line so you decide to calculate the average and the variability (variance) of their waiting times. To simplify the calculations, this problem uses only the following four waiting times (2, 4, 6 and 4 minutes). In normal practice, 30 or more waiting times should be used.

SOLUTION 14-1

An easy way to make these calculations is to set up the data in columns as follows:

Waiting times (X)	$(\bar{X} - X)$		$(\bar{X} - X)^2$	
2	4 – 2	= 2	2 × 2	= 4
4	4 – 4	= 0	0 × 0	= 0
6	4 – 6	= –2	(–2) × (–2)	= 4
4	4 – 4	= 0	0 × 0	= 0
Sum 16		0		8

The sum of the waiting times is 16 as shown in the first column. Therefore, the average waiting time is:

$$\text{Average } (\bar{X}) = \frac{\Sigma (X)}{n}$$

$$= \frac{(2 + 4 + 6 + 4)}{4}$$

$$= \frac{16}{4} \quad \text{(see column 1)}$$

$$= 4 \quad \text{(This number is used in the second column to represent } \bar{X}.)$$

$$\text{variance } (s)^2 = \frac{\Sigma(\bar{X} - X)^2}{(n - 1)}$$

$$\Sigma(\bar{X} - X)^2 = 8 \quad \text{(from the last column)}$$

Therefore,

$$\text{variance } (s)^2 = \frac{8}{(4 - 1)}$$

$$= \frac{8}{3}$$

$$= 2.67$$

The higher the variance, the more the spread of the data you are analyzing. In addition, if you know the variance you can calculate the standard deviation; if you know the average range for 21 or more constant-sized samples,[7] you can calculate the variance and the standard deviation. (Grant and Leavenworth[8] and Rosander[9] prefer 25 or more subgroups.) Procedures for making these calculations will be explained as you progress through this text.

Standard Deviation

The standard deviation is the square root of the variance. If the variance is 9, the standard deviation is the square root of 9, which equals 3. If the variance is 16, the standard deviation is the square root of 16, which is 4.

WHAT DOES STANDARD DEVIATION MEAN?

Without Gauss's discovery of the normal curve, Shewhart might never have developed control charts the way he did. According to Grant and Leavenworth,[10] "The basic probability distribution underlying the calculation of Shewhart control-chart limits for variables data is the normal or Gaussian distribution." When plotted on a frequency distribution chart, the normal curve is bell-shaped and looks like the one in Figure 14-1.

Figure 14-1 shows that with a normal curve 99.7% of the data falls within plus or minus 3 standard deviations of the mean; 95.4% of the data falls within plus or minus 2 standard deviations of the mean; 68.3% of the data falls within plus or minus 1 standard deviation of the mean.[11]

Most control charts have control limits that are also plus or minus 3 standard deviations from the mean.[12] This means that random data from a constant, perfectly centered, "normal" population will fall within the control limits 99.7% of the time. Since the probability of a random sample falling outside the control limits is so small, an investigation usually shows that data outside the limits does not belong to the same population as the rest of the data. Analyses of "abnormal" points often provide information on how to improve a process.

HISTOGRAMS

Histograms are frequency distribution charts; they are another way of evaluating variability. Histograms show frequency of occurrence plotted

Figure 14-1. **Areas Under The Normal Curve**

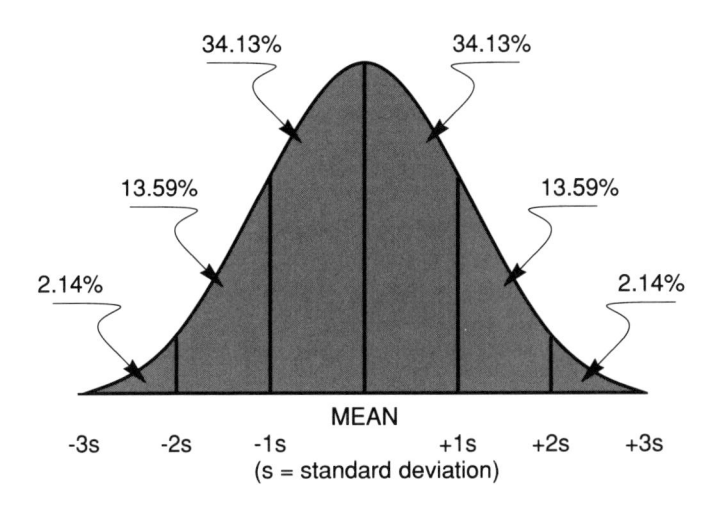

```
              34.13%    34.13%
        13.59%              13.59%
   2.14%                          2.14%

   -3s   -2s   -1s   MEAN   +1s   +2s   +3s
              (s = standard deviation)
```

68.3% of all values fall within ±1s of the mean.
95.4% of all values fall within ±2s of the mean.
99.7% of all values fall within ±3s of the mean.

against the variable being studied, such as backlog, time to complete a task, error rate, length of customer lines, time customers spend waiting in line, deviations from the budget or productivity. They are often used by troubleshooters to determine

- Whether distributions follow the normal curve
- Whether the data represents more than one population
- Whether a specification can be easily met

Normal Populations

Normal populations are similar to the one shown in Figure 14-1. To get such a smooth curve, however, you need a very large number of intervals (or classes) that are extremely small, plus extensive data. Most histograms have between 6 and 20 intervals,[13] and limited data. In addition, the intervals (or classes) are usually large enough to be obvious.

Figure 14-2 represents an idealized histogram for a normal population; it approximates a bell-shaped curve. Histograms as symmetrical and

164 QUALITY SERVICE PAYS: SIX KEYS TO SUCCESS!

Figure 14-2. **Frequency Distribution Chart: Productivity of Data-Entry Clerks (A Normal Distribution)**

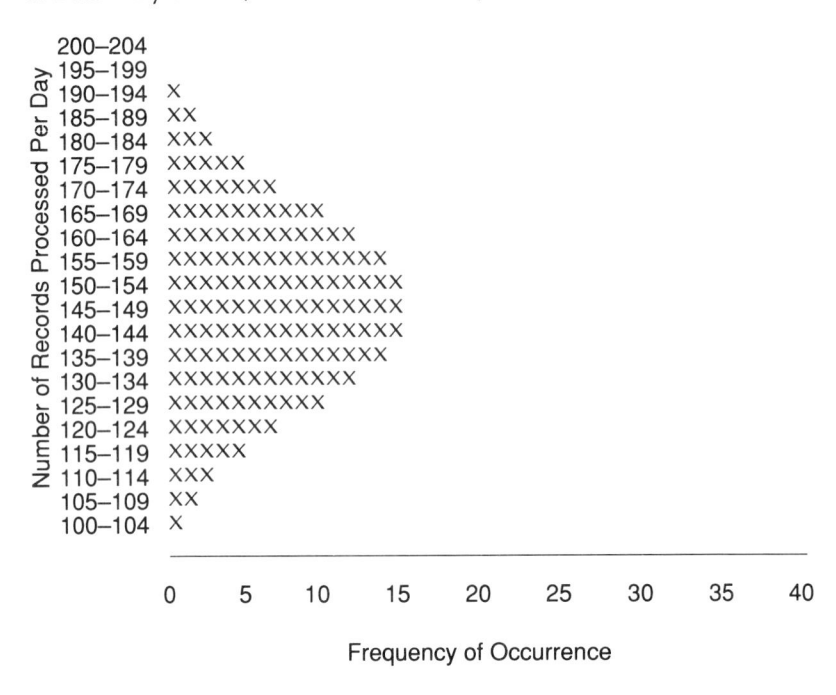

```
              200–204
              195–199
              190–194  X
              185–189  XX
              180–184  XXX
              175–179  XXXXX
              170–174  XXXXXXX
              165–169  XXXXXXXXX
              160–164  XXXXXXXXXXX
              155–159  XXXXXXXXXXXXX
              150–154  XXXXXXXXXXXXXX
              145–149  XXXXXXXXXXXXXX
              140–144  XXXXXXXXXXXXXX
              135–139  XXXXXXXXXXXXX
              130–134  XXXXXXXXXXX
              125–129  XXXXXXXXX
              120–124  XXXXXXX
              115–119  XXXXX
              110–114  XXX
              105–109  XX
              100–104  X

                       0    5    10   15   20   25   30   35   40
                                   Frequency of Occurrence
```

(Y-axis label: Number of Records Processed Per Day)

bell-shaped as the one in Figure 14-2 are not too common, especially when less data is available to plot. A few deviations from the normal curve are shown in Figures 14-3, 14-4 and 14-7.

Most histograms in this text show frequencies on the bottom of the chart instead of on the side; either approach is permissible. When computers are used to generate the histograms, it is more convenient to have the frequencies on the bottom; manually produced histograms often have them on the side.

Dual Populations

When two distinct populations are mixed together, the resulting histogram can look like the one in Figure 14-3.

Figure 14-3 represents the weekly error records of two distinctly different sets of technicians. The first averages a weekly error rate near 3.5%. The second averages a weekly error rate near 9%. This is called bimodal distribution; it has two distinct peaks or modes. The bimodal

Figure 14-3. Frequency Distribution Chart: Error Rates of Technicians (Trainees Included With Experienced Workers)

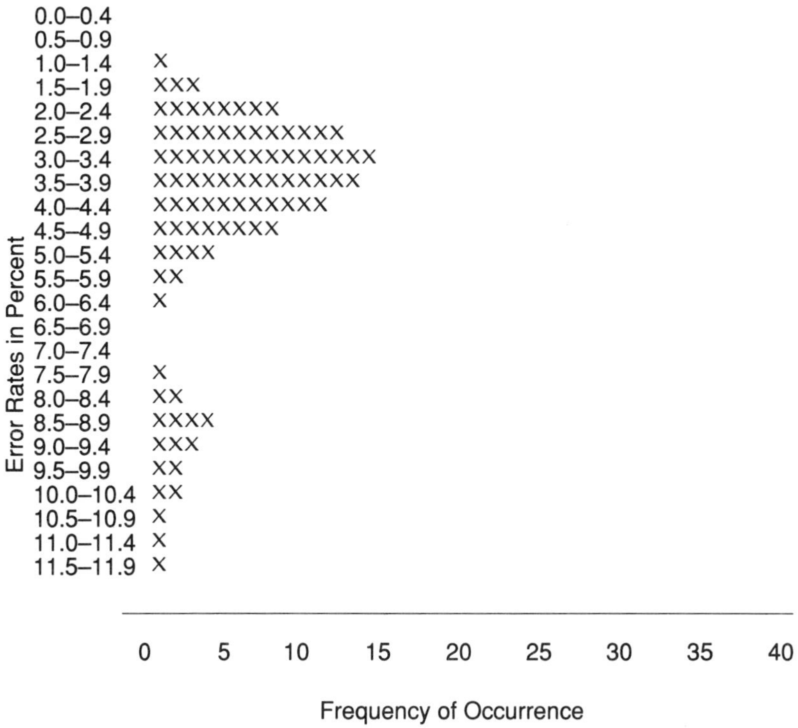

```
              0.0–0.4
              0.5–0.9
              1.0–1.4   X
              1.5–1.9   XXX
              2.0–2.4   XXXXXXXX
              2.5–2.9   XXXXXXXXXXXX
              3.0–3.4   XXXXXXXXXXXXXX
              3.5–3.9   XXXXXXXXXXXXX
              4.0–4.4   XXXXXXXXXXX
              4.5–4.9   XXXXXXXX
              5.0–5.4   XXXX
              5.5–5.9   XX
              6.0–6.4   X
              6.5–6.9
              7.0–7.4
              7.5–7.9   X
              8.0–8.4   XX
              8.5–8.9   XXXX
              9.0–9.4   XXX
              9.5–9.9   XX
             10.0–10.4  XX
             10.5–10.9  X
             11.0–11.4  X
             11.5–11.9  X
```
Error Rates in Percent

            0   5   10   15   20   25   30   35   40
                      Frequency of Occurrence

distribution of Figure 14-3 could be anticipated since information on the chart shows there are two separate populations present. Trainees make up one population; experienced workers make up the other. In my own work, I prefer to show trainees and experienced workers on different charts since trainees usually make more errors.

If the reason for a bimodal population is not known, you can benefit from the information supplied by the histogram; find out why there is a difference.

Another bimodal population is shown in Figure 14-4; this histogram is more typical. Most differences in populations that are plotted together are more subtle than Figure 14-3; most bimodal histograms show some overlap between the blended populations.

The chart in Figure 14-4 shows error rates for two different shifts. Assume, for illustration, an investigation showed that the average error rates of the day shift were lower than those of the swing shift. After looking at Figure 14-4, you could conclude that some of the day shift error rates were worse than some of the swing shift error rates. Otherwise, the two populations would be separated like those in Figure 14-3.

If you take a close look at Figures 14-3 and 14-4 you can see that the curves are not symmetrical. This is typical for attribute data that follows the binomial distribution; percentages and proportions don't often have symmetrical distributions unless the average percentage is 50 percent or the average proportion is 0.5.[10] An in-depth discussion on the binomial distribution, however, is beyond the scope of this book.

Histograms provide valuable information. If different populations are present, one of the populations is usually preferable to the other. With Figure 14-4, for instance, the lower error rates are definitely better. Based on this information, you might find that workers on one shift developed a better way of doing the job. Use this information; it normally pays for managers to find and implement improvements to the procedure or process—and to reward the innovative workers who developed them.

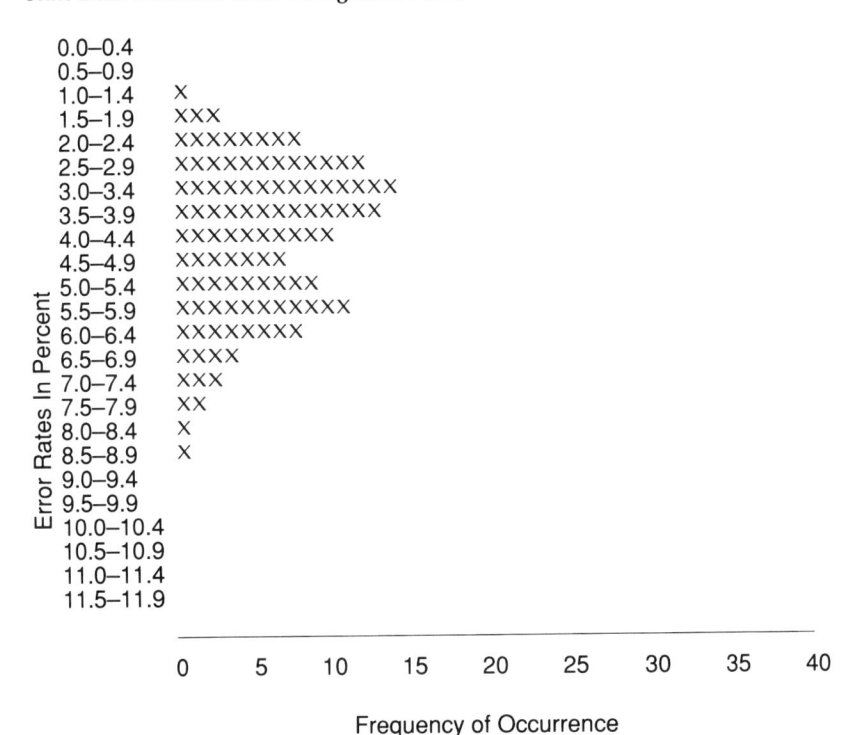

Figure 14-4. **Frequency Distribution Chart: Error Rates of Technicians (Day Shift Data Included With Swing Shift Data)**

```
                0.0–0.4
                0.5–0.9
                1.0–1.4    X
                1.5–1.9    XXX
                2.0–2.4    XXXXXXXX
                2.5–2.9    XXXXXXXXXXXX
                3.0–3.4    XXXXXXXXXXXXXX
                3.5–3.9    XXXXXXXXXXXXX
                4.0–4.4    XXXXXXXXXX
                4.5–4.9    XXXXXXX
                5.0–5.4    XXXXXXXXX
                5.5–5.9    XXXXXXXXXXX
                6.0–6.4    XXXXXXXX
                6.5–6.9    XXXX
                7.0–7.4    XXX
                7.5–7.9    XX
                8.0–8.4    X
                8.5–8.9    X
                9.0–9.4
                9.5–9.9
              10.0–10.4
              10.5–10.9
              11.0–11.4
              11.5–11.9
                         ┼────┼────┼────┼────┼────┼────┼────┼────┼
                         0    5   10   15   20   25   30   35   40
                                    Frequency of Occurrence
```

Error Rates In Percent

Figure 14-5. **Frequency Distribution Chart: Productivity of Data-Entry Clerks (A Normal Distribution)**

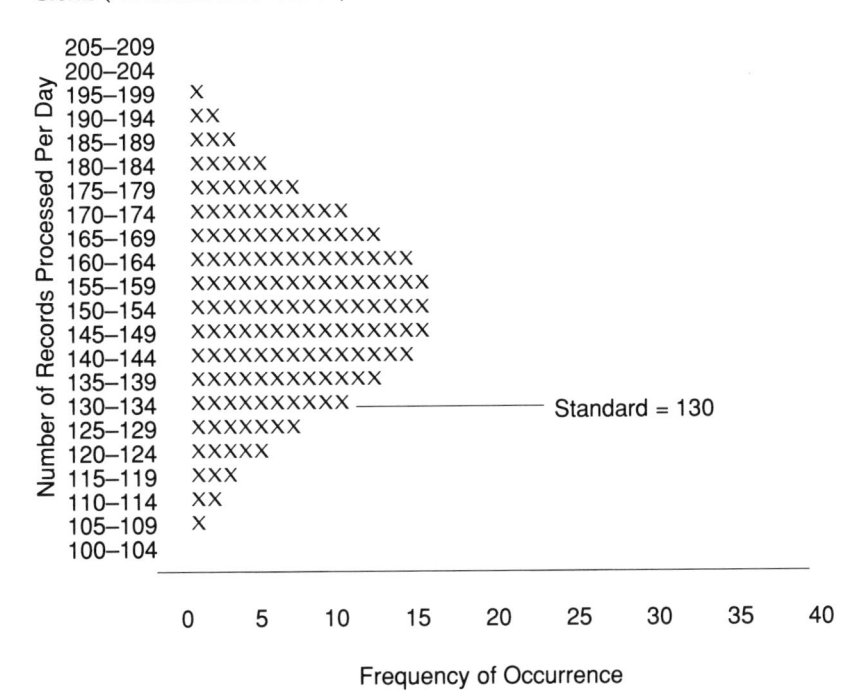

```
                     205-209
                     200-204
   ay              195-199   X
  D                190-194   XX
  er               185-189   XXX
  P                180-184   XXXXX
 ed                175-179   XXXXXX
ss                 170-174   XXXXXXXXXX
 e                 165-169   XXXXXXXXXXXX
 roc               160-164   XXXXXXXXXXXXXX
 P                 155-159   XXXXXXXXXXXXXXX
 s                 150-154   XXXXXXXXXXXXXXX
 rd                145-149   XXXXXXXXXXXXXXX
 co                140-144   XXXXXXXXXXXXXX
 Re                135-139   XXXXXXXXXXXX
 of                130-134   XXXXXXXXXX ————————— Standard = 130
 r                 125-129   XXXXXXX
 be                120-124   XXXXX
 um                115-119   XXX
 N                 110-114   XX
                   105-109   X
                   100-104
                           ┼────┼────┼────┼────┼────┼────┼────┼────┼
                           0    5   10   15   20   25   30   35   40

                                 Frequency of Occurrence
```

Meeting Specifications

You can also find histograms helpful when setting standards, specifications and performance requirements. As an example, the histogram in Figure 14-5 is often found where the standard is tighter than the capability of the system. When this situation is found, management must determine whether the standard is too tight. If relaxation of the requirements is not feasible, improvements need to be made to the system. This could involve additional training, improved procedures, better equipment or other management-controllable changes.

Histograms like the one in Figure 14-6 are often found where the standard is looser than the capability of the system. In many instances, it is desirable to tighten loose standards before the workers conclude that the requirements are not important and let their quality or productivity slip.

The distribution shown in Figure 14-7 can occur when worker peer pressure starts influencing productivity; all but five marks in the histogram are bunched just above the standard.

168   QUALITY SERVICE PAYS: SIX KEYS TO SUCCESS!

Figure 14-6. Frequency Distribution Chart: Productivity of Data-Entry Clerks, Normal Distribution (The Standard Appears to Be Too Loose)

```
Number of Records Processed Per Day
175–179
170–174
165–169  XXXXX
160–164  XXXXXXXXXXXXXXXXXXXXXXX
155–159  XXXXXXXXXXXXXXXXXXXXXXXXXXXXXX
150–154  XXXXXXXXXXXXXXXXXXXXXXXXXXXXXXXXX
145–149  XXXXXXXXXXXXXXXXXXXXXXX
140–144  XXXXX
135–139
130–134
125–129
120–124
115–119
110–114
105–109
100–104 ──────────────────────────Standard = 100
         ┼────┼────┼────┼────┼────┼────┼────┼────
         0    5   10   15   20   25   30   35   40
                    Frequency of Occurrence
```

Figure 14-7. Frequency Distribution Chart: Productivity of Data-Entry Clerks, a Truncated Distribution (Where Peer Pressure Could Be Influencing Productivity)

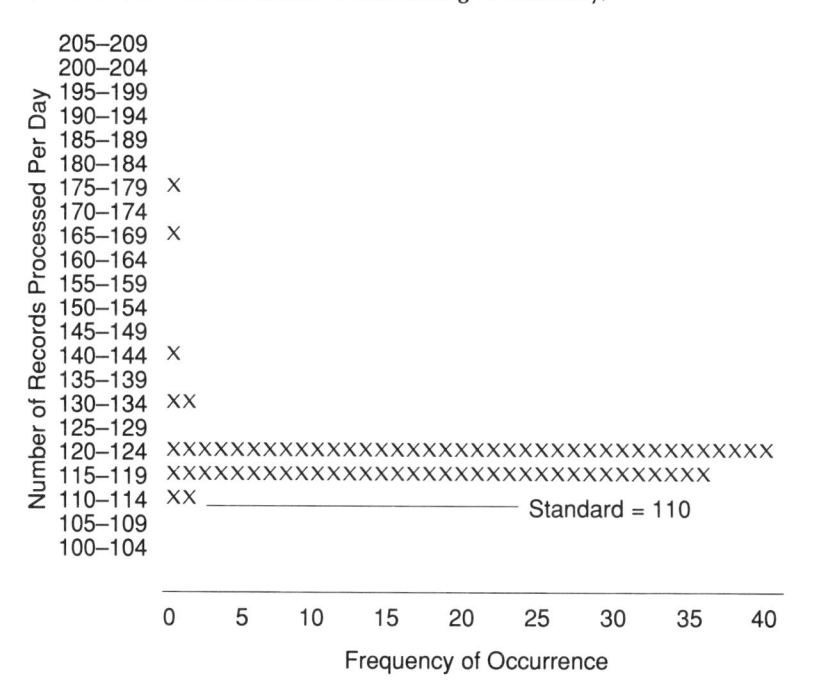

```
Number of Records Processed Per Day
205–209
200–204
195–199
190–194
185–189
180–184
175–179  X
170–174
165–169  X
160–164
155–159
150–154
145–149
140–144  X
135–139
130–134  XX
125–129
120–124  XXXXXXXXXXXXXXXXXXXXXXXXXXXXXXXXXXXXXXXX
115–119  XXXXXXXXXXXXXXXXXXXXXXXXXXXXXXXXXXXX
110–114  XX ─────────────────── Standard = 110
105–109
100–104
         ┼────┼────┼────┼────┼────┼────┼────┼────
         0    5   10   15   20   25   30   35   40
                    Frequency of Occurrence
```

After looking at Figure 14-7, you might conclude that the capability of the average worker was somewhere between 110 and 124 records per day. The chart, however, shows isolated performances as high as the 175–179 range; this implies that the average worker *capability* is quite a bit higher than the average worker *performance*. Peer pressure might be used to hold production down but there are often mavericks who refuse to go along with the group. If this is the case, corrective action should be initiated before the "outstanding" performers succumb to peer pressure.

Other explanations, however, are possible. The "maverick" data on the histogram could be due to a few workers discovering a better way of doing the job. They could also represent the performance of sloppy workers who put production ahead of quality. Never draw conclusions from the histogram until the true reasons for the "abnormal" distribution have been determined.

Histograms can give you information on the capability of the worker and the process. More information on worker and process capability will be covered in Chapter 17.

MULTI-VARI ANALYSIS

Once excessive variation is identified as a problem, an investigation should be initiated; Multi-Vari charts can be used for this task.[2,14,15] Multi-Vari charts were developed by Leonard A. Seder, who was exploring "the use of graphics in place of statistics."[14] The flexibility of the charts was anticipated by Seder back in 1950 when he wrote, "One of the chief virtues of the Multi-Vari Chart is that it lends itself admirably to the inclusion of additional specific sources of variation."[14] In its original form, within-piece, piece-to-piece and time-to-time variations in manufactured parts were emphasized. At that time, no attempt was made to introduce it to the service sector. It is, however, adaptable enough to be used in both areas.

A Multi-Vari chart, analyzing the quality of a group of data-entry clerks is shown in Figure 14-8. In this illustration, worker-to-worker, AM vs PM, and day-to-day variability are analyzed, and worker-to-worker variability appears to have the greatest impact.

In Figure 14-8, the best worker's performance for each period is shown as a small "o"; a falling vertical line connects it to another "o" representing the "worst worker's" performance for the same period. The longer the vertical line, the greater the difference between the performance of the best and the worst workers. The greatest difference for worker-to-worker quality shown in Figure 14-8 is for the PM period on Monday; the best worker's quality is 97.0% and the worst worker's quality is 92.0%. The total difference in worker-to-worker quality for the PM period on Monday is 5.0%. The average difference for the week is about 2.2%.

170   QUALITY SERVICE PAYS: SIX KEYS TO SUCCESS!

The "best worker" shown as an "o" at the top of the vertical line for one period can be the "worst worker" shown as an "o" at the bottom of the vertical line for another period.

Between the AM and PM vertical lines, "x" represents the group's average quality for the entire day. The "x" for Monday is above the midpoint for either the AM or PM line on that day. This indicates that the average worker was closer to the best worker and further from the worst.

The lowest daily average was the 96.0% reported for Monday; the highest daily average was the 97.5% reported for Wednesday. The difference was 1.5%, showing that the day-to-day average variability was less than the worker-to-worker variability.

The AM-VS-PM variability can be approximated by finding the difference between the average of the AM points and the average of the PM points. In Figure 14-8, the average AM-VS-PM variability was about 0.4%, which is less than either of the other sources of variability.

Figure 14-8. **Multi-Vari Chart: Worker Quality**

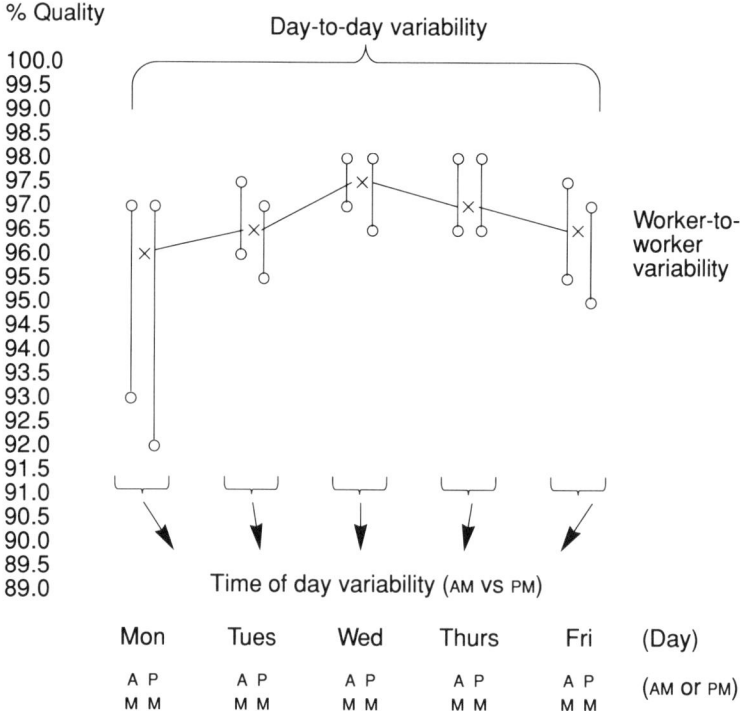

× = group average for the day
o = best or worst individual results for AM or PM

Figure 14-9. **Multi-Vari Study: Worker Quality**

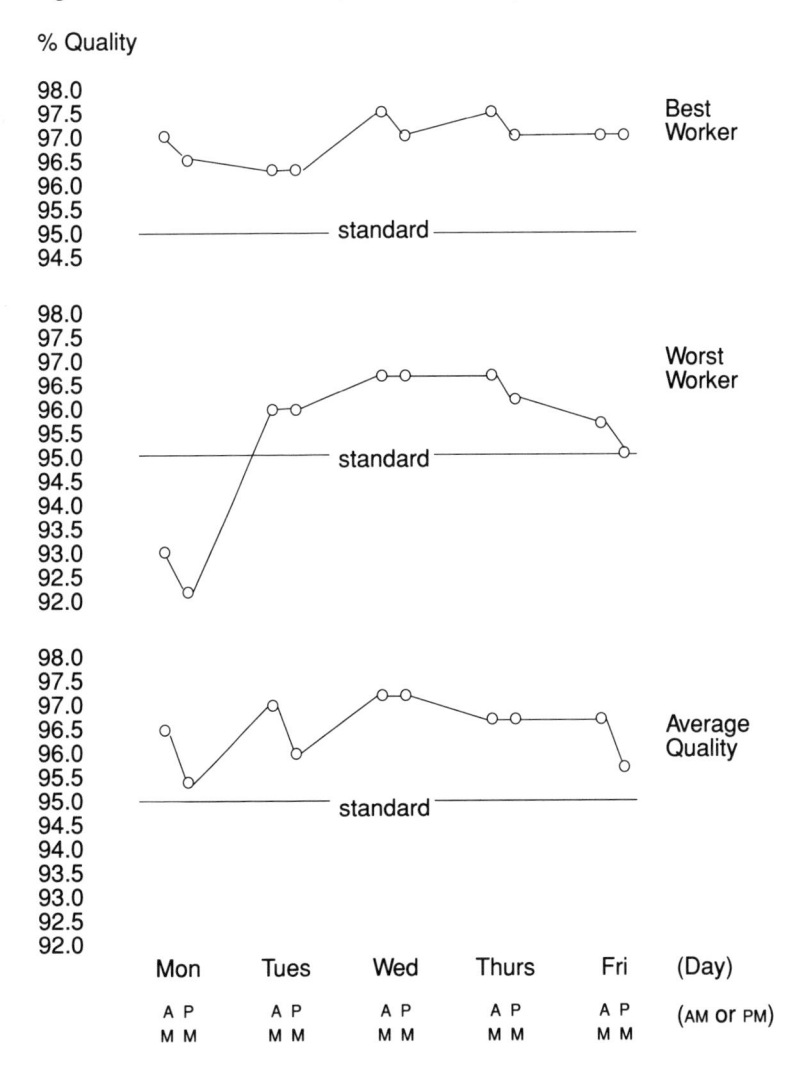

[Chart: Best Worker — values plotted around 96.5–97.5, above standard line at 95.0]

[Chart: Worst Worker — values ranging from 92.0 up to about 97.0, crossing standard line at 95.0]

[Chart: Average Quality — values plotted around 95.0–97.0, near standard line at 95.0]

Days: Mon, Tues, Wed, Thurs, Fri (AM or PM)

Based on the data shown in Figure 14-8, the supervisor might do Multi-Vari analyses on individuals within the organization. Figure 14-9 represents such a hypothetical analysis.

Figure 14-9 shows individual charts for the best worker, the worst worker and the average worker in the group. In this instance, the best and worst workers represent specific individuals and not composites. The best worker was well above the standard throughout the week. The worst worker was well below the standard for both AM and PM shifts on Monday, performed marginally on Friday and did well the rest of the week. The average quality for the group was above the standard for the week, although the "worst worker" did pull it down close to the standard during the Monday PM period.

Multi-Vari patterns, like those in Figures 14-8 and 14-9, are common when one worker pulls down the quality of the organization. Hypothetically, this could be due to excesses on the weekend. The "worst worker" appears to be capable of meeting the quality requirements; he or she just isn't up to par on Mondays. If the above explanation proves to be true, counseling or other corrective action might be warranted.

Multi-Vari charts can also be developed to evaluate the impact of variations in the type of work being processed, the equipment, the accuracy of inspectors or other variables that can contribute to changes in quality and productivity.

SUMMARY

In the utopia of some idealists, all work would be perfect; neither errors nor variability would exist. In the service sector, as in manufacturing, errors do occur—and so does variability. Sources of variability in the service sector include

- Person-to-person
- Project-to-project
- Time-to-time
- Equipment
- Process
- Environment
- Other hidden changes

Once you determine which of the above variables are contributing the most to errors and variability, you can plan corrective action. Most factors contributing to error rates are management controllable; managers, however, must be shown the problem before they can be expected to initiate corrective action.

FOOD FOR THOUGHT

The simplest, and possibly the most powerful, of the tools covered in this chapter is the histogram; the following can help you apply it to your work area.

1. Determine which area of your job has the most errors.
2. Take 30 samples of work from that area. Each sample should be the same size and should be large enough that at least one error would be expected.
3. Make a histogram showing number of errors per sample plotted against frequency of occurrence.
4. Determine:
    a. Is the distribution normal? If so, the area is probably "in statistical control." If you want to make improvements, you may have to improve the training, equipment or procedures.
    b. Is it bimodal? If so, you should determine what two populations are involved. Are different workers better trained, better equipped, using different procedures or operating in different environments?
    c. Do approximately 99.7% of the points meet your performance standard? If not, do you need to change the standard, make management-controllable improvements or just monitor the situation?

REFERENCES
1. Eugene L. Grant and Richard S. Leavenworth, *Statistical Quality Control,* 6th ed. (New York: McGraw-Hill, 1988), pp. 158–160.
2. Robert W. Traver, "Locating the Key Variable(s)," *39th Annual NEQCC Conference,* Windsor Locks, CT, October 9–11, 1985, pp. 31–41.
3. A. C. Rosander, *Applications of Quality Control in the Service Industries* (Milwaukee, WI: ASQC Quality Press, 1985), pp. 142–150.
4. W. Edwards Deming, *Out of the Crisis* (Cambridge, MA: Massachusetts Institute of Technology, 1986), p. 350.
5. Rosander, *Applications of Quality Control in the Service Industries,* pp. 112–116.
6. Edward M. Schrock and Henry L. Lefevre, *The Good and Bad News about Quality* (Milwaukee, WI: ASQC Quality Press, 1988), p. 67.
7. Ellis R. Ott, *Process Quality Control* (New York: McGraw-Hill, 1975), p. 28.
8. Grant and Leavenworth, *Statistical Quality Control,* p. 122.
9. Rosander, *Applications of Quality Control in the Service Industries,* p. 252.
10. Grant and Leavenworth, *Statistical Quality Control,* pp. 214–216.
11. Ott, *Process Quality Control,* p. 21.

12. Grant and Leavenworth, *Statistical Quality Control,* p. 670.
13. Elliot A. Tanis, *Statistics I: Descriptive Statistics and Probability* (New York: Harcourt Brace Jovanovich, 1987), p. 2.
14. Leonard A. Seder, "Diagnosis With Diagrams—Part I," *Industrial Quality Control,* January 1950, pp. 11–19.
15. J. M. Juran and Frank M. Gryna, *Juran's Quality Control Handbook,* 4th ed. (New York: McGraw-Hill, 1988), pp. 22.45, 24.5, 24.10.

Chapter 15

Control Charts for Variables

Control charts are similar to trend charts but go one step further; they help identify whether a process is in statistical control. If a process is not "in control," the reasons should be found and corrected.

Although both variables control charts and attributes control charts help control quality, each involves different assumptions and calculations; as a consequence, they deserve separate chapters.

Variables involve measurements like time, number-of-records-processed, backlog or volume-of-incoming-work; these data usually follow the normal curve. Attributes involve right-or-wrong and defect-or-no-defect judgments; they seldom follow the normal curve.

AVERAGE AND RANGE CHARTS

One of the most popular ways of plotting variables involves the average-and-range charts. They are also called the X-bar-and-R charts, X-and-R charts and Shewhart charts. Since the terms X-bar and R have limited meaning to nonstatisticians, they will be called average-and-range charts throughout most of this text. With formulas, however, abbreviations

Figure 15-1. **Control Chart: Response Time for Correspondence Statistically "In Control"**

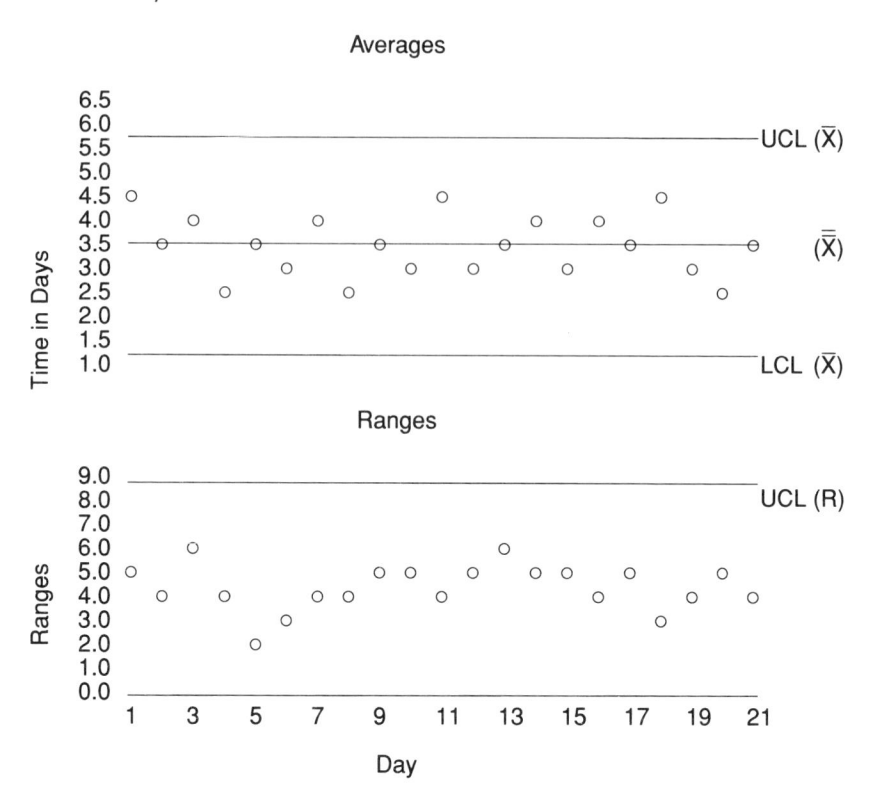

[Chart showing Averages (Time in Days) with UCL ($\bar{X}$), ($\bar{\bar{X}}$), and LCL ($\bar{X}$) lines, and Ranges chart with UCL (R) line, plotted across Days 1–21.]

NOTE: Each average contains five measurements.

and symbols are often necessary; some of the more important symbols include:

- $\bar{X}$ (average of the sample measurements)
- $\bar{\bar{X}}$ (average of the averages)
- R (range)
- $\bar{R}$ (average range)

Additional terms are covered in the definitions section of this chapter. Without abbreviations, one-line formulas can spread out over five or six lines; this can be confusing.

A typical average-and-range chart for a process that it statistically "in control" is shown in Figure 15-1.

Control Charts for Variables 177

Notice that the points shown in Figure 15-1 appear to be distributed randomly and there are no points outside the upper and lower control limits (UCL and LCL).

A typical average-and-range chart for a process that is statistically "out of control" is shown in Figure 15-2.

Notice that two points in Figure 15-2 are outside the control limits for the "average" chart and one point is above the control limit for "range."

The following sections include information on where these charts can be used, the meaning of the abbreviations and the procedures used in preparing the charts. They also elaborate on how to detect out-of-control conditions and what to do about them.

Figure 15-2. **Control Chart: Response Time for Correspondence Statistically "Out of Control"**

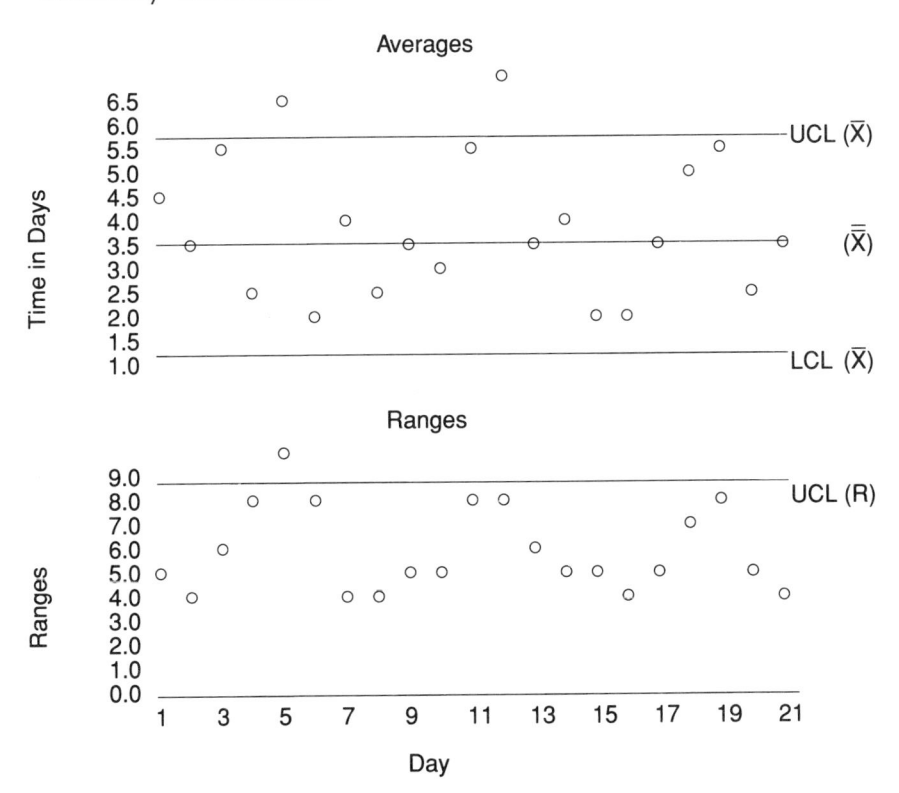

NOTE: Each average contains five measurements.

WHERE CAN AVERAGE-AND-RANGE CHARTS BE USED?

Average-and-range charts are often associated with manufacturing operations; production plants have used them for decades. Now, they are becoming popular in the service sector.

Huls[1] discusses using variables control charts for

- Response to mail requests
- Sales
- Production

Baker and Artinian[2] show how Windsor Export Supply used these charts to control the time taken to process invoices. They also used them to help analyze the number of cubic feet of material packed into shipping vans.

McCabe[3] used variables control charts to monitor:

- Time taken to reply to employee comments
- Time taken for pre-employment medical exams

He leaves off the "range" charts when monitoring the weight and delivery time of mail.[4]

Early and Dmytrow[5] show how the Bureau of Labor Statistics uses variables control charts for analyzing the time it takes to respond to field inquiries and for identifying the effect of process changes.

Affourtit[6] illustrates how control charts can be used to monitor:

- Absenteeism across an organization
- Absenteeism for different segments of an organization
- Task completion times

Rosander[7] shows how variables control charts can be used for testing a three-minute timer; he uses trend charts for monitoring the timeliness of city buses.

Control charts can be used to monitor and control almost any variable that can be measured. They are excellent for process control, defect prevention, performance monitoring and quality improvement. The above references document their use in the service sector. A review of problem areas within your own operation should identify many similar applications for these powerful tools.

Table 15-1. **Factors Used for Calculating Control Limits for Averages and Ranges**

	Factor For		
Sample Size	LCL (Averages) & UCL (Averages) (A2)	LCL (Ranges) (D3)	UCL (Ranges) (D4)
2	1.880	0	3.268
3	1.023	0	2.574
4	0.729	0	2.282
5	0.577	0	2.115
6	0.483	0	2.004
7	0.419	0.076	1.924
8	0.373	0.136	1.864
9	0.337	0.184	1.816
10	0.308	0.223	1.777

DEFINITIONS

Average-and-range charts are simple and easy to implement. They do, however, involve special terms not often used by managers in the service sector. Definitions of value to anyone setting up these charts include the following:

A2. The term "A2" represents a factor used when calculating control limits for an "average" control chart or X-bar chart or $\bar{X}$-chart. In this book, all three terms have the same meaning. In most instances, the term "average" will be used. Values for "A2" are shown in Table 15-1. You will need this information when you set up your own control charts.

D3. The term "D3" represents a factor used when calculating the lower control limit for a "range" or R chart. In this book, "range" and R have the same meaning. Values for "D3" are shown in Table 15-1.

D4. The term "D4" represents a factor used when calculating the upper control limit for a "range" or R chart. Values for "D4" are shown in Table 15-1.

Grand Average ($\bar{\bar{X}}$). The term "grand average" represents the average of a group of averages.

LCL(averages). This term represents the lower control limit for charts of averages or ranges. The formula is:

$$\text{LCL (averages)} = \text{grand average} - (A2 \times R\text{-average})$$

or

$$\text{LCL}(\bar{X}) = \bar{\bar{X}} - A2 \times \bar{R}$$

When the above formula is used to determine control limits, LCL($\bar{X}$) will be three standard deviations below the mean;[8] plotted points should not fall below the lower control limit more than 0.13 percent of the time, assuming your distribution is "normal" and your system is in statistical control. Refer to Chapter 14 for more detail on normal distributions.

LCL(*R*). The term "LCL(*R*)" represents the lower control limit for a range chart. The formula is:

$$\text{LCL }(R) = D3 \times R\text{-average}$$

or

$$\text{LCL}(R) = D3 \times \bar{R}$$

***n*.** The term *n* represents the sample size; it also refers to the number of measurements represented by each point on the chart.

***R*.** The term *R* refers to the range of measurements within a sample; the sample size is *n*.

$\bar{R}$ (*R*-average). The terms "*R*-average" and $\bar{R}$ represent the average range or the sum of the individual ranges divided by the number of ranges.

***s*.** The letter *s* represents the standard deviation. The term "standard deviation" is a statistic used to measure variability. Standard deviations were covered in Chapter 14.

Statisticians usually call *s* an *estimate* of the standard deviation and use the Greek term "sigma" for the true standard deviation of the entire population. The difference, however, is not critical to the average reader; it will not be explored in this text.

Standard deviation. See *s*.

UCL(averages). The term "UCL(averages)" represents the upper control limit for a chart of averages. The formula is:

$$\text{UCL (averages)} = \text{grand average} + (A2 \times \text{average range})$$

or

$$\text{UCL}(\bar{X}) = \bar{\bar{X}} + A2 \times \bar{R}$$

When the above formula is used to determine control limits, UCL($\bar{X}$) will be three standard deviations above the mean.[8] This means that a plotted point should not fall above the upper control limit more than 0.13 percent of the time, assuming the distribution is "normal" and the system is in statistical control. Refer to Chapter 14 for more details on "normal" distributions.

UCL(Ranges). The terms "UCL(Ranges)" and "UCL(R)" represent the upper control limit for a "range" chart. The formula is:

$$\text{UCL (Ranges)} = D_4 \times \text{average range}$$

or

$$\text{UCL}(R) = D_4 \times \bar{R}$$

X. The term X represents one measurement. It could be the time taken to process a single invoice, or the number of minutes a plane was late, or any similar measurement.

$\bar{X}$ (*X-average*). The term $\bar{X}$ or "X-average" refers to the average of n measurements taken for a sample. Each point plotted on an "average" control chart represents one X-average.

X-bar ($\bar{X}$). The term "X-bar" is the same as the terms "X-average" and $\bar{X}$.

$\bar{\bar{X}}$. See grand average.

In statistics, a letter with one bar above it usually represents an average; a letter with two bars over it represents the average of a number of averages. To calculate an average, add all the individual measurements in the sample and then divide by the number of measurements in the sample (n).

The values of A_2, D_3, and D_4 vary with the sample size. Refer to Table 15-1 when you need to use these factors.

SAMPLE SIZES

When setting up an average-and-range chart, one of the first decisions involves selecting the sample size to be used; once selected, it is seldom changed. If sample sizes were allowed to vary, data generated before each change would not compare with data generated after the change.

The smallest possible sample size for average-and-range charts is 2. If you had a sample size of 1, you couldn't calculate the range within that sample.

A sample size of 5 is common. Examples are shown in references (3), (4), (9), (10) and (11). The main advantage of this sample size is that calculations are easy. When computing averages, you can divide by 5 or multiply by 0.2.

A sample size of 4 is also common, as shown in references (7), (10) and

(11). Four unit samples are less expensive than 5 but the calculations are slower and the data is more scattered.

In some circumstances, a sample size of 10 is preferred.[4] Ten might be justified for high volume services and processes if the cost of inspection is low. Ott,[10] however, recommends you don't use sample sizes larger than 7 with variables control charts.

AVERAGE-AND-STANDARD-DEVIATION CHARTS

Average-and-standard-deviation charts use standard deviation in place of range to evaluate sample-to-sample variability. They are not very common, however, especially in the service sector. Why? Because standard deviation charts tend to give users a false sense of accuracy. Standard deviations are not much more discriminating than ranges when sample sizes are 5 or less. When sample sizes are larger, "average" charts tend to lose sensitivity. In support of "range" charts, Grant and Leavenworth[12] wrote: "In practical control-chart work in industry, R rather than s should nearly always be used as a measure of subgroup dispersion . . . partly because R is easier to find in hand calculation. Equally important is the advantage that R is easier to explain; almost everyone can understand range, whereas people with little background in statistics have difficulty understanding standard deviation."

RANGE AND AVERAGE CALCULATIONS

The easiest way to make range calculations is to line up the data by size and then subtract the smallest number from the largest; the result is the range. To calculate an average add all measurements in the sample and divide by the sample size.

PROBLEM 15-1

You have been getting complaints from your sales department about how long it takes to get an order processed. You decide to set up a control chart on this variable. The sample size you select is 5.

The first 5 orders you monitor take 5, 4, 6, 5 and 7 days. The second 5 orders take 6, 4, 4, 5 and 6 days. What are the ranges (R) and averages ($\bar{X}$) for these two sets of orders?

SOLUTION 15-1

Arrange the two sets of data in order:

$$\text{First set: } 4,5,5,6,7$$
$$\text{Second set: } 4,4,5,6,6$$

The range of the first group is: $7 - 4 = 3$
The range of the second group is: $6 - 4 = 2$
The average of the first group is:

$$\text{Average} = \frac{(4 + 5 + 5 + 6 + 7)}{5}$$

$$= \frac{27}{5}$$

$$= 5.4$$

The average of the second group is:

$$\text{Average} = \frac{(4 + 4 + 5 + 6 + 6)}{5}$$

$$= \frac{25}{5}$$

$$= 5.0$$

The following problem involves setting up a control chart from scratch. It has been simplified, however, to include only 10 points; Ott[13] recommends using more than 20 samples.

PROBLEM 15-2

The accounting department has complained about the excessive time spent processing invoices so you decide to set up a control chart on this variable. Five completed invoices will be selected at random each day; the time taken to process the invoices will be plotted on a control chart.

184   QUALITY SERVICE PAYS: SIX KEYS TO SUCCESS!

Results of the first ten days showed the following information:

Day	Days to Complete Processing
1	10 9 6 9 8
2	12 6 10 8 9
3	9 8 9 6 10
4	8 7 9 8 8
5	9 10 9 8 11
6	6 7 9 8 5
7	11 7 10 9 10
8	9 11 9 13 8
9	8 9 6 11 6
10	9 6 7 6 9

Using the above information, set up a control chart that includes upper and lower control limits for both the averages and the ranges.

SOLUTION 15-2

The first step is to calculate the averages and ranges for each of the ten samples. In this case, an average is the sum of the five measurements from a sample, divided by the sample size. The range is the difference between the highest and lowest values in the sample.

The average range ($\bar{R}$) and the grand average ($\bar{\bar{X}}$) also have to be calculated. The average range is the sum of the ranges divided by the number of samples. The grand average is the sum of the averages divided by the number of samples; in this case, there are ten samples.

Results of the calculations follow:

Day	Days to Complete Processing (Daily sample = 5 invoices)	Range (R)	Average ($\bar{X}$)
1	10 9 6 9 8	4	8.4
2	12 6 10 8 9	6	9.0
3	9 8 9 6 10	4	8.4
4	8 7 9 8 8	2	8.0
5	9 10 9 8 11	3	9.4
6	6 7 9 8 5	4	7.0
7	11 7 10 9 10	4	9.4
8	9 11 9 13 8	5	10.0
9	8 9 6 11 6	5	8.0
10	9 6 7 6 9	3	7.4
Total		40	85.0

$$\text{Average range} = \frac{40}{10} = 4$$

$$\text{Grand average} = \frac{85}{10} = 8.5$$

The next step is to calculate the control limits.

$$\begin{aligned}
\text{LCL (averages)} &= \text{Grand average} - (A2 \times R\text{-average}) \\
&= 8.5 - .577 \times 4 \\
&= 8.5 - 2.3 \\
&= 6.2
\end{aligned}$$

The value of "A2" comes from Table 15-1, using a sample size of 5.

$$\begin{aligned}
\text{UCL (averages)} &= \text{Grand average} + (A2 \times R\text{-average}) \\
&= 8.5 + .577 \times 4 \\
&= 8.5 + 2.3 \\
&= 10.8
\end{aligned}$$

$$\begin{aligned}
\text{LCL (R)} &= D3 \times R\text{-average} \\
&= 0 \times 4 \\
&= 0
\end{aligned}$$

$$\begin{aligned}
\text{UCL (R)} &= D4 \times R\text{-average} \\
&= 2.115 \times 4 \\
&= 8.5
\end{aligned}$$

The values of "D3" and "D4" come from Table 15-1, using a sample size of 5 because each daily sample contained five invoices.

The calculations are complete. The final job is to make a control chart using the results of the calculations shown above. Figure 15-3 shows the resulting average-and-range chart.

All of the averages and ranges in Figure 15-3 are randomly distributed between the upper and lower control limits. This implies that the process is in statistical control. An in-control condition, however, would not be present if the points were not distributed randomly. Some criteria used to identify nonrandom distributions include the following:

- There is a distinct trend up or down.
- Two successive points are near one of the control limits.
- Seven successive points are on the same side of the center line of the control chart.
- Ten of 11 successive points are on the same side of the center line.

186   QUALITY SERVICE PAYS: SIX KEYS TO SUCCESS!

Figure 15-3. **Control Chart: Time to Process Invoices**

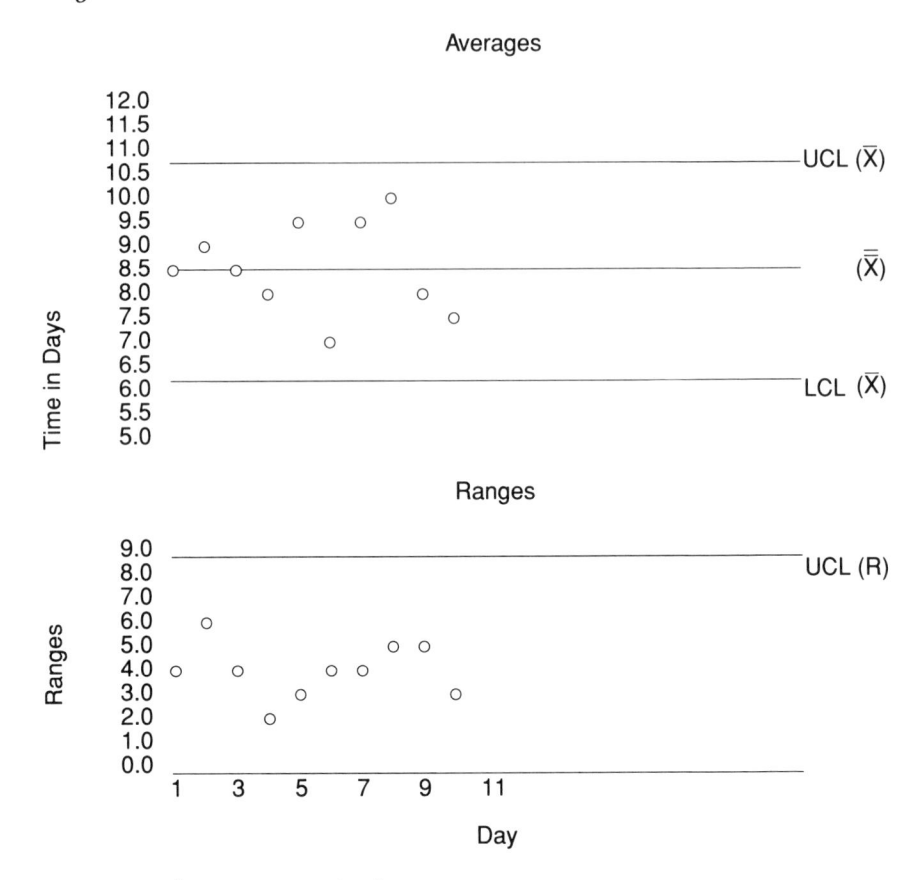

NOTE: Each average contains five measurements.

When one of these conditions occurs, it is wise to investigate. As an example, suppose "the time required to respond to customer complaints" showed 7 successive points on the *low* side of the mean. You would want to find out what happened, making sure the quicker response times were not due to sloppy work or inadequate research. On the other hand, new and better procedures or equipment could have been introduced. When improvements in the system are identified, make them official. After the change is implemented, plot an additional 21 (or more) new points; if the system appears to be in statistical control, calculate new control limits.

When a process is running smoothly, practically all of the points are scattered randomly within the control limits. There is only a 0.3 percent chance that a random point will fall outside the two control limits; 0.13

percent can be expected above the upper control limit and 0.13 percent can be expected below the lower control limit, unless there is an assignable cause. As a consequence, these maverick points should be investigated; they are probably not due to chance. Once the cause is identified, corrective action should be initiated to prevent recurrence.

Being in "statistical control" indicates that the system is running smoothly; it doesn't mean that improvements can't be made. In some cases, data that is "in statistical control" lulls organizations into complacency even though system improvements are needed to make the organization competitive.

If the time to process invoices is causing problems with the customers, despite the system being "in statistical control," improvements should be made to the system. Possible changes include the following:

- Using computers to automate the process
- Reducing the number of steps required
- Improving the invoice forms
- Developing a better training program

All of the above items fall within the control of management, not the workers. In many instances, however, the workers can help identify which of the above responses would do the most good. They may also have ideas about which steps can be eliminated, how invoice forms can be simplified and what types of training would be most useful.

TREND CHARTS VS AVERAGE-AND-RANGE CHARTS

Most trend charts identify the appropriate standard; most average-and-range charts don't. On the other hand, average-and-range charts have control limits; trend charts don't. Despite these differences, most of the chart patterns identified in Chapter 13 apply to average-and-range charts. Here are some examples:

- Average-and-range charts with a process in statistical control resemble the "Happy Days" pattern (Figure 13-1). All points for both the "average" and the "range" charts would fall inside the control limits in a random manner.
- Average-and-range charts having many points outside the control limits often resemble the "Yo-Yo" pattern (Figure 13-2), or the "Sad Sack" pattern (Figure 13-5). Major problems would appear to exist. If both the "average" and the "range" charts have numerous points outside the control limits, the process has probably been changed; find out why. If the "average" chart has many points outside the control

limits but the "range" chart does not, you may have an "Early Warning," or "Get Well," or "Jump-Shift" pattern. If the "range" chart has points outside the control limits but the "average" chart does not, heed the warning—the "average" chart will probably follow.
- Average-and-range charts with a distinct drift might resemble the "Early Warning" pattern (Figure 13-3), or the "Get Well" pattern (Figure 13-4); they should be investigated unless the reason for the drift is known and considered acceptable.
- Average-and-range charts with little or no variation might resemble the "Why Plot?" pattern (Figure 13-6). With this pattern, the "average" charts use a small fraction of the space between the upper and lower control limits; they show little scatter. In addition, the "range" plots normally hug the bottom of the "range" chart; when there's little variation in the averages there should be little variation between individual measurements. This type of chart can occur when the process or the inspection procedures have undergone major changes; a process that shows no variability is often one that is not being properly inspected. "Why Plot?" patterns shouldn't survive long. The reason for the reduced variation should be detected or new control limits calculated or both.
- An "average" chart with a pronounced shift in the averages might resemble the "Jump-Shift" pattern (Figure 13-7). When this occurs, the "range" chart often shows a large increase at the same time, even though points on the "average" chart may stay between the control limits. Whether or not the control limits are breached on either chart, the reason for the shift should be determined. Average-and-range charts require the assumption that you have a normal population. The presence of a "Jump-Shift" pattern indicates the presence of a bimodal or multimodal distribution. Identify the different populations; then, if possible, get rid of all but one.

RANGE CHARTS

Range charts are normally used to identify within-sample or short-term variability. When a range exceeds the upper control limit, excessive short-term variability exists and should be investigated. There are times when range charts tip you off to problems before the average charts show you are out of statistical control. The earlier you know a problem exists, the quicker you can correct it; the quicker you correct it, the less it usually costs.

When the sample size is less than 7, a range chart will have an upper control limit [UCL(R)] but no lower control limit [LCL(R)]—see Table 15-1.

DEFECT PREVENTION

The current trend in quality assurance is to stress defect prevention rather than defect identification. The concept is, "You can't inspect quality into a product or service." Control charts can help prevent or reduce defects. By using them, you can anticipate and avoid many problems. They are also good for identifying the effectiveness of changes. If a new data-entry form is developed to improve data-entry production, control charts on productivity can help verify its effectiveness; when there is a difference, a "Jump-Shift" pattern will develop. If a new safety program has been introduced, control charts on the number of lost-time accidents can be used to monitor its effectiveness. Control charts are simple but powerful tools and are getting increased recognition in the service sector.

SUMMARY

Control charts are good for monitoring and controlling variables—even in the service sector. References (1) through (7) illustrate their potential use. References (7) through (10) provide additional information on the theory behind them.

Food for Thought

Develop a control chart on the time it takes to process your mail. The time spent in a day would be an individual value (X). The average time-per-day during a week would be the value you would plot on your "average" chart. The differences between the least time-per-day and the most time-per-day during each week would be the range you would plot. This exercise can help you answer the following questions.

1. Do you spend a lot of time on the mail?
2. Does the time you spend vary quite a bit?
3. Is variability increased by letting mail pile up?

4. Is the time spent influenced by junk mail?
5. How can you reduce the time spent?

REFERENCES
1. Rebecca Lee Huls, "Dedication to Quality Spans All Industries," *ASQC Quality Congress Transactions,* May 4–6, 1987, pp. 90–95.
2. E. M. Baker and H. L. Artinian, "The Deming Philosophy of Continuing Improvement in a Service Organization," *Quality Progress,* June 1985, pp. 61–69.
3. W. J. McCabe, "Improving Quality and Cutting Costs in a Service Organization," *Quality Progress,* June 1985, pp. 85–89.
4. W. J. McCabe, "Quality Methods Applied to the Business Process," *ASQC Quality Congress Transactions,* May 19–21, 1986, pp. 429–436.
5. John F. Early and Eric D. Dmytrow, "Managing Information in the CPI," *ASQC Quality Congress Transactions,* May 19–21, 1986, pp. 2–9.
6. B. B. Affourtit, "Statistical Process Control (SPC) Implementation—Common Misconceptions," *ASQC Quality Congress Transactions,* May 19–21, 1986, pp. 440–445.
7. A. C. Rosander, *Applications of Quality Control in the Service Industries* (Milwaukee, WI: ASQC Quality Press, 1985), pp. 248–266.
8. Eugene L. Grant and Richard S. Leavenworth, *Statistical Quality Control,* 6th ed. (New York: McGraw-Hill, 1988), pp. 214–216.
9. State University of Iowa Section, ASQC, *Quality Control Training Manual,* 2d ed. 1965, Chapters 4–10.
10. Ellis R. Ott, *Process Quality Control* (New York: McGraw-Hill, 1975), pp. 44–68.
11. Western Electric Company, AT&T, *Statistical Quality Control Handbook,* 11th ed. (Charlotte, NC: Delmar Printing, 1985), pp. 12–31.
12. Grant and Leavenworth, *Statistical Quality Control,* p. 81.
13. Ott, *Process Quality Control,* p. 28.

Chapter 16

Control Charts for Attributes

Attributes control charts are similar to the average-and-range charts covered in Chapter 15. Both are control charts. Both usually have upper control limits three standard deviations above the mean. Both usually have lower control limits three standard deviations below the mean. Both help identify trends. Both help control and improve processes.

Here are some differences between them:

- Attributes control charts use attributes in place of variables.
- Attributes control charts don't include range data.
- Attributes control charts usually have sample sizes greater than 100;[1] variables control charts usually have sample sizes less than 10.[2]
- Attributes and variables have different abbreviations, and different formulas for calculating control limits.

Figure 16-1 shows a typical attributes control chart.

Figure 16-1. p-Control Chart: Clerical Error Rate—Proportion Nonconforming; Sample Size (n) = 200

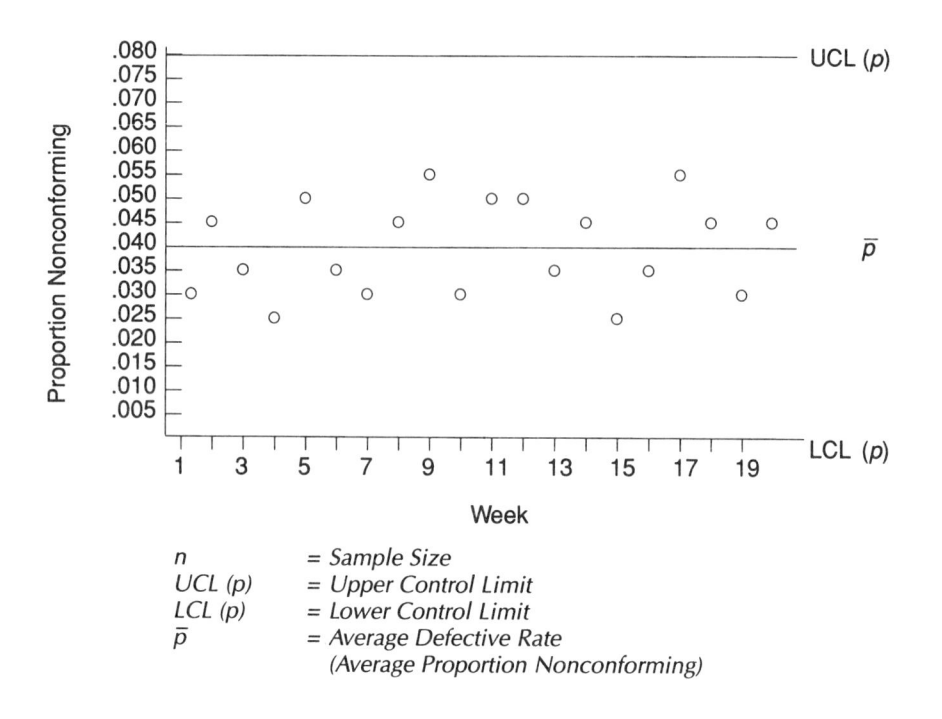

```
n         = Sample Size
UCL (p)   = Upper Control Limit
LCL (p)   = Lower Control Limit
p̄         = Average Defective Rate
            (Average Proportion Nonconforming)
```

WHY DO ATTRIBUTES CHARTS REQUIRE LARGER SAMPLES?

Attributes usually follow a binomial rather than a normal distribution. The two distributions, however, approximate each other when the attribute sample sizes are large and the average attribute value ($\bar{p}$) approaches 0.5. According to Grant and Leavenworth,[1] "if n (the sample size) is large enough—say in the hundreds or more—the normal curve may be used for a wide range of values of p and will give an approximation to the binomial that is good enough for practical purposes."

The sample sizes for attributes control charts are usually larger than the sample sizes for variables control charts. The cost of inspecting a unit within an attribute sample, however, is usually lower than the cost of inspecting a unit within a variables sample. As a consequence there is no consistent cost advantage for either approach.

ABBREVIATIONS

The letter n represents the sample size, just as it did with variables charts. The letter p (lowercase) represents a proportion but P (uppercase) represents a percentage. If your sample size is 100 and you find 5 rejections (nonconforming units), the value of p is:

$$p = \frac{\text{number nonconforming}}{\text{sample size}}$$
$$= 5/100$$
$$= .05$$

The value of P (percent) is:

$$P = p \times 100$$
$$= 5 \text{ percent}$$

In formulas, variables are usually represented by X; attributes are usually represented by either p for proportions or P for percentages. The average of several p measurements is $\bar{p}$ and the average of several P measurements is $\bar{P}$. Both follow the convention, "A letter or abbreviation with a bar above it is an average; one with two bars above it is a grand average or the average of a number averages."

The first part of this chapter will be devoted to p-charts and P-charts, since they are the most common attribute charts used in the service sector. P-charts are essentially the same as p-charts except the data and formulas are expressed in percentages instead of proportions.

We will cover np-charts and c-charts at the end of the chapter.

APPLICATIONS

Examples of p-chart applications for the service sector include the following:

Huls[3] discusses using p-charts to control:

- Proportion of mail requests answered on time
- Proportion of transactions handled properly

Bajaria and Copp[4] used p-charts to control process output.

Duncan[5] recommends p-charts for controlling "fraction nonconforming" and "fraction rejected."

Rosander[6] suggests p-charts for:

- Errors in typing
- Errors in filling mail orders
- Errors in key-punch coding
- Errors in transcribing data

Examples of P-chart applications for the service sector include the following:

Lawson[7] used P-charts to control:

- Percentage of commercial loan notes not properly completed
- Percentage of time that systems are on line
- Percentage of items missing from statements
- Percentage of errors in money transfers

McCabe[8] used P-charts to control the errors of buyers. He also used them for purchase order errors.[9]

Other typical services can be monitored with p-charts and P-charts including:

- *Airline landings*: Are they late?
- *Rental cars*: Are they cleaned properly?
- *Sales contacts*: Was a sale made?
- *Freight bills*: Were there errors?
- *Invoices*: Were they right?
- *Documents*: Were they misfiled?
- *Newspapers*: Were they delivered on time?
- *Design changes*: Were they rejected?
- *Billings*: Were there any errors?
- *Shipments*: Were they on time?
- *Mail*: Was it addressed properly?
- *Hamburgers*: Were they cold?
- *Hotel rooms*: Were they prepared properly?
- *Customer service*: Was it acceptable?
- *Transactions of a bank teller*: Were they right?
- *Letters*: Were the formats and spelling correct?

The most difficult task you face when introducing charts involves deciding what to plot. Examples in this book will give you an idea of how others have used them. The best applications for your department, however, must be determined by those familiar with your operation.

WHAT CAN ATTRIBUTES CONTROL CHARTS TELL YOU?

Assume that ABC Airline's upper control limit for late flights is five percent. If six percent of their flights are late this month, they are statistically out of control. When this situation is discovered, management should be alerted and reasons for the problem should be investigated. The probability of there being no assignable cause approaches one chance out of a thousand based on the assumption that the distribution is approximately normal (see Chapter 14). Details on calculating control limits for attribute charts are shown later in this chapter.

Control charts tell you whether a process is running smoothly or whether something has changed. Being in statistical control, however, doesn't necessarily mean that no opportunity for improvement exists. You may have to improve your process capability and adjust your control limits in order to be competitive.

Assume, for example, that you are monitoring freight billings and your lower control limit for billing errors is four percent. Then, during June, your error rate drops to two percent. Here, the control chart signals a change; an unexpected improvement has taken place. This is the flip side of control charts; they not only help spot problems, they also help identify process improvements.

In both situations, supervision should be alerted. In this case it is important to know what improvements were made in the freight billing operation. For example, an error-prone clerk could have gone on vacation. New computer equipment could have been added to eliminate errors in the calculations. Edits could have been added to the old computer program; edits help identify errors in data at the time they are entered into the computer. Another possibility is that someone in the office developed a better method of billing customers. Once improvements are identified and verified, they should be incorporated into the system.

- If the absence of an error-prone clerk made things better, reasons for the clerk's high error rate should be studied. It is possible that additional training is all that's needed.
- If computer equipment or program edits contributed to the reduction in errors, similar improvements should be considered in other parts of the company.

- If better ways of doing the work are found and verified, they should become part of the standard procedure.

There's another alternative that should be explored. The reviewers may have relaxed, allowing more errors to slip through undetected.

p-CHARTS

When service companies turn to control charts, they usually start by monitoring error rates. The term "error rates" covers a broad assortment of items including slipped schedules, substandard work, inadequate service and other good-vs-bad evaluations. The *p*-chart is a popular tool for monitoring and controlling these activities.

Use *p*-charts to help you evaluate the overall quality of your product or service. Was it good or bad? Was the flight on time or late? Was the letter typed properly or did it have to be redone? With *p*-charts, each entry is shown as a proportion (percent divided by 100).

You may also consider *P*-charts, which involve percentages in place of proportions. Some authors use the lowercase *p* when proportions are used and the uppercase *P* when percentages are used.[10] Others use the lowercase *p* for both proportions and percentages[11,12]

Calculating Proportions

Attribute control charts can be developed for percent defective (*P*) or proportion defective (*p*). The difference is in the formulas used to calculate the control limits. The first part of this section stresses proportions. The *p* value for defectives, expressed as a proportion is

$$\frac{\text{Number of defectives}}{\text{Number evaluated}}$$

If you already have data in the form of percentages, divide the numbers by 100 to get proportions.

PROBLEM 16-1

In the month of July, bank teller Caron King processed 1000 transactions for her bank. During this period, she made 2 faulty transactions that had to be corrected before the accounts would balance. What defective rate or *p*-value did she have?

SOLUTION 16-1

e = the number of incorrect transactions
 = 2
n = the number of transactions in the sample
 = 1000

$$p = \frac{e}{n} \quad \text{(where } p \text{ is expressed as a proportion)}$$

$$= \frac{2}{1000}$$

$$= .002$$

Calculating Averages ($\bar{p}$)

The first step in setting up a *p*-chart is to calculate the average value of *p*. The formula is $\bar{p}$ = the sum of the incorrect transactions divided by the sum of the samples, or,

$$\bar{p} = \frac{\Sigma(e)}{\Sigma(n)}$$

where $\Sigma(e)$ is the sum of the errors or other items being measured, and $\Sigma(n)$ is the total number of units sampled.

If all the samples are the same size, the value of $\bar{p}$ can be calculated by adding all of the values for *p* and dividing by the number of samples.

PROBLEM 16-2

You've been having problems in your shipping department; too many deliveries went to wrong addresses. In addition, too many customers have been complaining about receiving the wrong merchandise. As a consequence, you made a trend chart for monitoring progress.

A shipment is considered to be a single defective if there is an error in the address, if there is an error in the contents or if both are wrong.

You now have data for 6 weeks. You want to set up a tentative control chart on the shipping operation, even though you realize that you will need more than 20 samples (weeks) of data for a more permanent evaluation.[13]

Your data shows:

Week	Shipments Inspected (n)	Defective Shipments Found (e)
1	100	10
2	100	12
3	100	16
4	100	12
5	100	16
6	100	12

Find the average error rate.

SOLUTION 16-2

Add the columns to get values for n(total) and e(total). Also calculate the weekly values of p.

Week	Shipments Inspected (n)	Defective Shipments Found (e)	Error Rate $\left(p = \frac{e}{n}\right)$
1	100	10	.10
2	100	12	.12
3	100	16	.16
4	100	12	.12
5	100	16	.16
6	100	12	.12
Total	600	78	.78

$n \text{ (total)} = 600$

$e \text{ (total)} = 78$

$$\bar{p} = \frac{\Sigma(e)}{\Sigma(n)}$$

$$= \frac{78}{600}$$

$$= .13$$

In this case, we could have added the six values of p and divided by 6. The results would still be .13. If the sample sizes varied from week to week, however, this would not have been the case.

Ideally, each weekly sample should be the same size. Grant and Leavenworth,[14] however, acknowledge that "where the variation in subgroup size is not too great (for example, where the maximum and minimum subgroups are not more than 25% away from the average) it often may be good enough for practical purposes to establish a single set of control limits based on the expected average subgroup size."

Calculating Control Limits

The control limits for a p-chart are:

$$\text{upper control limit (UCL)} = \bar{p} + 3\sqrt{\frac{\bar{p}(1-\bar{p})}{n}}$$

and

$$\text{lower control limit (LCL)} = \bar{p} - 3\sqrt{\frac{\bar{p}(1-\bar{p})}{n}}$$

where:

$\bar{p}$ = average error rate (as a proportion).
n = sample size. If samples vary slightly, use the average sample size.

PROBLEM 16-3

Using data from Problem 16-2, calculate the upper control limit (UCL) and the lower control limit (LCL) for the shipping operation.

SOLUTION 16-3

Here are the data need to solve this problem:

Average fraction defective ($\bar{p}$) = .13 (see Problem 16-2)

Average sample size (n) = 100

upper control limit (UCL) = $\bar{p} + 3\sqrt{\dfrac{\bar{p}(1-\bar{p})}{n}}$

$= .13 + 3\sqrt{\dfrac{.13(1-.13)}{100}}$

$= .13 + 3\sqrt{\dfrac{.13 \times .87}{100}}$

$= .13 + 3\sqrt{.001131}$

$= .13 + 3 \times .03363$
$= .13 + .10$
$= .23$

lower control limit (LCL) = $\bar{p} - 3\sqrt{\dfrac{\bar{p}(1-\bar{p})}{n}}$

$= .13 - 3\sqrt{\dfrac{.13(1-.13)}{100}}$

$= .13 - 3\sqrt{\dfrac{.13 \times .87}{100}}$

$= .13 - 3\sqrt{.001131}$

$= .13 - 3 \times .03363$
$= .13 - .10$
$= .03$

The upper control limit is normally three standard deviations above the average; the lower control limit is normally three standard deviations below. This means that very few points will fall outside the two control limits without an assignable cause. Control charts tell you when to look for assignable causes.

Plotting Control Charts

Having computed the average ($\bar{p}$), the upper control limit (UCL) and the lower control limit (LCL), the next step is plotting a control chart. Figure 16-2 is a chart using the data listed in Problem 16-2 and the control limits calculated in Problem 16-3.

In Figure 16-2, all six weeks are within the upper and lower control limits. In view of the small number of points on the chart, it is difficult to identify chart patterns like those discussed under trend charts and average-and-range charts. The same patterns, however, are also applicable

Figure 16-2. p-Control Chart: Shipments — Proportion Nonconforming; Sample Size (n) = 100

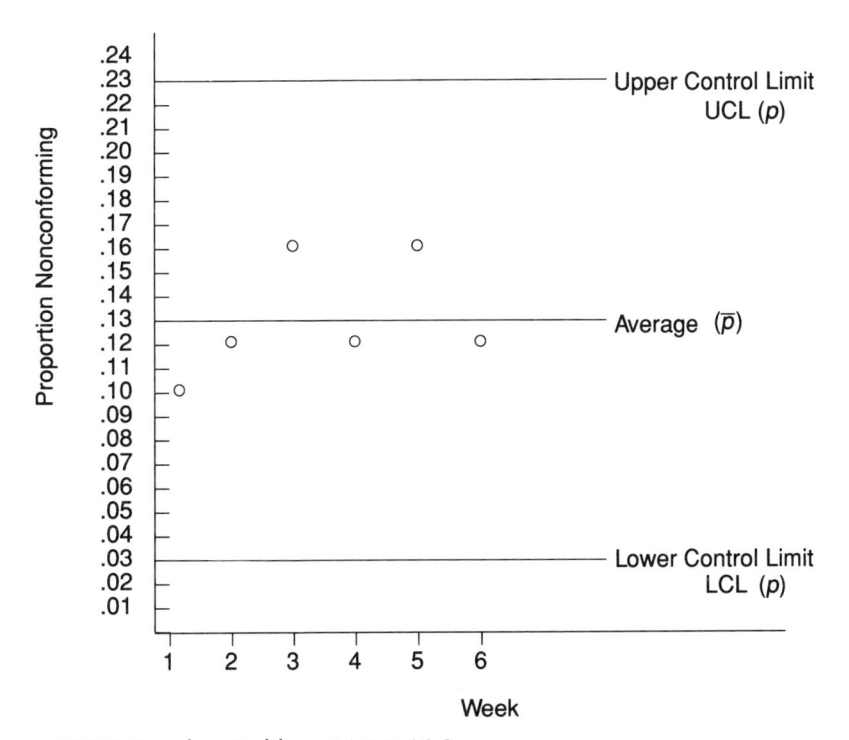

NOTE: Based on Problems 16-2 & 16-3.

to attributes control charts and are apt to be detected after more points become available. The small number of points also make the control limits in Figure 16-2 quite tentative; the control limits should be recalculated after 21 or more points become available.[13]

Values for the upper control limit and the lower control limit are constant as long as the average ($\bar{p}$), the sample size, the people and the process don't change.

Working with Percentages

Problem 16-4 uses data from Problem 16-2. This approach is intended to facilitate step-by-step comparisons between calculations for p-charts and P-charts.

PROBLEM 16-4

After Figure 16-2 was presented to the boss, she decided that proportions might be harder to evaluate than percentages. As a consequence, she asked that everything be converted. Now we need to redo the calculations and make a P-chart using the same data we had in Problem 16-2.

SOLUTION 16-4

First, convert the p numbers to P.

Week	Defective Rate, p as a proportion	Defective Rate, P as a percentage ($P = p \times 100$)
1	.10	10
2	.12	12
3	.16	16
4	.12	12
5	.16	16
6	.12	12
Total	.78	78

$$\bar{P} = \frac{78}{6}$$
$$= 13\%$$

Now, recalculate the control limits.

$$\text{Average error rate } (\bar{P}) = 13\%$$
$$\text{Average sample size } (n) = 100$$

The new formula for UCL is:

$$\text{upper control limit (UCL)} \atop \text{(percents)} \quad = \bar{P} + 3\sqrt{\frac{\bar{P}(100 - \bar{P})}{n}}$$

$$= 13 + 3\sqrt{\frac{13(100-13)}{100}}$$

$$= 13 + 3\sqrt{\frac{13 \times 87}{100}}$$

$$= 13 + 3\sqrt{11.31}$$

$$= 13 + 3 \times 3.363$$

$$= 13 + 10$$

$$= 23 \text{ percent}$$

The new formula for LCL is:

$$\text{lower control limit (LCL)} = \bar{P} - 3\sqrt{\frac{\bar{P}(100 - \bar{P})}{n}}$$

$$= 13 - 3\sqrt{\frac{13(100-13)}{100}}$$

$$= 13 - 3\sqrt{\frac{13 \times 87}{100}}$$

$$= 13 - 3\sqrt{11.31}$$

$$= 13 - 3 \times 3.363$$

$$= 13 - 10$$

$$= 3 \text{ percent}$$

The *P*-chart for this problem is shown in Figure 16-3.

Figure 16-3. **P-Control Chart: Shipments — Percent Nonconforming Sample Size (*n*) = 100**

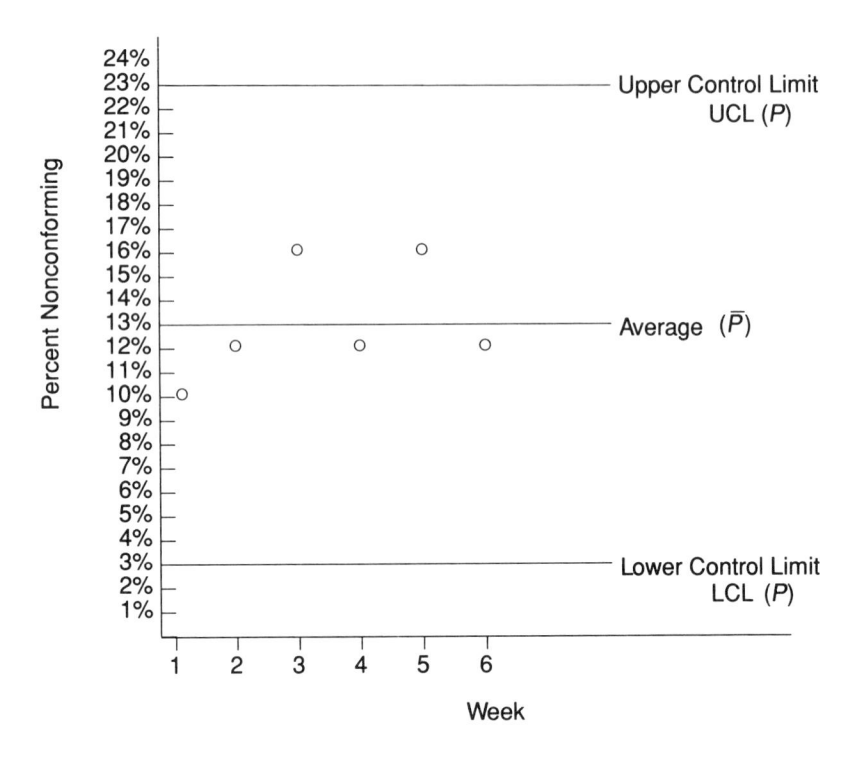

NOTE: Based on Problem 16-4.

A comparison of Figure 16-3 with Figure 16-2 shows that the only differences between the *p*-chart and the *P*-chart is the location of the decimal points.

np-CHARTS

There are times when management is interested in the number of errors rather than the proportion or percentage. When this occurs, *np*-charts can be used. Artinian and Baker,[15] for example, use *np*-charts for the number of claims at an order processing center.

With a given set of data, *np*-charts provide the same chart patterns as *p*- and *P*-charts; *np*-charts, however, have two advantages. First, many managers like them; it pays to please the boss. Second, they require fewer calculations; you just count the number of defectives or nonconforming units. It isn't necessary to calculate proportions or percentages for each sample.

The main disadvantage of *np*-charts is they require a constant sample size. With *np*-charts, allowing sample sizes to fluctuate would be like giving all college students the same math proficiency exam without considering the student's major or class level. With students, the Ph.D.-candidate math majors would have an advantage over the beginning English majors. With *np*-charts, the smallest samples would contain the fewest number of errors (everything else being equal).

Here are the formulas for *np* control limits:

$$\text{UCL } (np) = n\bar{p} + 3\sqrt{n\bar{p}(1-\bar{p})}$$

$$\text{LCL } (np) = n\bar{p} - 3\sqrt{n\bar{p}(1-\bar{p})}$$

Problem 16-5 illustrates how *np*-charts can be set up with the same data used in Problems 16-2 and 16-4.

PROBLEM 16-5

Figure 16-3 was presented to the boss the day after she went to a seminar where *np*-charts were discussed. She wondered whether *np*-charts might be easier to understand than either *p*-charts or *P*-charts. To find out, she asked that everything be converted a second time. Now we need to redo the calculations to make an *np*-chart based on data used in Problem 16-2.

SOLUTION 16-5

Week	Shipments Inspected (n)	Defective Shipments Found
1	100	10
2	100	12
3	100	16
4	100	12
5	100	16
6	100	12
Total	600	78

$n\bar{p}$ = average number of defects found

$$= \frac{78}{6}$$

$$= 13$$

$$\bar{p} = \frac{\text{total defects found}}{\text{total inspected}}$$

$$= \frac{78}{600}$$

$$= .13$$

$$\text{UCL } n\bar{p} = n\bar{p} + 3\sqrt{n\bar{p}(1-\bar{p})}$$

$$= 13 + 3\sqrt{13(1-.13)}$$

$$= 13 + 3\sqrt{11.31}$$

$$= 13 + 3 \times 3.363$$

$$= 13 + 10$$

$$= 23$$

$$\text{LCL } n\bar{p} = n\bar{p} - 3\sqrt{n\bar{p}(1-\bar{p})}$$

But

$$3\sqrt{n\bar{p}(1-\bar{p})} = 10$$

as shown above. Therefore,

$$\text{LCL } (np) = 13 - 10$$
$$= 3$$

The *np*-chart presented to the boss is shown in Figure 16-4. Note the similarities between the *np*-chart and the *P*-chart (Figure 16-3).

Figure 16-4. np-Control Chart: Shipments — Number Nonconforming Sample Size (n) = 100

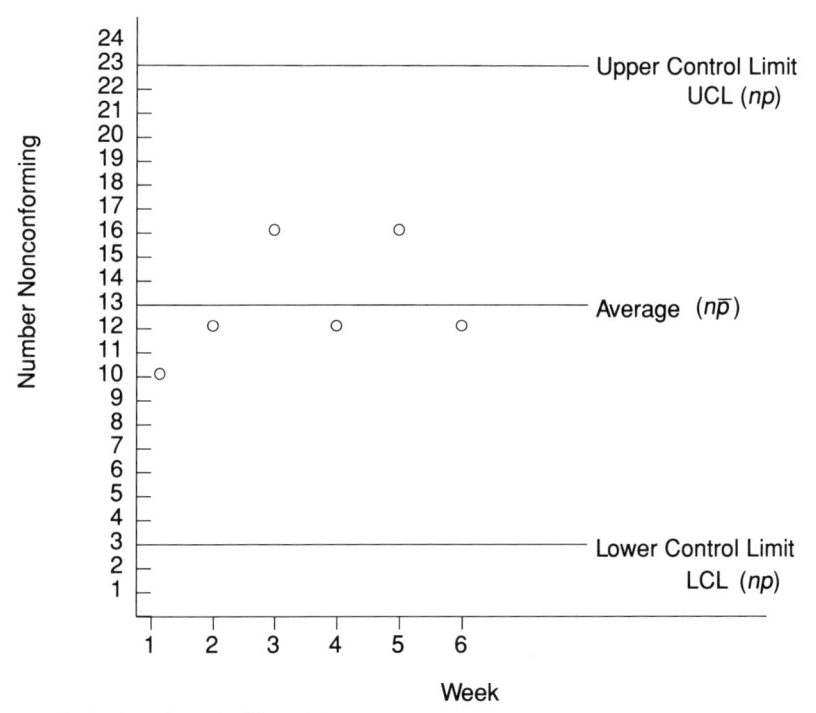

```
         24
         23 ─────────────────────────── Upper Control Limit
         22                                UCL (np)
         21
         20
         19
         18
         17
         16         o         o
         15
         14
         13 ─────────────────────────── Average (np̄)
         12    o         o         o
         11
         10 o
Number    9
Nonconforming 8
          7
          6
          5
          4
          3 ─────────────────────────── Lower Control Limit
          2                                LCL (np)
          1
            1    2    3    4    5    6
                       Week
```

NOTE: Based on Problem 16-5.

c-CHARTS

Although c-charts are used in the service sector, they are not as easy to interpret as average-and-range charts. The c-charts follow a Poisson distribution, which is not symmetrical.[17] Average-and-range charts assume a normal distribution, which is symmetrical, while p- and P-charts approximate a normal distribution as long as the sample sizes are large and the values of p are not too small. As a consequence, with c-charts you can't be sure that only one point out of a thousand will be above the upper control limit. Nor can you assume that one point out of a thousand will be below the lower control limit. As long as these shortcomings are known and accepted, however, c-charts can be used effectively. The probability of points being outside the two control limits is still quite small—and they should be investigated.

A typical *c*-chart is shown in Figure 16-5.

Figure 16-5. **Typical *c*-Control Chart: Errors Per 5 Database Files Sample Size (*n*) = 5 Database Files**

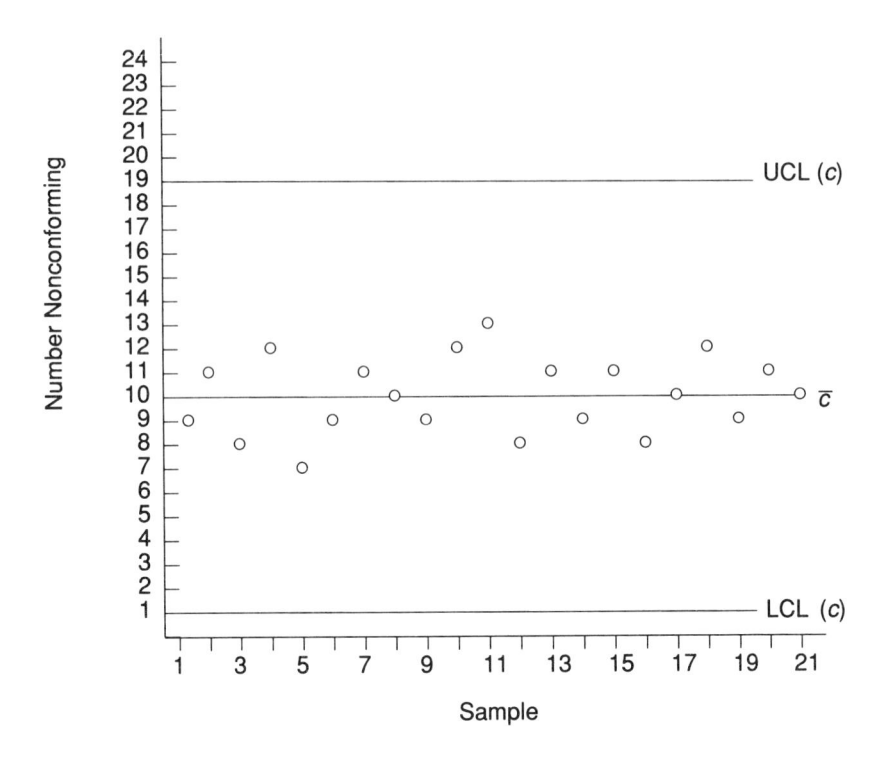

Although *c*-charts are much like *np*-charts they measure defects or errors rather than the defectives or number of units that are nonconforming. McCabe[17] used *c*-charts to study "problems per move" reported by customers after being relocated by a contractor. Rosander,[16] on the other hand, used *c*-charts to control errors made by document transcribers.

Here are the formulas for *c*-chart control limits:

$$UCL(c) = \bar{c} + 3\sqrt{\bar{c}}$$
$$LCL(c) = \bar{c} - 3\sqrt{\bar{c}}$$

Problem 16-6 illustrates how *c*-charts can be set up.

PROBLEM 16-6

The typing pool in a large company was having quality problems and decided to set up control charts on their operation. Few documents went through the first draft with no errors, and some had many mistakes. As a consequence, the typing pool's customers were complaining about having to do excessive proofing. The pool's supervisor decided to plot "errors per ten pages of typing" for each typist. The choice of this type of c-chart was based on the need to differentiate between documents that had a single error and those that had many.

Construct a preliminary c-chart from the following performance data, keeping in mind that new control limits will be needed after 21 or more points are available.

Day	Errors/10 pages of typing
1	11
2	13
3	10
4	10
5	12
6	10
7	16
8	9
9	8
10	11

SOLUTION 16-7

The first step is to calculate $\bar{c}$. Then calculate the two control limits.

Day	Errors/10 pages of typing
1	11
2	13
3	10
4	10
5	12
6	10
7	16
8	9
9	8
10	11
Total	110

$$\bar{c} = \text{average number of errors per sample}$$

$$= \frac{\text{total number of errors}}{\text{number of samples}}$$

$$= \frac{110}{10}$$

$$= 11$$

$$\text{UCL}(c) = \bar{c} + 3\sqrt{\bar{c}}$$

$$= 11 + 3\sqrt{11}$$

$$= 11 + 3 \times 3.3166$$
$$= 11 + 10$$
$$= 21$$

$$\text{LCL}(c) = \bar{c} - 3\sqrt{\bar{c}}$$

$$= 11 - 3\sqrt{11}$$
$$= 11 - 3 \times 3.3166$$
$$= 11 - 10$$
$$= 1$$

The results of the above calculations are shown in Figure 16-6.

SUMMARY

P-charts, *p*-charts, *np*-charts and *c*-charts are all attributes control charts. The choice of which to use is often dictated by the personal preferences of the people involved; however, there are exceptions:
1. If the sample size is allowed to vary, *c*-charts and *np*-charts can be misleading. With *P*-charts and *p*-charts, some variation is permitted as long as the extreme sample sizes are within 25% of the mean.[14]
2. *P*-charts and *p*-charts work best with sample sizes above 100 units; the larger the sample size, the closer the data approximates a normal distribution.

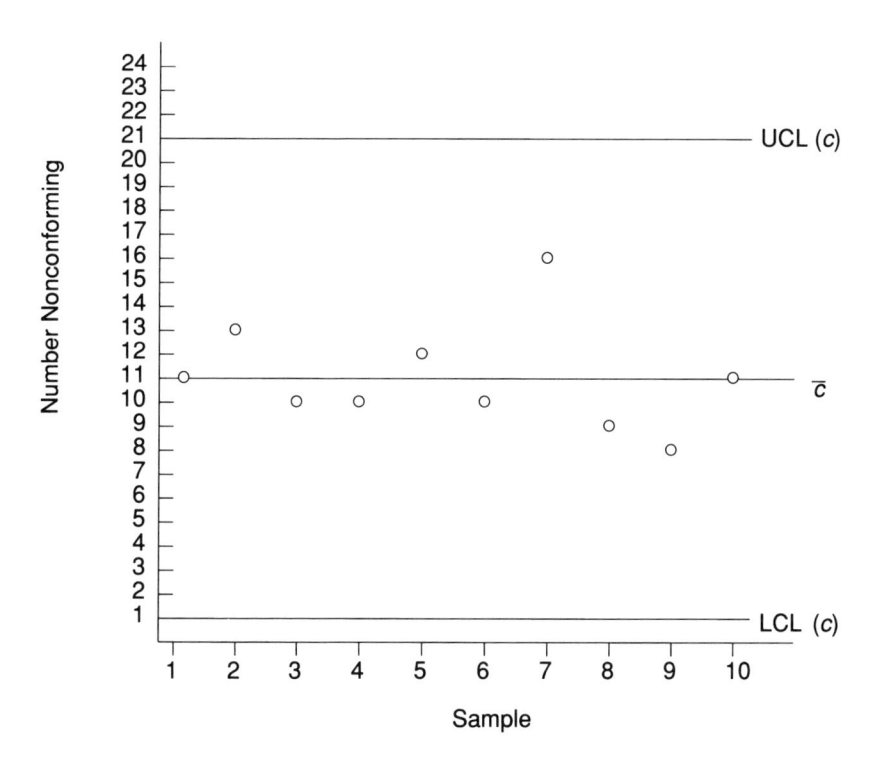

Figure 16-6. c-Control Chart: Errors Per 10 Pages of Typing
Sample Size (N) = 10 Pages of Typing

NOTE: Based on Problem 16-7.

3. P-charts, p-charts and np-charts are used to monitor and control defectives; c-charts are used to monitor and control defects. A defective can have more than one defect or nonconforming attribute.

FOOD FOR THOUGHT

Make a c-chart on the errors you find in correspondence passing over your desk. In order to keep things simple, consider each page a sample. If you find three spelling errors and one obvious erasure on the first page, the c value for that page is four.

Since this is only an exercise, limit the plot to 10 samples. In practice, however, you would want at least 21 points before fixing control limits. After completing the chart, answer the following questions:

1. Were all of the points in statistical control (i.e., distributed within the control limits in a random manner)?
2. If you find points out of statistical control, did they all represent the work of a single individual?
3. Did you expect to find as many errors as you did?

REFERENCES
1. Eugene L. Grant and Richard S. Leavenworth, *Statistical Quality Control*, 6th ed. (New York: McGraw-Hill, 1988), p. 216.
2. Ellis R. Ott, *Process Quality Control* (New York: McGraw-Hill, 1975), p. 45.
3. Rebecca Lee Huls, "Dedication to Quality Spans All Industries," *ASQC Quality Congress Transactions*, May 4–6, 1987, pp. 90–95.
4. H. J. Bajaria and R. P. Copp, "Quality Improvement: In Front of Live Problems," *ASQC Quality Congress Transactions*, May 9–11, 1988, pp. 170–179.
5. Acheson J. Duncan, *Quality Control and Industrial Statistics*, 5th ed. (Homewood, IL: Irwin, 1986), pp. 422–433.
6. A. C. Rosander, *Applications of Quality Control in the Service Industries* (Milwaukee, WI: ASQC Quality Press, 1985), pp. 253.
7. Barry Lawson, "Bank Management Acceptance and Use of Simplified Quality Control Techniques," *Administrative Applications Division 1978 Yearbook*, pp. 58–70.
8. W. J. McCabe, "Improving the Business Process," *ASQC Quality Congress Transactions*, May 9–11, 1988, pp. 344–351.
9. W. J. McCabe, "Quality Methods Applied to the Business Process," *ASQC Quality Congress Transactions*, May 19–21, 1986, pp. 429–436.
10. Ott, *Process Quality Control*, p. 73.
11. State University of Iowa Section, ASQC, *Quality Control Training Manual*, 2d ed. 1965, p. 74.
12. Armand V. Feigenbaum, *Total Quality Control* (New York: McGraw-Hill, 1983), p. 435.
13. Ott, *Process Quality Control*, p. 28.
14. Grant and Leavenworth, *Statistical Quality Control*, p. 248.
15. H. L. M. Artinian and Edward M. Baker, "Improving Quality: the Critical Hidden Line," *ASQC Quality Congress Transactions*, May 9–11, 1988, pp. 109–113.

16. Grant and Leavenworth, *Statistical Quality Control*, p. 276.
17. W. J. McCabe, "Improving Quality and Cutting Costs in a Service Organization," *Quality Progress*, June 1985, pp. 85–89.
18. Rosander, *Applications of Quality Control in the Service Industries*, p. 256.

Chapter 17

Capability Studies

Capability studies are being discovered by the service sector; they help blind managers see. When managers set standards and specifications without knowing the capability of their process, they're flying blind like injured bats with damaged radar. In other words, capability studies guide management to meaningful, objective standards, making the dart-board approach obsolete.

Latzko,[1] gives capability studies priority when he says, "The function of clerical quality control is to first determine the process capability; second, to identify any outlier clerk."

WHAT ARE CAPABILITY STUDIES?

Hy Pitt[2] wrote that process capability studies are tools that help you "determine the inherent, or built-in, variability of the process, devoid of assignable causes." He also noted that process capability shouldn't be confused with process performance, which he defines as "the actual performance of the process, which may include assignable causes that make the variability greater than what is inherent in the process."

ANSI/ASQC A1-1987[3] says that process capability is a "statistical measure of the inherent process variability for a given characteristic."

Feigenbaum[4] identified some limitations of capability studies when he wrote, "To be meaningful, a process capability must be stated with respect to a given set of specifically listed process factors." In other words, if you change the process or procedure, you should run a new process capability study. Changing the scope of the study can also change the results. As an example, you can determine the process capability for a group of technicians doing travel pay calculations according to one specific procedure. You can also determine the process capability of each individual within the same group, using the same procedure. The results for individuals, however, will seldom be the same as the results for the group because the sample sizes will normally be different; a change in the sample size requires a change in the process capability calculations (see Problems 17-1 and 17-2).

WHY RUN CAPABILITY STUDIES?

Reasons for running capability studies include the following:

- To determine the natural process limits (NPL)
- To determine the capability of the group
- To set standards and specifications
- To determine the capability of individual workers
- To help identify and eliminate "unnatural" variation

Natural process limits (NPL). According to ANSI, the natural process limits (NPL) are the "limits which include a stated fraction of the individuals in a population . . . . They are mostly used to compare the natural capability of the process to tolerance limits."[5] ANSI also states: "For populations with a Normal (Gaussian) Distribution, the normal process limits ordinarily will be at +/- 3 standard deviations." Note the similarity between the natural process limits (NPL) and the control limits discussed in the chapters on control charts. They are both +/- 3 standard deviations from the mean.

When you know the natural process limits, you know the capability your process has after all "unnatural" sources of variation are removed—in other words, you know your process capability under the conditions of the study. Knowing the NPL is important. As Hy Pitt[2] says, "Running a process, without knowledge of its ability to meet specifications, is a risky business and is a severe handicap to the quality performance of the company."

The capability of the group. When you know the capability of the group, you can use that information for setting standards for the group.

Standards and specifications. In the past, standards and specifications have been set by a multitude of criteria ranging from scientific wild guesses to capability studies. The latter is preferable. If you don't know what your processes, procedures and people are capable of doing, you have no idea how close they are to their current potential. Standards should not be too loose nor too difficult. If they are too loose, workers are not challenged. If they are too difficult, workers find them impossible and quit trying.

Many standards are based on presumed need with no regard for capability. For example, Dmytrow[6] documents a Bureau of Labor Statistics data-input operation where the standard wasn't being met 40 percent of the time. Intensive troubleshooting led to system changes that reduced the figure to 20 percent nonconforming; the standard still demanded more than the improved process capability could provide. It's highly unlikely that capability studies were used to set the standard; it must have been based on presumed need.

The capability of individual workers. Once you know the capability of the group, it often helps to determine the capability of individuals. Then you can identify which workers are helping and which are hurting the group's performance. In the service sector, variation in the capability of individuals often has a greater impact on quality than it does in the manufacturing sector. At the Air Reserve Personnel Center, for example, I noted a tenfold difference between the error rates of my best and my worst technicians; I never noted a comparable difference in the manufacturing sector.

When service organizations run capability studies on individuals, they can identify outstanding as well as marginal workers. Armed with this information, they can work with both. Supervision can determine what the better employees are doing right; in many instances, they develop techniques that are better than the "official" ones. Those techniques should be investigated. In some instances, their adoption will raise the capability of the entire group. With marginal workers, supervision can determine what they are doing wrong and help them correct it.

Identifying and eliminating "unnatural" variation. This is a major factor in process improvement. Typical causes of "unnatural" variation include:

- Improperly or inadequately trained personnel
- Faulty equipment (like a typewriter that stutters)
- Unclear procedures
- Confusing forms
- Poor working conditions (light, temperature, humidity, noise, etc.)

PREPARATION FOR CAPABILITY STUDIES

The first step in preparing for a capability study is to determine whether the system is in statistical control. The most common tools used for this task are histograms and control charts.

Histograms were covered in Chapter 14; they give a good indication of whether the population is normal. They also help determine whether the system is out of statistical control. If you have a normal population, the histogram will have a symmetrical, bell-shaped curve. If you have a bimodal population, or one that shows other gross variations from a bell-shaped curve, investigate. If possible, eliminate multiple procedures and other unnecessary sources of variation before the capability study is started.

Control charts are also excellent tools for showing whether you are in statistical control, which is a prerequisite to running capability studies. If the control charts show points outside the control limits or an excessive number of points on one side of the mean or a distinct trend, corrective action should be initiated before the capability test is started.

IMPLEMENTING A CAPABILITY STUDY (ATTRIBUTES)

In the service sector, it is frequently necessary to set standards for error rates. It is usually unprofitable, however, to set these performance criteria without knowing the capability of the process and the individuals doing the work.

Steps for implementing capability studies (attributes) include the following:

- Ensure that the process is in statistical control.
- Select personnel to participate in the study.
- Document conditions of the test.
- Run the test.
- Analyze the data.

Ensuring statistical control. The best way to evaluate whether a process is in statistical control is to prepare a control chart; with error rates, a P-chart is appropriate. Procedures for determining whether these charts are "in statistical control" were covered in the last chapter.

If a histogram is used to supplement the control chart, expect a slightly unsymmetrical distribution; attribute analyses usually produce histograms that are tilted to one side or skewed. This deviation from a bell-shaped curve is usually acceptable, however, as long as samples contain 100 units or more.[7] Chapter 14 contains more details on histograms.

Selecting personnel. Personnel selected for a capability study should be representative workers who are familiar with the procedure to be used. Don't pick unrepresentative workers. This rule can eliminate trainees whose work hasn't reached a steady state. It can also screen those on probation for poor performance; if their production were acceptable, they wouldn't be on probation. Even sick employees might be removed from the test; those who are ailing seldom operate at their true capability. Why screen participants? Because the objective of the study is to determine process capability, not process performance.

Inspectors who review the work should also be selected with care; you want the results to reflect actual quality, not presumed quality.

Documenting conditions. Record names of personnel working on the test, including the inspectors and the supervisors. Also, document what procedures and equipment will be used. Then keep everything as stable as possible. With a computer-input study, for example, introduction of a new computer terminal might invalidate the test; it takes time to get acquainted with new equipment. With clerical operations, a new supervisor might influence the clerk's performance. New input forms or new data-entry formats have similar unsettling effects on workers. Changes occurring during the test should be thoroughly documented; their impact can be evaluated after the test is over.

Running the test. Capability studies are often run on "typical" test data where each participant has identical work. This enables supervision to evaluate the process in a controlled but representative work situation. The environment should also be controlled. Don't conduct capability studies when the environment, equipment, procedures or process are not representative and stable. In addition, don't run them in the middle of crises or when unusual work loads are being processed.

At least 100 pieces of production are normally required when attributes, like error rates, are involved. With rapid, easy-to-inspect operations, the best sample size might exceed 500 units. The test should be long enough to cover a normal day's operation. A week's work is even better since it keeps the data from being biased by "time of the day" or "day of the week." Many workers are more accurate during certain parts of the day or days of the week.

Analyzing the data. Procedures for analyzing the data are shown in the next section of this chapter.

Expanding the testing. Some quality professionals prefer to convert capability studies into Multi-Vari tests (see Chapter 14). To do this, they use "typical" data that has been specifically selected for the test. Each worker completes the same representative batch of work, making it possible to evaluate the worker-to-worker variability. They also evaluate the repeatability of each individual's work by having the task performed more than once. In addition, they evaluate time-to-time variability, comparing morning error rates with afternoon error rates and Monday's error rates with performances recorded on other days of the week.

CALCULATING THE PROCESS CAPABILITY OF GROUPS

In many service areas, the first priority is to determine the process capability of the organization as a whole. Having this information, management can set performance standards for the organization's average. These standards, however, should not be applied to individuals within the organization.

Problem 17-1 shows how standards can be set for groups. Problem 17-2 shows how they can be used in both cases; only the calculations and the subsequent NPL limits are different.

PROBLEM 17-1

Ten data-entry clerks in the quality division were given 200 "typical production records" to enter into the Quality Information System. Once one clerk was through, the records were erased. Then another was given an identical assignment.

Results of the study showed that the average error rate for the group was 5 percent. What was the process capability (NPL) for the group average?

SOLUTION 17-1

There are ten data-entry clerks in the group. Since each completed 200 records, the sample size *for the group* is 2000.
Given:

$$\text{Error rate} = \bar{P} = 5 \text{ percent}$$
$$\text{Sample size} = n = 2000$$
$$\text{Standard deviation} = s = \text{unknown}$$

$$s = \sqrt{\frac{\bar{P}(100 - \bar{P})}{n}}$$

$$s = \sqrt{\frac{5(100-5)}{2000}}$$

$$s = \sqrt{\frac{475}{2000}}$$

$$s = \sqrt{.237}$$

$$s = .49$$

natural process limits = $\bar{P} \pm 3s$
lower limit = $5 - 3 \times .49$
= $5 - 1.5$
= 3.5%
upper limit = $5 + 3 \times .49$
= $5 + 1.5$
= 6.5%

Based on these data, the organization can be expected to maintain a group error rate between 3.5% and 6.5% most of the time. Group performance outside these limits should be investigated.

The main difference between process capabilities (NPL) and control limits (see Chapter 16) is in the gathering of data. With the capability study, the test was closely controlled to keep out extraneous variables. With control limit calculations, the data came from normal production.

CALCULATING PERFORMANCE STANDARDS FOR INDIVIDUALS

The above analysis is for a service operation where 200 units per individual make a reasonable sample: a sample that can be obtained in a week or less and one that exceeds 100 units. It also assumes interest in evaluating the average capability of the group as a whole.

Capability studies also help set standards for individuals. The data developed in Problem 17-1 can be used for both; only the sample sizes and calculations have to change. The difference in the results stems from the natural process limits fluctuating as the sample sizes vary.

PROBLEM 17-2

After determining the natural process limits for the group as a whole, you decide you want to set a standard for individuals within the organization. You have already run the capability study; new calculations are all that are needed at this point. What standards would you set for individuals using data listed in Problem 17-1?

SOLUTION 17-2

Given:

$$\text{Error rate} = \bar{P} = 5 \text{ percent}$$
$$\text{sample size} = n = 200$$
$$\text{standard deviation} = s = \text{unknown}$$

$$s = \sqrt{\frac{\bar{P}(100 - \bar{P})}{n}}$$

$$s = \sqrt{\frac{5(100 - 5)}{200}}$$

$$s = \sqrt{\frac{475}{200}}$$

$$s = \sqrt{2.375}$$

$$s = 1.5411$$

$$\text{natural process limits} = \bar{P} \pm 3s$$
$$\text{lower limit} = 5 - 3 \times 1.5411$$
$$= 5 - 4.6$$
$$= 0.4\%$$
$$\text{upper limit} = 5 + 3 \times 1.5411$$
$$= 5 + 4.6$$
$$= 9.6\%$$

Based on these data, individuals within the organization can be expected to maintain an average error rate between 0.4% and 9.6% most of the time.

Therefore, you would probably use the upper limit (9.6%) for the performance standard; you should look for problems whenever anyone exceeds this limit. You should also look for process improvements whenever anyone has an error rate under 0.4%.

PROBLEM 17-3

Jimmy Jones took part in the capability study discussed in Problems 17-1 and 17-2. His error rate for the 200 records was 10 percent. Based on this information, what steps would you take?

SOLUTION 17-3

Since Jimmy Jones had a 10-percent error rate, his work was outside the natural process limits for individuals. Latzko[1] would refer to Jimmy as an outlier, and recommend that the natural process limits be recalculated, omitting Jones's data from the analysis. When there are outliers, he says, "the true quality attainable by a clerical department is often far better than what is represented by the basic process average."[8]

What is an outlier? Here, we define it as any point that doesn't fit within the natural process limits; by this definition, Jones is an outlier and the natural process limits should be recalculated excluding the Jones data.

It would be desirable to find the reason for Mr. Jones's performance being outside the natural process limits. Jones might be in over his head—or relatively new to the job—or poorly trained—or unhappy—or suffering from eye problems. His performance was not compatible with the capability of the group. It is up to the supervisor to find out why and correct the problem.

SPECIAL TEST CASES

In these problems, we had the organization use a special set of "typical" work assignments. Some organizations may resist accumulating special test cases; the use of routine production samples cuts the cost of testing. Use of production data, however, reduces the amount of information gained. If each individual runs different test cases, it is difficult to tell whether the people identified as outliers are actually less proficient or are given tougher work assignments.

Does the concept of using capability studies to monitor the performance of individuals sound too theoretical? It shouldn't. While at Irving Trust, Latzko[9] ran weekly computer reports comparing the quality of clerks with the process capability for their assignments. Those who were more than three standard deviations from "normal" were monitored.[10] He found the system very effective.

PROCESS CAPABILITY STUDIES FOR VARIABLES

This chapter stressed process capability studies for attributes, not variables; attribute analyses are much more common in the service sector. Moreover, process capability studies for variables have been thoroughly documented in many other books [references (11) through (15)].

In both attributes and variables studies, the natural process limits are normally set at +/– 3 standard deviations around the process mean. In addition, neither attributes nor variables studies should be run until "controllable" sources of variation are removed and the process is in statistical control.

The main differences between attributes and variables capability studies are with the sample sizes and the methods of calculating the standard deviations. For more details, refer to Chapters 14, 15, and 16.

SUMMARY

The capability study is an excellent tool for determining the current capability of groups and individuals. Capability studies can be used to set standards and to identify superior workers as well as those who are marginal.

Process capability studies are not limited to manufacturing operations; nor are they limited to error-rate analyses. They are also useful for evaluating the productivity of workers and many other attributes. They are appropriate almost any place where objective standards are required.

Capability studies reveal the capability of people, equipment, processes and procedures—under the conditions of the test. If the natural process limits they identify are loose and cause customer dissatisfaction, improvements need to be made to the system. People can be given more training or guidance, inefficient equipment can be replaced, outdated processes or procedures can be improved. These, and many other options, are management controllable.

FOOD FOR THOUGHT

Review the service operations in your department. Then estimate:

1. Which operations cost you the most in proofing, checking, redoing and undetected errors?
2. Do you know the average error rates of each employee working on that operation?
3. Do you have performance standards for that operation? If so:
   a. How were they set?
   b. Are they being met?
   c. Have you thought of running capability studies?

REFERENCES

1. William J. Latzko, *Quality and Productivity for Bankers and Financial Managers* (Milwaukee, WI: ASQC Quality Press, 1986), pp. 61–62.
2. Hy Pitt, "A Modern Strategy for Process Improvement," *Quality Progress,* May 1985, pp. 22–28.
3. *American National Standard ANSI/ASQC A1-1987* (Milwaukee, WI: American Society for Quality Control, 1987), pp. 16–17.
4. Armand V. Feigenbaum, *Total Quality Control,* 3rd ed. (New York: McGraw-Hill, 1983), p. 779.
5. *American National Standard ANSI/ASQC A1-1987,* p. 8.
6. Eric D. Dmytrow, "Assessing Process Capability in the Federal Government," *Quality Progress,* October 1985, pp. 35–40.
7. Eugene L. Grant and Richard S. Leavenworth, *Statistical Quality Control,* 6th ed. (New York: McGraw-Hill, 1988), pp. 216.
8. William J. Latzko, "Process Capability in Administrative Applications," *Quality Progress,* June 1985, pp. 70–73.
9. William J. Latzko, "A Quality Control System for Banks," *Bank Administration,* November 1972, p. 21.
10. William J. Latzko, "Quality Control in Banking," unpublished.
11. Edward M. Schrock and Henry L. Lefevre, *The Good and the Bad News about Quality* (Milwaukee, WI: ASQC Quality Press, 1988), Chapter 20.
12. Western Electric Company, AT&T, *Statistical Quality Control Handbook,* 11th ed. (Charlotte, NC: Delmar Printing Company, 1985), pp. 56–74.
13. David M. Rinderknecht, "Setting Up a Capability Study," *Quality,* October 1975, pp. 20–22.
14. Grant and Leavenworth, *Statistical Quality Control,* pp. 154–177.
15. Feigenbaum, *Total Quality Control,* pp. 779–797.

Chapter 18

Choosing the Right Process or Product

Choosing the right process or product can be an art or a science. Normally, it's in between. When decision making is treated as an art, beauty is in the eye of the beholder. Sometimes, however, the beholder has a thoroughly trained eye and can make accurate, spontaneous decisions.

Many experienced managers are experts at subjective decision making. When potential disaster threatens, they act promptly without waiting for conclusive data. When the smoke clears, some have subordinates evaluate the decisions statistically.

How do they succeed despite their subjectivity? Some managers have a wealth of experience and an outstanding memory; they know what worked in the past and are able to apply this knowledge to current problems.

Subjective decisions are allowable when indecisiveness can be costly or fatal. They should not be relied on, however, if other timely options are available. In many cases, controlled experiments are a timely and much less risky alternative. In the service sector, controlled experiments are in the early stages of development. Many of the tools used with high-volume manufacturing, however, are applicable. Some of these techniques include:

- Control charts[1,2]
- Ends Tests[3]
- Tukey-Duckworth Test[4-6]

USING CONTROL CHARTS TO EVALUATE PROCESSES

According to Affourtit:[1] "A control chart allows the user to assess the effect of deliberately introduced changes, and will also reveal unexpected and unforeseen sources of variation." McCabe[2] used the control-chart approach when working on mail room efficiency.

A typical application of control charts for troubleshooting is shown in Figure 18-1.

One glance at the "Jump-Shift" pattern in Figure 18-1 is enough to convince most engineers that a change has taken place. It is highly unlikely that chance variation caused the four points on the control chart to drop below the lower control limit; Chapters 14 and 16 showed that the probability of a single random point falling below the lower control limit by chance is roughly one chance out of a thousand.

The vertical line in Figure 18-1 marks the time that the system for routing delivery trucks changed; the shift in delivery times happened simultaneously. If the test was run properly, it is very likely that the change in routing caused the improvement in delivery times. In most instances, this conclusion would be correct. It is possible, however, that other changes occurred at the same time. For example, there could have been a change in drivers. That is why you won't get the most out of the control-chart approach unless you minimize changes in variables that are not part of the study. This warning also applies to other "controlled" experiments.

Control charts help evaluate process adjustments. They also help detect unexpected changes. On the other hand, they are less effective at estimating the probability that the change was effective. This is where designed experiments like Ends Tests and Tukey-Duckworth analyses come in.

Advantages of designed experiments include the following:

- They are normally controlled, reducing the risk that external variables will cause confusion.
- They are normally run in random order, reducing the risk of time-related changes influencing the results.

Controls. When experiments are not controlled, the results can be influenced by variables that are not monitored. In some cases, a variable

Figure 18-1. Control Chart: Average Time for Truck Delivery (Days)

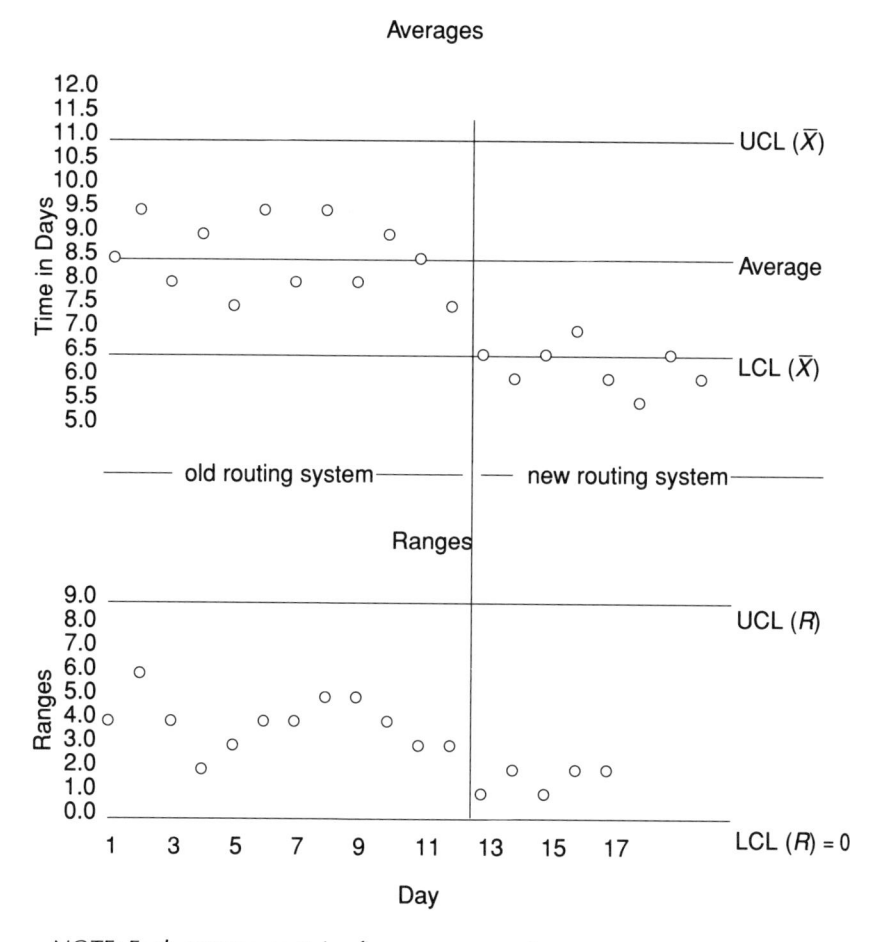

NOTE: Each average contains five measurements.

that was not considered critical has a greater influence than expected. In others, the Hawthorne Effect comes into play. The term "Hawthorne Effect" refers to the influence of special attention given to participants in an experiment. At times, the tests create enough interest that those involved do better work than usual. This, in turn, can affect the results.

Random sequence. When the sequence of the tests is randomized, the probability of excessive influence from extraneous or time-related changes is reduced.

THE ENDS TEST

One of the simplest forms of designed experiments is the Ends Test.[3] It was developed by Dorian Shainin when he was working for Rath & Strong, a large consulting company.

The Ends Test was designed to help people make decisions about two methods, processes or materials; it helps answer the questions "Which is better?" and "How much confidence should you have in the conclusion?"

Dorian Shainin[3] recommended selecting a confidence level of 99 percent if the consequences of a wrong decision were "very critical." He recommended a 95-percent confidence if the consequences were "important." He recommended 90-percent confidence if they were moderate and a 75- to 80-percent confidence if the consequences were slight. A 90-percent confidence means the decision should be right approximately 90 percent of the time and wrong approximately 10 percent of the time.

Different users have different definitions of the terms "very critical," "important," "moderate" and "slight"; take this difference into consideration when selecting your own confidence level.

Sample Sizes for the Ends Test

One of the first steps in conducting an Ends Test is to select sample sizes for the two processes, procedures or materials to be compared; they don't have to be equal.

Data for some of the confidence levels and their required sample sizes are shown in Figure 18-2.[3]

Reference (3) has additional options that veteran experimenters may wish to explore. They were omitted from this chapter in order to keep things simple.

Running an Ends Test

When running an Ends Test, the first step is to determine how important it is to be right. With this knowledge, you will know which section of Figure 18-2 to use when selecting your sample size.

The second step is to determine the sample sizes for the two conditions being tested. If the cost and availability of both procedures or products are approximately the same, choose sample sizes that are similar. If one

Figure 18-2. **Sample Sizes to Use With Ends Tests**

Confidence for Decision	Sample Size for First Process	Sample Size for Second Process
99 percent	2 3 4	13 7 5
95 percent	1 2 3	19 5 3
90 percent	1 2	9 3

Source: See reference (3). Reprinted with permission from the American Society for Quality Control, Milwaukee, Wisconsin.

condition is more expensive or harder to obtain, choose its sample size from the column marked "First Process."

The third step is to determine the test conditions. Well-run tests are planned so that unnecessary changes are minimized.

The fourth step is to determine the order of the tests. The sequence should be random, giving each test an equal chance of being run first or second or third. Be sure that tests involving the first condition are not all scheduled ahead of the second test condition, and vice versa. This way, time-related trends and unpredictable external changes will not have an excessive influence on the outcome of the test. Procedures for randomizing the order of testing were explained in Chapter 6.

The fifth step is to run the test, recording all unexpected occurrences. In some cases, changes in variables not being tested make the test invalid; the work must then be repeated.

The sixth step is to analyze the results. When the test is based on Figure 18-2, the product or procedure with all test results better than the competition is judged better—under the conditions of the test. The confidence warranted in that judgment is shown in the "Confidence for Decision" column of Figure 18-2. No clear-cut decision can be made unless all tests involving the preferred condition come out better than the best test of the competition. Another rule that often takes precedence is "Do the results make sense?" If the common sense rule isn't met, it is usually preferable to conduct additional testing to verify the results.

PROBLEM 18-1

Your department has been entering payroll data into the computer via a number of terminals. A vendor has been trying to sell you an optical character reader (OCR) that will eliminate manual input; the OCR reads data directly from the data input forms.

You know that the OCR will speed up data entry but you are concerned about its accuracy. In order to make an objective decision, you set up an Ends Test to determine whether the OCR will create more data input errors than you are getting now. You believe the decision is "important" but not "very critical."

Results of this Ends Test were:

Day	Time	Type of Input	Error Rate
Monday	Morning	Manual	4.2%
Monday	Afternoon	OCR	3.6%
Tuesday	Morning	OCR	3.3%
Tuesday	Afternoon	Manual	5.5%
Wednesday	Morning	Manual	4.8%
Wednesday	Afternoon	OCR	3.7%

Identify the confidence level and justify the sample size and sequence of testing shown above. Then discuss the conditions of the test.

Can you think of any foreseeable observations you might want to record? What decision does the Ends Test favor?

SOLUTION 18-1

Confidence levels. How important is the decision? In this case, it is "important" but not "very critical." Based on this judgment, a 95-percent confidence was used.

Sample sizes. The smallest number of tests shown in Figure 18-2 for a 95-percent confidence level is six—three using the OCR and three using manual input. This test plan would be the most economical assuming the cost of running an OCR test is close to the cost of running a manual-input test. There is one additional advantage in using equal sample sizes; you can use the same input data for both sets of tests. This eliminates a variable that could have a significant effect on the outcome. Some data is more difficult to input; some is less.

Sequence. When selecting your test sequence, time of day may be an important variable. As a consequence, at least one of the manual input tests should be scheduled in the morning and at least one in the afternoon. The same holds true for the OCR tests. In the morning, the workers may be alert. In the afternoon, the temperatures may be higher and excessive heat can affect the accuracy of both people and equipment.

To speed up the test, payroll data was divided into three segments, each having the same number of entries. The first segment was run on Monday, the second on Tuesday and the third on Wednesday.

Test conditions. One type of variation has been eliminated; identical data will be used in both parts of the test. Another variable involves the personnel chosen to input the data manually. In order to have typical results, the data-entry personnel should be representative. Don't run the test when your best clerks are on vacation and don't use new trainees. In addition, you may not want to tell the data-input team that a test is being run; this information could influence the workers' performance.

Observations. In order to identify observations of possible value, assume the records show that the best data-entry clerk went home sick during the middle of the last test. If this had occurred, it should have been recorded.

Analysis. The next step is to arrange the test data in order of the error rates. Then, it becomes:

Day	Time	Type of Input	Error Rate
Tuesday	Morning	OCR	3.3%
Monday	Afternoon	OCR	3.6%
Wednesday	Afternoon	OCR	3.7%
Monday	Morning	Manual	4.2%
Wednesday	Morning	Manual	4.8%
Tuesday	Afternoon	Manual	5.5%

The table above shows that even the worst OCR error rate was better than the best manual-entry error rate. Therefore you can say, with a confidence of at least 95 percent, that the accuracy of the OCR system was better than the accuracy of the manual-entry system (refer to Figure 18-2).

If the worst OCR error rate had been worse than the best manual error rate, there would have been an overlap, and you could not have justified a 95-percent confidence that the OCR method was more accurate. This would mean the results were inconclusive—under the conditions and requirements of the test. Inconclusive results often favor one of the methods tested but they do not give you the confidence specified when you set up the test.

If all OCR error rates were worse than the worst manual-entry rate, you would have a 95-percent confidence that the manual method was best.

In this test, the absence of the data-entry clerk who became sick on Wednesday had no apparent effect on the results of the test. The recording of this information, however, was important; it would have helped explain the distortion had the manual-entry error rates for Wednesday been inconsistent with the rest of the data.

This problem does not imply that all OCR data-entry systems are more accurate than all manual data-entry systems. It only applies to the specific OCR and manual data-entry systems used in the test.

PROBLEM 18-2

The chief administrator at a hospital received a large number of complaints about errors in the patient admission forms. Social Security numbers were missing, addresses were incorrect and writing was often illegible.

The administrator decided to try continuous sampling to see if it would help improve quality in this area. A group of five clerks were chosen and trained in the continuous sampling system. Their error rates and production were monitored; both showed unfavorable results at first. In a week, however, the learning curve came into play; they started to improve. After two months, the improvements levelled off. At this time, the error rates were better than they were before continuous sampling was introduced.

The administrator decided to run an Ends Test to see if continuous sampling was responsible for the improvement in quality. The criterion she set was that continuous sampling would be dropped unless it led to error rates that were at least one percent lower than those of the previous system.

The consequences of making a wrong decision were considered important but not critical.

Decisions made before running the test included the following:

Confidence Level. Since the decision was important but not critical, a 95-percent confidence level was chosen.

Sample Size. After looking at Figure 18-2, the administrator was torn between testing each method for three weeks or having two weeks of continuous sampling and five weeks of the old method. Because of the extra work continuous sampling made for the shift supervisors, the administrator decided to give it only two weeks.

Test Conditions. The most important test condition was to ensure that the new procedure was thoroughly understood before the test was started. That is why the training preceded the test and continued until production and quality had stabilized. The test wouldn't be fair if the participants were still on the steep slope of their learning curves at the time the test was run.

Sequence. In this experiment, each week was considered a separate test and random sequencing was required. A typical random order would be:

Week	Inspection System
1	old
2	new
3	old
4	old
5	new
6	old
7	old

Observations. During this test, it was noted that the technicians grumbled every time they went on the new method (continuous sampling).
Results:

Week	Inspection System	Error Rate	Adjusted Error Rate (1% added to the new system)
1	old	5.0%	5.0%
2	new	2.7%	3.7%
3	old	5.4%	5.4%
4	old	5.1%	5.1%
5	new	3.0%	4.0%
6	old	5.7%	5.7%
7	old	4.9%	4.9%

Based on the above data, do you have the specified confidence that the continuous sampling method improved quality by at least 1 percent?

SOLUTION 18-2

In order to evaluate the tests it is necessary to arrange the data according to error rates. In this instance, however, 1 percent was added to each of the new-method error rates; nothing less than a 1-percent improvement was considered acceptable. The adjustments are shown in the last column.

The rearranged list, with the lowest error rates on top, now shows:

Week	Inspection System	Error Rate	Adjusted Error Rate (1% added to the new system)
2	new	2.7%	3.7%
5	new	3.0%	4.0%
7	old	4.9%	4.9%
1	old	5.0%	5.0%
4	old	5.1%	5.1%
3	old	5.4%	5.4%
6	old	5.7%	5.7%

Again, all of the tests using the new method show lower error rates than the best test using the old method—even though a 1-percent handicap was added to all of the error rates of the new system. Therefore, continuous sampling (the new method) passed the test; it gave the administrator a 95-percent confidence that continuous sampling would reduce sampling errors by at least 1 percent. If one or more of the new-method tests had an error rate of 4.0 percent or more, the new method would not have passed the test (4.0 + 1.0 = 5.0). Then the administrator would not have a 95-percent confidence that the new method was at least 1 percent better than the old; results would have been inconclusive.

Other factors, however, would have to be considered before making a permanent change. One of those factors was the observation indicating worker resistance to the continuous sampling system. Another variable to consider would be productivity. What impact did the new system have on the ability of the existing staff to get the job done?

Critique of Ends Testing

Ends testing is a simple technique for selecting the better of two systems, processes, procedures, tools or materials. Conditions, however, have to be rigidly controlled and conclusions should not be extrapolated beyond the items and conditions of the test.

THE TUKEY-DUCKWORTH TEST

Another method of making decisions was developed by John W. Tukey.[4-6] It is called Tukey's Two-sample Test to Duckworth's Specifications,[4] or the Tukey-Duckworth Test.

Here are the steps in the Tukey-Duckworth Test:

Choosing the Right Process or Product 237

1. Run the tests in a random sequence, using precautions discussed under Ends testing.
2. Arrange the tests in the order of their results with the best results on top. Similar procedures were used with the Ends Tests.
3. Determine whether the test condition at the top of the list is the same as the one at the bottom. If this occurs, stop; the significance, if any, is less than 90 percent.
4. Starting at the top, go down the list until you reach a change in the system, procedure, tool, or material being tested. Then count the number of tests above that point.
5. Starting at the bottom, reverse the process.
6. Add the results of steps 4 and 5.
7. Compare the result from step 6 with Figure 18-3. If the sum at step 6 is 6, the approximate risk is 9 percent or less. If the sum is 7 or more, the approximate risk is 5 percent or less. If the sum is 10 or more, the risk is 1 percent or less.

Figure 18-3. **Critical Values of the Tukey-Duckworth Sum**

Approximate Risk	Count at Step 6
9 Percent	6
5 Percent	7
1 Percent	10
0.1 Percent	13

Source: See Reference (4). Reprinted with permission from the American Society for Quality Control, Milwaukee, Wisconsin.

These are the conditions for the Tukey-Duckworth Test:

- The largest and the smallest test results can't come from the same test condition.
- The ratio of the larger sample size to the smaller sample size should not be greater than 4:3.
- Test conditions should be controlled, just as they were with the Ends Test.
- The sequence of testing should be random.
- Unusual occurrences during the test should be recorded and reviewed after the test.

PROBLEM 18-3

Data-entry clerks were having difficulty putting information into the company's personnel database. They blamed their problems on the incompatibility of the incoming data forms and the format that came up on the computer screen.

Computer programmers, working with the data-input clerks, developed a new screen that looked better. Before wiping out the old screen, however, supervision decided to run tests to compare the new with the old.

Results of the test were:

Test Sequence	Type of Screen	Error Rates
1	old	4.5%
2	old	4.7%
3	new	2.9%
4	old	3.5%
5	new	3.6%
6	new	3.1%
7	old	4.1%
8	new	2.6%
9	old	5.6%
10	new	3.3%

What is the approximate risk of switching to the new computer terminal screen?

SOLUTION 18-3

The above data shows that the sequence of the tests is random. It also shows that there are five tests with the old screen and five tests with the new. This meets the requirements that the ratio of the larger sample size to the smaller is less than 4:3.

The first step is to rearrange the data according to error rates. The new order is:

Test Sequence	Type of Screen	Error Rates
8	new	2.6%
3	new	2.9%
6	new	3.1%
10	new	3.3%
4	old	3.5%

Choosing the Right Process or Product 239

Test Sequence	Type of Screen	Error Rate
5	new	3.6%
7	old	4.1%
1	old	4.5%
2	old	4.7%
9	old	5.6%

There are 4 "new methods" on top of the list. Therefore, step 4 adds up to 4.

There are also 4 "old methods" below the lowest "new." Therefore, step 5 adds up to 4 also.

The sum obtained during step 6 is 8 (4 + 4 = 8).

Figure 18-3 shows a risk of less than 5 percent when the sum of steps 4 and 5 is 8. Based on this data, if you choose the new screen, the chance of being wrong is less than 5 percent.

SUMMARY

Control charts have many uses, including comparing two processes, procedures or materials; they also help control operations.

The Ends Test and the Tukey-Duckworth Test are similar and have a single function; they compare processes, procedures and materials. Both are quick and easy methods for determining the probability of a decision being correct—as long as only two choices are being considered. More complex decisions require more complex experiments.

FOOD FOR THOUGHT

Family members are usually prompt to give you feedback on which foods they like best. Most pets, however, are not as good at communicating. Are you buying the brand they like best, or the one you prefer because of price, label or advertising pitch? To answer this question objectively, run your own series of tests on two different brands of pet food.

- For the Ends Test, use 3 servings of each brand.
- For the Tukey-Duckworth Test, use 4 servings of each.
- Keep as many variables constant as possible, including feed time, quantity of food, bowl and time between feedings.

- Sequence tests randomly; at a bare minimum, alternate between brands.
- Minimize disturbances during feed time.
- Make an evaluation based on some pet-pleaser criterion like "time it took to empty the bowl" or "amount left after 15 minutes."

Was there a clear winner, or were the tests inconclusive?

Did the results of the Ends Test confirm the results of the Tukey-Duckworth Test? With the Ends Test, no-overlap would give you a 95-percent confidence. With the Tukey-Duckworth Test, a score of 7 or 8 would give you a comparable 5-percent risk.

REFERENCES

1. B. B. Affourtit, "Statistical Process Control (SPC) Implementation—Common Misconceptions," *ASQC Quality Congress Transactions,* May 19–21, 1986, pp. 440–445.
2. William J. McCabe, "Quality Methods Applied to the Business Process," *ASQC Quality Congress Transactions,* May 19–21, 1986, pp. 429–436.
3. Dorian Shainin, "How to Calculate the Risk of a Decision," *Quality Progress,* August 1968.
4. Ellis R. Ott, *Process Quality Control* (New York: McGraw-Hill, 1975), pp. 210–212.
5. John W. Tukey, "A Quick, Compact, Two-sample Test to Duckworth's Specifications," *Technometrics,* Vol. 1, No. 1, February 1959, pp. 31–48.
6. Bradford S. Brown, "Quick Ways Statistics Can Help You," *Chemical Engineering,* September 4, 1961, pp. 137–143.

Chapter 19

Efficiency and Problem Solving

Before *The One Minute Manager,* back in the days when paperbacks cost $2.45, James McCay[1] wrote, "Would you like to be able to read 50,000 words a minute? There are many times when it is easy to do this if you know how. All you have to be able to do is recognize within one minute that a 50,000 word book does not suit your purposes, and decide not to read it." Efficient quality assurance is similar to efficient reading. If you're working on the wrong projects, having phenomenal speed and superior tools won't solve your problems; it will only help you waste time more efficiently.

This chapter discusses a good tool for picking the right project—the Pareto chart. Then it covers other ways of improving quality and efficiency.

PARETO CHARTS

It seldom pays to spend a million dollars to solve a nickel-and-dime problem. Efficient problem solving involves identifying the problems that are likely to provide the best payoff—or the biggest bang per buck. That is where the Pareto chart comes in; it helps you set priorities.

The Pareto principle is based on the observations of an Italian sociologist and economist, Vilfredo Pareto (1848–1923). It has been interpreted to mean that "80% of the problem comes from 20% of the causes."[2]

The concept has been expanded to include the following:

- 20% of the people create 80% of the errors.
- 20% of the projects show 80% of the cost overruns.
- 20% of the problems have 80% of the potential savings.

Bill Latzko credits Juran with the terms "vital few" for the 20% and "trivial many" for the rest.[2]

How do you find the vital few? Ishikawa[3] recommends gathering people familiar with the problem and conducting a brainstorming session. Then he recommends statistically analyzing the suggested solutions and checking them "scientifically and rationally against the data available." Ishikawa uses Pareto charts to help identify which problems should be brainstormed.

Many engineers use Pareto charts to identify the most common or the most costly problem in the department; then they work on that problem. Overall-cost Pareto charts are also good during the early phases of a quality improvement study. To use this approach, determine the cost of all functions within the department using budget data verified by monthly accounting reports. Then create a bar graph, like the one in Figure 19-1, showing the most costly functions on the left and the least costly on the right. The result is an overall-cost Pareto chart.

All else being equal, the most expensive function will harbor the greatest potential savings. Analyze this function thoroughly, exposing it to one or more of the tools covered in this book or in other books on problem solving. Once you have reduced waste and improved quality in the first function, move to the second, then the third, then the fourth. Problem solving tools that can help you, in addition to those covered in previous chapters, include:

- Flow charts[4–8]
- Why-Why diagrams[9]
- Ishikawa diagrams[3, 10–17]
- Cross-functional management[18,19]

FLOW CHARTS

How often do you review your administrative functions? Annually? Every two years? Never? Every job should be reviewed from time to time to see if new tools are available or the workplace has changed. If a flow chart

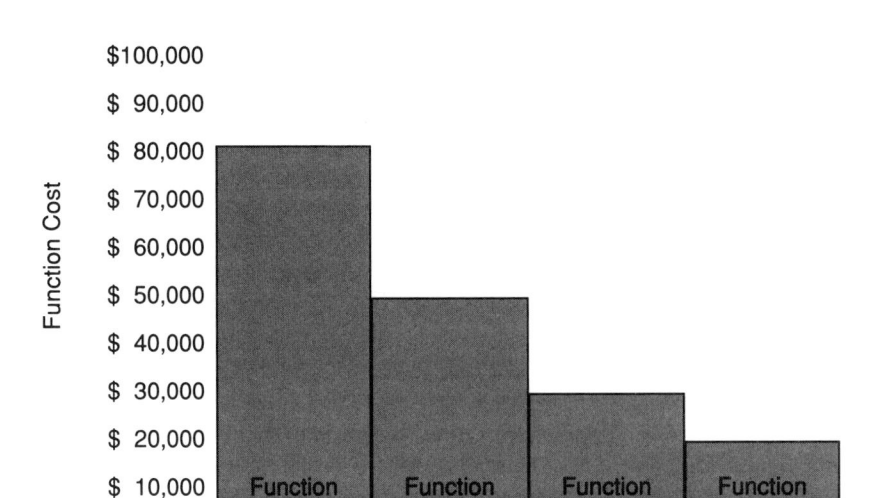

Figure 19-1. **Pareto Chart: Function Costs**

[Bar chart showing Function #1 at $80,000, Function #2 at $50,000, Function #3 at $30,000, and Function #4 at $20,000, with Function Cost on the y-axis ranging from $10,000 to $100,000.]

exists, study it for possible improvements. If there is no flow chart, make one. A typical example is shown in Figure 19-2.

Once you and your people have reviewed your charts, ask the following questions, making sure those performing the function are included in the discussion.

- Does the flow chart reflect what's going on? Processes change and people develop shortcuts. If beneficial changes have occurred, the flow chart should reflect them.
- Are steps missing? People making flow charts occasionally leave something out.
- Can steps be eliminated? Make sure they are not needed before dropping them from the procedure.
- Should steps be automated? In many cases, automation improves efficiency and reduces errors.
- Should any automated steps revert to manual? At times, automation makes things worse. When that happens, admit the mistake and return to the old way of doing things. If it doesn't pay for itself, get rid of it.
- Is the work flow smooth and logical? If not, why not? Can it be improved?

Figure 19-2. **Original Flow Chart for Processing a Letter**

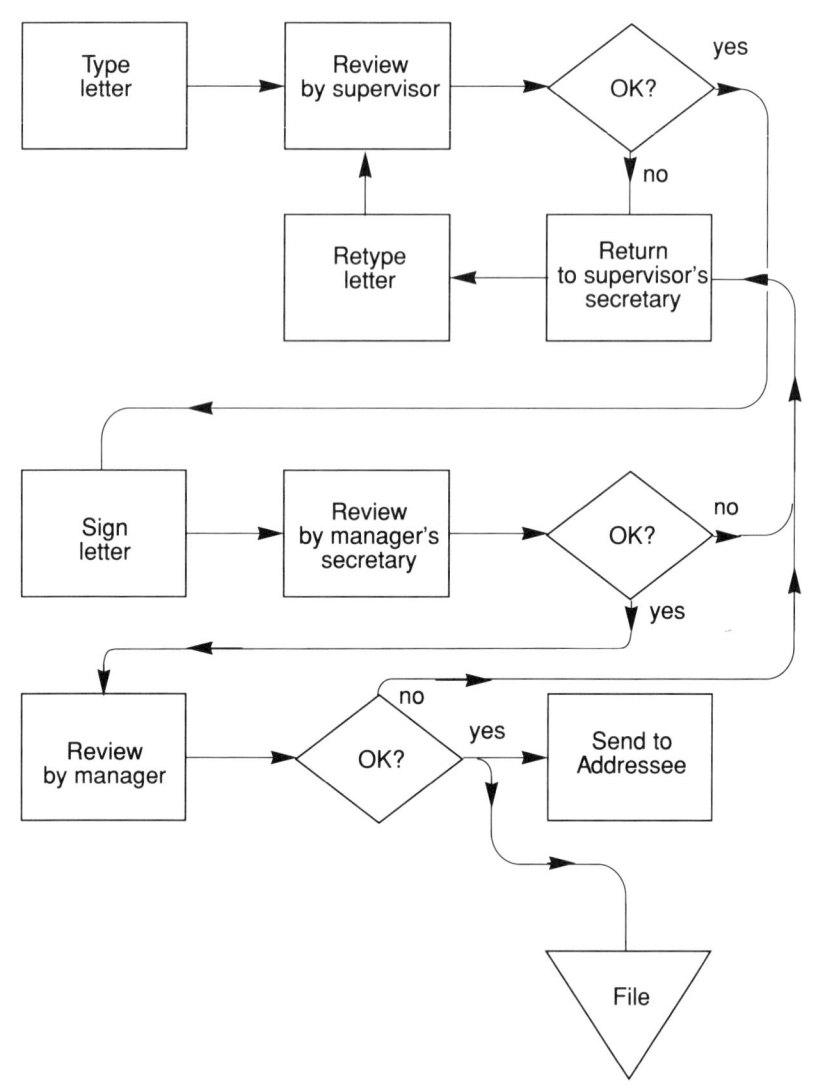

Figure 19-2 is a flow chart for typing, reviewing and mailing letters. Does it look appropriate for your office? Can you improve it?

The first step in Figure 19-2 shows that a letter is typed. Then, it is reviewed by the supervisor. If the supervisor wants changes, the letter is returned to the typist and the process is started over at square one. If the supervisor finds no reason to make a change, he signs it and sends it to the manager's secretary who also reviews it.

Similar options are found when the manager's secretary reviews the letter and when the manager reviews it. Flow charts, like the one in Figure 19-2, can tip you off to potential savings and quality improvements at several levels of the organization.

After reviewing Figure 19-2, you might ask: "Why do they have so many review cycles? Each time a reviewer gets the document, new pet requirements can be imposed; typists, supervisors, secretaries and managers can make changes based on their own concepts and personalities. The typists could be spending more time redoing letters than typing originals. In addition, the supervisors, managers and secretaries shouldn't get tied up with redundant editing when they could be involved in more productive work."

The above comments make sense. An alternative flow chart is shown in Figure 19-3.

Should management inspect the spelling and grammar of subordinates? The flow chart in Figure 19-3 implies that the answer is "no." Here, the supervisor reviews correspondence to ensure that the typist didn't misinterpret the handwriting. Then, sampling is used to maintain the proper level of quality. Procedures for sampling were covered in Chapters 6 and 7.

The flow chart in Figure 19-3 has two advantages:

1. It eliminates two levels of review.
2. It makes the typist and supervisor responsible for their own quality.

The above example explains how flow charts can be used to help visualize process flow. In many cases, they also help identify inefficiencies and sources of errors that can be eliminated. Here are some additional illustrations of flow charts used in the service sector:

- Huls[4] used them to show the work flow in marketing and sales.
- Aubrey[5] used them to clarify the way banks handle encoding checks.
- Latzko[6] used them to analyze "why individual errors get fixed but not prevented." He also used them to show how error rates were reduced in a bank environment.
- Stoeger[7] used them to clarify different design processes.
- Shertz[8] used them to clarify the rate-quoting process for a truck line.

According to Aubrey,[5] "A completed flow chart is a graphic representation of the sequence of events in any process. It gives a step-by-step detailed record of the order in which work is done to facilitate analysis."

Figure 19-3. **Alternative Flow Chart for Processing a Letter**

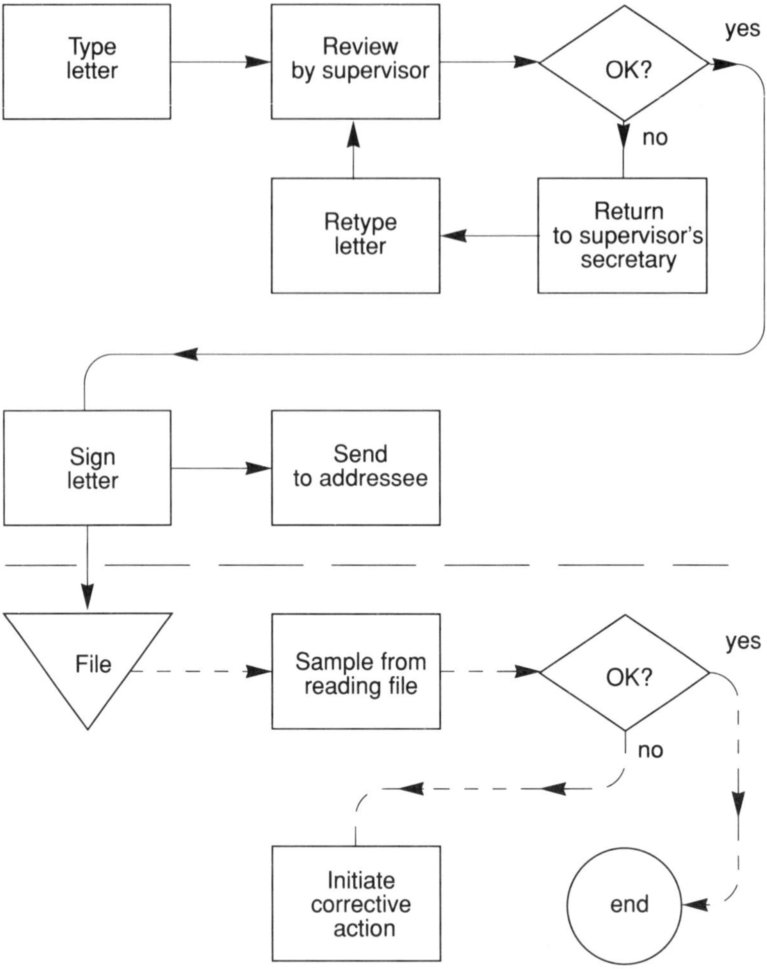

NOTE: Steps involving sampling are shown with dashed lines.

WHY-WHY DIAGRAMS

Why-Why diagrams can be used to justify the removal or retention of steps in a flow chart. At each activity in the process, ask the question

"Why is that step there?" If you can't come up with a good answer, get rid of it.

The main use for Why-Why diagrams is to organize your thinking; you can also use them for solving problems. The steps are:

1. Describe the problem.
2. Ask, "Why does the problem exist?" Write down the reasons.
3. Use the statements in step 2 to define new problems. Then ask, "Why do those problems exist?"
4. The questioning is repeated until each chain ends in a reason for the original condition occurring.

Figure 19-4 shows a typical Why-Why diagram.

Figure 19-4. **Why-Why Diagram**

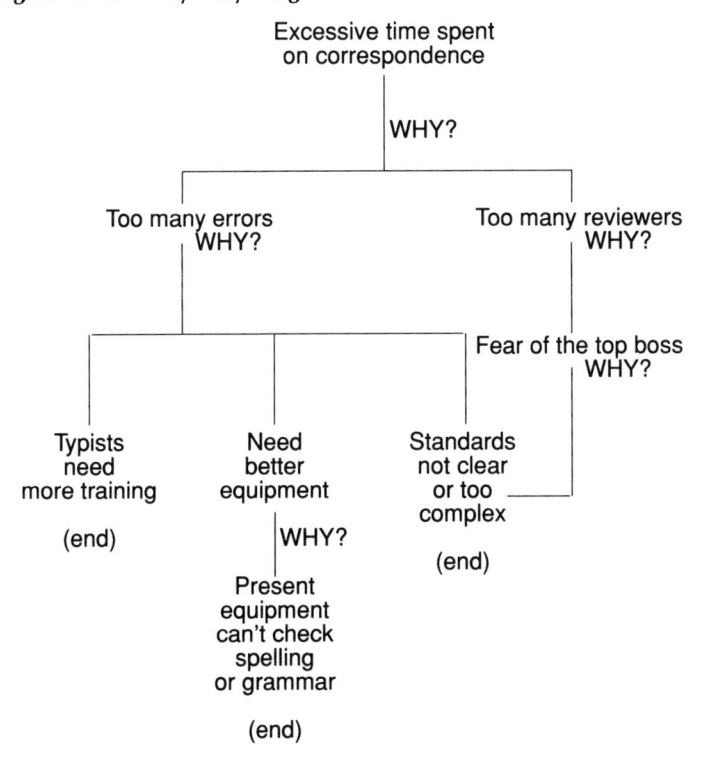

```
                    Excessive time spent
                    on correspondence
                           |
                          WHY?
              ┌────────────┴────────────┐
        Too many errors            Too many reviewers
           WHY?                         WHY?
    ┌────────┼────────┐                  │
                              Fear of the top boss
                                    WHY?
    │        │        │
 Typists   Need    Standards
  need    better   not clear
more      equipment or too ─────┘
training            complex
 (end)     WHY?    (end)
            │
         Present
        equipment
        can't check
         spelling
        or grammar
           (end)
```

The problem identified in Figure 19-4 is that excessive time is spent on the correspondence function—this includes management time (proofing) as well as clerical time (typing). Reasons shown on the chart are "too many errors" and "too many reviewers."

Why were there too many errors? The responses of the hypothetical "brainstorming team" were: "Typists need more training" and "Need better equipment," plus "Standards not clear, or too complex."

Response to the problem "Typists need more training" is up to management; this chain in the Why-Why diagram can be terminated at this point—unless you want to bring budgets into the analysis.

"Need better equipment" requires additional information so another "Why?" is asked. The response shown in Figure 19-4 is "Present equipment can't check spelling or grammar." At this point, the chain is terminated; action is up to management. Is the "excessive" time spent on correspondence serious enough to warrant replacing the typewriters with personal computers or other equipment that can check spelling and grammar?

"Standards not clear or too complex" is again up to management; this chain can be terminated. Either management can have the standards simplified and clarified or they can put up with the confusion.

The branch in the chain that states there are "too many reviewers" needs the clarification of another "Why?" The answer given by the brainstormers was "Fear of the top boss." In this organization, it might appear that the entire chain of command got pneumonia every time the top boss sneezed. Or, no one knew exactly what the top boss wanted—and they were afraid to ask. Fear promotes inefficiency. It is probable that the top boss would be happy to accept a less complex and confusing standard if it were properly presented.

According to Bailie,[9] "Why-Why diagrams help problem-solving groups to recognize the broad network of problem sources, their interrelationship, and the most promising directions to take in pursuing long- and short-range solutions."

ISHIKAWA, FISHBONE OR CAUSE-AND-EFFECT DIAGRAMS

Ishikawa, fishbone or cause-and-effect diagrams provide a different way of organizing the thinking of problem-solving groups. They are called Ishikawa diagrams because they were developed by Kaoru Ishikawa of Japan.[3] They are called fishbone diagrams because of their appearance. They are called cause-and-effect diagrams because of their function. A typical cause-and-effect diagram is shown in Figure 19-5.

Cause-and-effect diagrams, like Why-Why diagrams, are usually developed during brainstorm sessions where on-the-job workers are

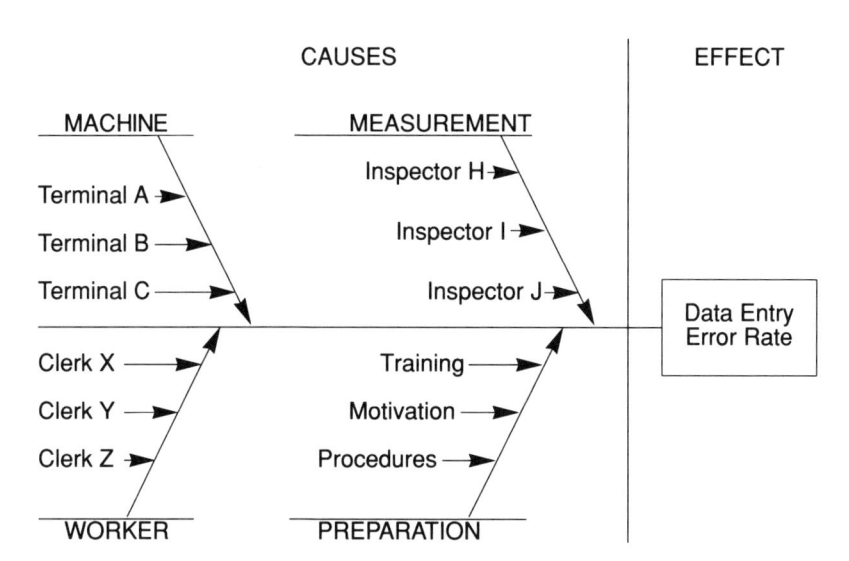

Figure 19-5. Cause-and-Effect Diagram (Ishikawa Diagram)

```
                    CAUSES                    |    EFFECT

    MACHINE              MEASUREMENT
                        Inspector H
  Terminal A
                        Inspector I
  Terminal B
  Terminal C            Inspector J
                                              ┌──────────────┐
                                              │ Data Entry   │
  Clerk X               Training              │ Error Rate   │
                                              └──────────────┘
  Clerk Y               Motivation
  Clerk Z               Procedures
  ─────────             ──────────────
   WORKER                PREPARATION
```

important contributors. The first step is to determine the problem you want to analyze; this will take care of the "effect" side of the diagram. The second step is to identify major contributors to the problem such as machines, measurements, workers and preparation. Then you should identify factors that fall under each of the major classifications and attach them to their "major" limb.

Jane Jackson, for instance, could have used Figure 19-5 to solve a data-entry problem. Jane's group identified four major limbs—machines, measurements, workers and preparation. Then she used a Pareto diagram to show which of the major limbs was causing the data-entry-error problem. Jane's group found that the "worker" limb was the biggest contributor; another Pareto chart helped identify which worker—it was Jack Smith (clerk Y). At this point, control charts were used to determine whether the process was statistically in control; it was. Then Jane ran a capability study and determined that Jack Smith was "an outlier"—Jack's error rate was outside the upper natural process limit. Discussion with Jack brought out the fact that he had been added to the data-entry team with little formal training and he was confused about some of the codes used by the system. Additional training corrected the problem.

Cause-and-effect diagrams are not used by themselves; their greatest strength is in helping to organize the group's thinking. Major elements contributing to the problem are laid out in chart form. If the chart doesn't help solve the problem, it is possible that at least one "branch" or "twig" is missing. Group discussions, featuring the people involved, can usually identify it.

Examples of cause-and-effect diagrams in the service sector include the following:

- Affourtit[10] used one to help analyze the motivational climate process.
- Young and Kennedy[11] used one to help analyze "quality of nonmanufacturing staff support and general services."
- Thornton[12] used one to determine "causes of lot number errors."
- Scholtes and Hacquebord[13] used one to show how to get "a good start for the transformation to a quality organization."
- Jones and McBride[14] used one to help reduce slow deliveries.
- Berger[15] used one when discussing "human resource tools for quality improvement."
- Harrington[16] used one to help identify factors contributing to "errors in engineering changes."
- Ryan[17] used one to illustrate "the role of information in quality and productivity improvement."

CROSS-FUNCTIONAL MANAGEMENT

Cross-Functional Analysis (CFA) fits under the cross-functional management umbrella; it is a technique developed by General Electric for reducing redundancy.[18] The activities of each functional organization are classified as unique, or containing duplication, or redundant or overlapping the work of others. Where duplication is found, it is justified or eliminated. Removal of duplication and overlapping responsibilities frequently leads to improved quality; when prime responsibility is not clear, key elements affecting quality can slip through the cracks. By reducing redundancy, you can make more funds and personnel available for quality improvement projects.

Ishikawa[19] looks at cross-functional management in a broader sense. He says: "In accordance with the functions to be managed, the company must establish cross-function committees. For example, a cross-function committee on quality assurance may be established. The chairman must be a senior managing director who is in charge of that function." The job of the cross-function committee on quality is to ensure that quality problems are treated from a company-wide view. In Japan, cross-function committees are not limited to quality. Separate committees often address other functions such as cost, technology, production, marketing and personnel.

Cross-functional management, however, is not just a tool for efficiency and problem solving; it is a management system.

SUMMARY

Important tools for improving quality, upgrading efficiency and solving critical problems include:

- Control charts (Chapters 15 and 16)
- Capability studies (Chapter 17)
- Designed experiments (Chapter 18)
- Pareto charts (this chapter)
- Flow charts (this chapter)
- Why-Why diagrams (this chapter)
- Cause-and-effect diagrams (this chapter)
- Cross-functional management (this chapter)

Try each of these tools from time to time. Then, when the need arises, you will be able to select the one that meets your requirements. Tools can be explained by books; they can't be mastered, however, unless they are used.

FOOD FOR THOUGHT

Make a Pareto chart of the functions within your department, basing it on your budget. Then make a flow chart of the function involving the largest scheduled expenditures.

1. Does the flow chart reflect what's going on?
2. Are steps missing?
3. Can steps be eliminated?
4. Should steps be automated?
5. Should any automated steps revert to manual?
6. Is the work flow smooth and logical?

REFERENCES

1. James T. McCay, *The Management of Time* (Englewood Cliffs, NJ: Prentice-Hall, 1959), p. 142.
2. William J. Latzko, *Quality and Productivity for Bankers and Financial Managers* (Milwaukee, WI: ASQC Quality Press, 1986), p. 157.
3. Kaoru Ishikawa, *What is Total Quality Control?—The Japanese Way* (Englewood Cliffs, NJ: Prentice-Hall, 1985), pp. 63–64.
4. Rebecca Lee Huls, "Dedication to Quality Spans All Industries," *ASQC Quality Congress Transactions,* May 4–6, 1987, pp. 90–95.
5. Charles A. Aubrey, II, *Quality Management in Financial Services* (Wheaton, IL: Hitchcock Publishing, 1985), p. 13.
6. Latzko, *Quality and Productivity for Bankers and Financial Managers,* pp. 66, 91.
7. Kenneth J. Stoeger, "Ohmeda Design Assurance Process," *Rocky Mountain Quality Conference Transactions,* June 16–17, 1987, p. 224.
8. Robert S. Shertz, "Effecting a Quality Plan of Action," *Quality,* January 1988, p. 59.
9. Howard H. Bailie, "Organize Your Thinking with a Why-Why Diagram," *Quality Progress,* December 1985, pp. 22–24.
10. Thomas D. Affourtit, "Control Charts for Motivational Climate Analysis," *ASQC Quality Control Transactions,* May 19–21, 1986, pp. 378–385.
11. Barbara J. Young and David A. Kennedy, "Process Control in Staff Arenas," *ASQC Quality Control Transactions,* May 19–21, 1986, pp. 418–428.
12. Manly P. Thornton, "SPC for Administration Systems," *ASQC Quality Control Transactions,* May 4–6, 1987, pp. 287–292.
13. Peter Scholtes and Heero Hacquebord, "A Practical Approach to Quality," *ASQC Quality Control Transactions,* May 4–6, 1987, pp. 202–222.
14. Lewis N. Jones and Ronald C. McBride, "Team Approach to Problem Solving, TAPS," *ASQC Quality Control Transactions,* May 4–6, 1987, pp. 139–147.
15. John A. Berger, "Human Resources Tools for Quality Improvement," *Quality Progress,* August 1985, pp. 21-28.
16. H. James Harrington, *The Improvement Process; How America's Leading Companies Improve Quality* (New York: McGraw-Hill, 1987), p. 218.
17. John Ryan, "Divisions and Technical Committees Look Toward the Future," *Quality Progress,* April 1987, pp. 36–39.
18. Brian K. Higgins, "The Source of Quality Improvement—The White-Collar Worker," *Rocky Mountain Quality Conference Proceedings,* June 7–8, 1988, pp. 475–483.
19. Ishikawa, *What is Total Quality Control?—The Japanese Way,* pp. 113–119.

Chapter 20

Key 4: Understanding Automation

"Love 'Em or Hate 'Em—Here Come the Computers." Where did that quote come from? Steve Finn, editor of the *Quality Control Supervisor's Bulletin,* used it for the title of an article I wrote.[1] His observation couldn't have been more appropriate. Computers are here to stay. Those who don't understand them are like tug boat captains trying to race a speed boat—they don't have the right equipment.

A LITTLE HISTORY

The era of tedious calculations and repetitive number crunching is reminiscent of the days of Charles Dickens, Ebenezer Scrooge and *A Christmas Carol.* At that time, according to Dickens, low-paid clerks with green eyeshades handled the payroll, accounting and routine statistical calculations. Now, computers do most of the number crunching.

When I started my career with Union Oil Company, regression analyses were run by hand; the work was tedious and errors were common. Soon, however, there was a calculator on every statistician's desk. This made the work faster and errors less frequent, but problems persisted.

By the time I went to work for Aerojet, statisticians were developing statistical work sheets; technicians filled in the blanks. Still, a lengthy regression analysis would take a day or more.

Now, computers do most of the work; data-entry clerks and optical character recognition (OCR) units feed most of the computers. In the retail area, data fed to many cash registers is automatically transmitted to computer memory; routine human intervention is becoming minimal. In addition, calculations are becoming faster, errors are becoming fewer and statisticians are spending more of their time planning, analyzing, reviewing and writing reports.

With the coming of desktop computers, old jobs are changing and new jobs are surfacing. Computer programmers and analysts were unheard of in 1945. Now, they are found in almost every major company. Most exceptions hire outside organizations to do their programming—and sometimes their computing. Computers are the fourth key to quality service; those who use their output should understand their benefits, their shortcomings and the jargon that surrounds them.

A PEEK AT WHAT'S AHEAD

Although an in-depth knowledge of computers is beyond the scope of this book, the next three chapters will give you an exposure to the field. Material covered includes

- An introduction to the jargon that surrounds computers
- Techniques for justifying their purchase
- Ideas about controlling database quality

Chapter 21 defines some of the technical terms used by computer professionals. Programmers and analysts use the words fluently and often expect outsiders to know what they're talking about. Outsiders call the jargon "computerese" and are bewildered by the large number of odd-sounding phrases. For self-protection, it often pays to develop an understanding of this somewhat technical language. Mastery of the terms covered in this book will not make you a programmer or an analyst; this knowledge will, however, help you understand what the specialists are talking about. Literacy in the field of computers is becoming more and more necessary.[2]

Chapter 22 covers some of the fundamentals of planning for a computer—and then justifying it.[3] Those who want to make computers into status symbols will waste time and money. Those who buy first and plan later will have similar problems. Here are some questions to ask before getting a computer for your department:

- Will the computer pay for itself in three years?
- How much help will you get from the data-processing people?
- What are the advantages and disadvantages of having your own programmers?
- Can you buy commercial programs that will do the work you need?

These questions will be discussed in Chapter 22.

Chapter 23 takes a look at database quality assurance. Databases are becoming more and more important in business. In the past, computer professionals were given the responsibility for assuring the accuracy of these computerized files. In some cases, however, the computer people had a vested interest in the results of their evaluations. As a consequence, some of them reported exceptional quality levels where poor quality existed. Having system programmers solely responsible for the accuracy of their database is similar to having football coaches referee championship games when their own teams are playing. In these circumstances, the coaches are not likely to be impartial third parties—neither are computer professionals evaluating systems their friends designed. In other words, don't have a "chocoholic" guarding the chocolates.

FOOD FOR THOUGHT

Review the background of computer experts and quality assurance professionals working with your department. Then answer the following questions:

- How many of the quality assurance professionals have an in-depth understanding of computers?
- How many of the computer experts understand sampling and other quality assurance tools?
- Can the computer people and the quality assurance staff understand each other when discussing software and database quality—or do they speak different languages and live in different worlds?
- What is the background of those monitoring the quality of your software and your database?

REFERENCES

1. Henry L. Lefevre, "Love 'Em or Hate 'Em—Here Come the Computers," *Quality Control Supervisor's Bulletin,* June 25, 1985, pp. 1–2.
2. Henry L. Lefevre, "Computer Literacy," *Quality,* September 1983, p. 90.
3. Henry L. Lefevre, "A Computer in Every Office," *The Press,* July 1982, pp. 6–13.

Chapter 21

Computer Basics

Want to improve quality in the service sector? If so, learn computer basics. Then try automating your routine mathematical and clerical work. Computers normally reduce the errors; they also speed things up. This is good, since timeliness and low error rates contribute to quality. Computers, however are not cure-alls; they can be abused, misused and forced to hurt your profits. Knowledge of the potential risks and rewards of automation is vital.

COMPUTERS CAN IMPROVE QUALITY AND PRODUCTIVITY

When I was working for Aerojet General Corporation in Sacramento, California, I had my first exposure to electronic data processing. The company purchased an IBM 1130 computer and allowed the engineers to use it. Many of us jumped at the chance since it enabled us to run statistical calculations in less than two hours. The computer wasn't that slow; the lines were that long. During the late 1960s, waiting for feedback from computers was like waiting for a snail to get motivated. The fastest results we could get from the big units were available in two days—and that took a priority.

By 1967, Aerojet had lost a Poseidon contract they were counting on. Soon budgets got smaller and talented workers were laid off; we had to compensate. Whenever we were forced to cut a technician, we put the work on the computer. Soon, our staff was cut in half but we were doing the same amount of work and our quality improved; the computer made few errors as long as we programmed it properly and fed it the right data.

Our work at the Air Force Accounting and Finance Center (AFAFC) provides another example of how computers can reduce costs and improve quality. At AFAFC, we saved $50,000 per year by computerizing three report-generator programs.[1,2] We also implemented a program for forecasting funds disbursements; it saved even more. In both cases, the use of computers improved quality as well as productivity. The Apple II computer system we used cost less than $4,000.

Back in 1982, it was estimated that businesses could make computers pay for themselves if the time they were spending on routine manual calculations exceeded 10 hours per week.[3] Now, computers can be justified with even smaller work loads; comparable systems cost less and wages cost more. These savings can't be achieved, however, unless someone in the group understands computers; in many organizations, no one does.

COMPUTERS CAN BE LIABILITIES

The examples above show how automation can improve both productivity and quality. Computers, however, can also be liabilities; a lot depends on how they are used.

One executive prided himself on his ability to select the right subordinates—and let them handle the details. Because he himself had no knowledge of computers, however, the experts he selected had limited familiarity with automation. As a consequence, his computer projects were unrealistic; the schedules he set were impossible. The available funds were wasted; in time he became disillusioned with automation. Had he taken the time to find out what computers could and couldn't do, he would have had more realistic expectations. In addition, he would have improved his chances of selecting competent people to manage his computer function. For those who don't do their homework, computers can be a liability.

UNDERSTANDING THE LANGUAGE

When working with computers, it helps to learn their jargon, idiosyncrasies, strengths and shortcomings. It is the responsibility of managers to achieve computer literacy so they won't expect computers, programmers or analysts to do the impossible. In addition, they won't be snowed by computer professionals quite as often.[4-7]

Negotiating with programmers and analysts without learning their language, "computerese," is like ordering a five-course meal in France without understanding French. The story is told of a quality engineer who assumed that all French could speak English. When he ordered dinner at an out-of-the-way restaurant near Paris he had difficulty making himself understood. Not to let ignorance spoil his supper, he ordered anyway—guessing, pointing and hoping. When the meal arrived, he was served deep fried snails, marinated squid and chocolate covered grasshoppers. At this point, he could either eat or go hungry. The unfortunate engineer went away with a gurgling stomach that was unresponsive to Tums and a Visa bill that was too big for his expense account.

The following definitions introduce you to "computerese." This jargon is ever-changing and the learning process is never-ending; in time, you will need to know much more. To keep from falling behind, read specialized material that is devoted to automation; you can never know too much about a technical subject.

DEFINITIONS

Computers are involved in major segments of most service industries. When living in the land of these electronic monsters, it is helpful to master a few basic definitions.

Analysts. Computer analysts are interpreters, planners and designers. They convert the needs of the user into computerese (the jargon of programmers). Then they help plan and design programs, develop specifications and draw flow charts. The best analysts usually have experience in the user's area as well as in programming.

Assembler Language. Assembler language (also called assembly language) is a programming language used by professional programmers who are looking for computer efficiency and speed. Few amateurs master it.

BASIC. BASIC is the computer language used by most amateur programmers. It became prominent when time-sharing computer systems were introduced. At present, it comes with most personal computers. BASIC is similar to FORTRAN, a computer language used by many large-model computer programmers. Both BASIC and FORTRAN are considered scientific programming languages although they can be used in business applications.

COBOL. COBOL is one of the most popular business languages. It is used on most large computers; it is seldom used on personal or desktop units.

Computerese. Computerese is a slang term for the jargon used by computer specialists. Many of the terms shown here belong in the computerese dictionary.

CPU. CPU or central processing unit is where the computer makes decisions and does its calculations after getting detailed instructions from a computer program. Many texts divide computer operations into three steps: input, processing and output. CPUs handle the processing part. The term "CPU" is used with large computers more than it is with personal and desktop units.

CRT. Technically, a CRT is a cathode ray tube. The screens of TV sets and the display screens of most data-input terminals are CRTs. Some users, however, refer to the whole data input station as a CRT.

Database. A database is the computer's version of a library. Most databases contain large volumes of information that can be retrieved, reviewed or processed as necessary. Typical databases include: Quality Information Systems, Management Information Systems and Personnel Information Systems. Some computer databases, like SOURCE, are available to the public. They are run by private companies that charge customers for retrieving, processing or storing information. Many other databases are developed and maintained by companies for their own use.[8]

Disk Drive. A disk drive is a device or piece of hardware used to store programs and data. When working with large computers, the term "disk drive" is seldom qualified. With personal computers, the terms "hard disk drive" and "floppy disk drive" are often used. The functions of all three are the same; the sizes and mechanisms are different.

Edits. Edits are instructions inserted into computer programs that help screen out or edit bad data. As an example, a computer program could have an edit to reject all attempts to enter a "current date" that is less than 1989 or greater than 1999.[9]

EDP. EDP is the abbreviation for Electronic Data Processing; it refers to processing data via a computer.

EDP Auditors. EDP auditors are individuals who review, monitor and audit electronic data processing operations. In other words, they handle the quality control function for data processing. Most EDP auditors know a lot about computers; some know very little about sampling and quality control.

Firmware. Programs that are a permanent part of the computer are called firmware (see ROM).

Floppy Disk. A floppy disk is a storage unit about the size of a 45-rpm phonograph record; some of the newer units are even smaller. Floppy disks are placed into a floppy disk drive when needed. When programs for personal computers are stored on disks, the programs are called software; when permanently stored in the computer, they are called firmware.

Floppy Disk Drive. A floppy disk drive is a device for reading information off floppy disks—it can also add information to floppies. Every personal computer should have at least one floppy disk drive. Some sophisticated computer programs require two disk drives—the second, however, can be a "hard disk" (see hard disk drives).

Flow Chart. Flow charts show the sequence and relationships of steps in a series of processes. When used by analysts and programmers, they show the steps, relationships and logic of computer programs.

FORTRAN. FORTRAN is a computer language similar to BASIC—but more complicated and powerful. It is normally used on large computers for "scientific" work.

Hard Disk Drive. Hard disk drives are storage devices used by personal computers. Their capacities usually run between 20 and 40 million characters although smaller and larger units can be found. Once a hard disk drive is full, you normally have to erase programs or data to make room for more. Few hard disk drives currently on the personal computer market have removable disks. They are, however, being developed; at least one is being marketed.

Hardware. Hardware refers to the computers themselves—the things you can see and touch. The term includes the computers, their input devices like disk and tape drives and output devices like printers. Computer programs, on the other hand, are usually called software.

Input. Input is data and information fed to a computer through an input device such as an OCR, disk, terminal or modem. The basic functions of a computer are: *input* the data, *process* it and then *output* it to a output device like a printer or terminal. Sending data to a storage device, like a disk, is also considered output.

Keypunch. A keypunch machine is a typewriter-like device used to punch holes in computers cards. The cards are the type that you shouldn't "bend, spindle, fold or mutilate." Keypunch systems are rapidly being replaced by terminals and other devices that feed data directly to the computer.

LAN. The term LAN is an abbreviation for Local Area Network. As the name implies, a LAN is a computer network with limited distance between the units. Like other networks, the interconnected units usually share hardware and software.

Mainframe. Large, top-of-the-line computers are called mainframes; many cost over a million dollars. As a consequence, only professional programmers are allowed to program them; if there are exceptions, there shouldn't be. Mainframe computers work with the speed of hyperactive electricity. Still, they almost always have a backlog of priority jobs. The individual user often waits days before getting results from a program, and months before getting a simple program change.

Memory. Computer memory refers to storage of information. A computer's memory can include information stored on disks, hard disks, floppy disks, storage tapes, ROM, RAM and a few other less common storage devices. "Programs" are used to instruct computers to read data from input devices or memory, process it and transfer it to storage or output devices.

MICR. MICR refers to Magnetic Ink Character Recognition devices. These units are used primarily by financial institutions, like banks, for reading data off checks. The information is then fed to a computer.

Microcomputer. Microcomputers are the same as home computers, desktop computers or personal computers. At first most of them were bought for homes and small businesses. As they became more powerful, however, they started invading large corporations and government offices. Prices range from under $1000 to over $10,000. Microcomputers are becoming popular in corporate America because they produce results quickly and stay within the control of user organizations. A statistician can run regression analyses in minutes. A manager can have simple changes in a program implemented in hours; complex changes take days or weeks.

Minicomputer. Minicomputers are the next step up from microcomputers. Minicomputers, like the IBM system 36, are big enough to require an operator. They are too small and inefficient, however, to compete with the mainframes for heavy-duty jobs. Most minicomputers get their information from a network of input terminals. Many also use tape drives, disks, card readers, MICRs and OCRs for input.

Modem. A modem is a device used to help computers talk to each other. The information is usually transmitted over telephone lines.

Network. A network is a number of terminals or small computers hooked up together. They frequently share mass-storage, printing and CPU equipment.

OCR. OCR is an abbreviation for optical character recognition equipment. An OCR device reads characters directly from a document, providing input for a computer.

Output. Output is information fed from a computer to an output device such as a printer or terminal. *Output* is the last of the basic functions of a computer. The others are *input*, where the data is fed to the computer, and *process*, where the computer manipulates the data (sorts, calculates, edits, etc.).

PC. See personal computer.

Peripherals. These are the elements of computer hardware that have nothing to do with the computations. Printers, disk drives, input terminals, optical character recognition equipment (OCRs) and tape drives are typical peripherals.

Personal Computer. A personal computer (PC) is a microcomputer. The term desktop computer is also used.

Programmers. Programmers are people who write the programs that tell computers what to do. Computers are fast, but they don't have minds of their own.

Punched Cards. Punched cards are cards with holes in them that provide information for computers. They are the product of keypunch machines. During the late 1940s punched cards were in the forefront of data automation. Now, they are being replaced by computer terminals and other devices that feed data directly to the computers.

RAM. RAM is Random Access Memory. When you ask computer sales personnel about the capacity of a computer, they normally tell you how much random access memory it has. A computer with 256K memory will have approximately 256,000 characters (bytes) of memory. A character is a letter, a single digit number or a symbol. The letter K represents 1000: 16K = 16,000; 32K = 32,000.

ROM. ROM is Read Only Memory. Computer designers place frequently used instructions on these computer chips in order to make computers faster. These instructions can be read by computers but can't be changed by them. Computer programs stored in ROM are called firmware.

Software. Software refers to the programs that tell the computers what to do. Computers do nothing without being told; if you want them to do things right, you have to give them very detailed instructions in the form of computer programs.

Tape. Computer tape (also called magnetic tape) is plastic tape having a magnetic surface for storing data in code; the tape itself can look like an oversized version of the tape in a recorder cassette, but it is too large to be conveniently packaged that way. Computer tape is normally wound on reels similar to those used with motion picture film. The biggest advantage of computer tapes is that they provide cheap mass storage. Their biggest disadvantage is that they are normally read sequentially from beginning to end; when they have to back up they slow down the reading or recording process. During their infancy, many personal computers used cassette-packaged magnetic tapes. They were slower and less reliable than disks, however, and were seldom used by experienced computer buffs.

Tape Drive. Tape drives are the equipment used to read data from a computer tape or write data on it.

Terminals. Computer terminals look like personal computers. Normally, both have TV-type screens and input keyboards. Terminals can be connected to personal computers, minicomputers or mainframes. Some of them are "intelligent," meaning they edit information before forwarding it to the computer. When used with minis and mainframe computers, a number of terminals are usually connected to a single computer.

Time-sharing Systems. Time-sharing computers are systems that allow a number of users at different terminals to execute programs concurrently. Most networks are time-share systems.

Word Processing. Word processing is the creation of correspondence and reports using a word processor. Most word processors are computers built specifically for writing, editing, correcting and printing correspondence. Most personal computers are capable of acting as efficient word processors—all they need are the appropriate computer programs (software). Few dedicated word processors, however, are capable of acting like efficient computers because they are too specialized. Many minicomputers also provide word processing capabilities for their work stations and terminals.

These definitions cover only a few common terms that are specific to the world of computers. Many additional definitions can be found in references (10) through (14).

SUMMARY

Computers are invading the service industries. To keep up with the competition, it is necessary to know a little about them. Those who leave computers and computer software to the specialists generally get what the specialists are willing to give them. Those who understand computer basics have a better chance of getting what they need.

Many computer specialists insist on speaking in their own tongue. If you can't understand them, you had better learn their dialect. Your future may be at stake.

Food for Thought

Visit a computer store in your area and show an interest in buying one. Immediately after leaving, try to answer these questions:

- Did the clerk speak in plain English or a blend of English and computerese?
- How many of the terms defined above did the clerk use when trying to make the sale?

REFERENCES
1. Henry L. Lefevre, "Productivity—Microcomputers and the Government," *ASQC Quality Congress Transactions,* May 3–5, 1982, pp. 305–307.
2. Henry L. Lefevre, "One Personal Computer Boosts Accounting Productivity 1,000 percent!" *Productivity Improvement Bulletin,* April 25, 1986, pp. 4–5.
3. Henry L. Lefevre, "A Computer in Every Office," *The Press,* July 1982, pp. 6–13.
4. Henry L. Lefevre, "Computer Literacy," *Quality,* September 1983, p. 90.
5. Henry L. Lefevre, "Love 'Em or Hate 'Em—Here Come the Computers," *Quality Control Supervisor's Bulletin,* June 25, 1985, pp. 1–2.
6. Henry L. Lefevre, "Computers—Are They QA's Patron Saint or Satan?" *Midwest Regional Quality Control Conference,* Minneapolis, 1970.
7. Henry L. Lefevre, "Time-share Computer Training . . . In Industry," *Journal of Data Education,* January 1969, pp. 12–13.
8. Henry L. Lefevre, "Quality Control and Database Management Systems," *ASQC Technical Conference Transactions,* May 9–10, 1978, pp. 371–374.
9. Henry L. Lefevre, "Deliver Yourself From Documentation Devils," *Personal Computing,* June 1982, pp. 85–86.
10. Robert A. Stern and Nancy Stern, *An Introduction to Computers and Information Processing* (New York: Wiley, 1982), pp. 617–627.
11. Donald D. Spencer, *Spencer's Computer Dictionary for Everyone* (New York: Scribner's, 1985).

12. Jerry M. Rosenberg, *Dictionary of Computers, Data Processing & Telecommunications* (New York: Wiley, 1984).
13. Douglas Downing and Michael Covington, *Dictionary of Computer Terms* (New York: Barron's, 1986).
14. James Hall-Sheehy, *Computer Basics For Human Resource Professionals* (New York: Wiley, 1986).

Chapter 22

As Literacy Approaches, Questions Multiply

Computers are interesting to read about, especially the success stories. But have you ever asked, "Does a desktop computer belong in *my* department?" The answer is complex; you need to know whether a computer can save *your* department money. If the answer is yes, you should think about its care, nourishment and software. To help prepare, consider the following questions:

1. Will it pay for itself?
2. What support services are available?
3. Is commercial software handy?
4. Should your computer department do the programming?
5. Should your own department do the programming?

The following sections will help you find answers that apply to your own operation; answers that are appropriate for you may not apply to other organizations in the company.

WILL IT PAY FOR ITSELF?

Many managers request computers because "the office down the hall has one"; computers become status symbols. When this happens, the equipment is seldom used effectively. Unless managers have objective guidelines for justifying equipment, they often find desktop computers easier to request than to use. As stated in *Fortune* magazine,[1] "In most cases managers do not scrutinize before they automate."

Although guidelines vary from company to company, a common method of justification requires that a computer pay for itself in three years. To make this evaluation, calculate the *Current-Cost-Per-Year* of the work you want to computerize. Until you identify potential applications, you shouldn't think of automating. From the Current-Cost-Per-Year figure, subtract the *Cost of Maintaining* the computer system; this includes data-input and programmer salaries as well as maintenance costs. Call the result the *Net Savings Per Year*.

Next, calculate the cost of buying the system and making it operational; include the computer, installation, training and software. Call this the *Total Cost*.

Divide the Net Savings Per Year into the Total Cost to get the number of years it will take the computer to pay for itself.

PROBLEM 22-1

You believe your statistical group is not providing quality service; it is too slow and makes too many errors. You consider buying a desktop computer to do the routine calculations and you want to know how long it will take before the computer pays for itself; this figure is called the payback. Supporting data includes the following:

Cost of running statistical calculations now:	
1 technician × $20,000 per year	$20,000
Cost of running calculations via computer:	
0.2 data-input clerk × $15,000 per year	(3,000)
Cost of programmer (not applicable—	
statistical software is available):	0
Cost of service contract for the equipment (per year):	(600)
Cost of computer system	(3,500)
Cost of statistical software	(200)
Cost of setup and training	(800)

Based on the above data, how long would it take for the desktop computer to pay for itself?

SOLUTION 22-1

Current cost per year:		$20,000
Expected cost per year of new system:		
Clerk running computer:	$3,000	
Service contract:	600	
Total:	$3,600	(3,600)
Net savings per year:		$16,400
Cost of computer system:	$3,500	
Cost of software:	200	
Cost of setup and training:	800	
Total cost:	$4,500	

Years for computer to pay for itself = Total cost / Net savings per year
= $4,500 / $16,400
= .27 years
= 3.2 months

In this instance, the computer is expected to pay for itself in slightly more than three months; the requirement of keeping the payback under three years has been met. The benefits of reduced error rates were considered intangible and were not included in the calculations. These savings are not unusual for computer applications when commercial software is available—if the store-bought programs don't need modification.[2-4]

Once you have a computer or word processor, you might wonder whether it's time to buy another. William Kreykenbohm[5] says that one way to determine the cost-effectiveness of word processors is to make a series of random, unannounced observations of the units. (This approach can be called time sampling or work sampling.) Kreykenbohm concluded that it is being used "fairly effectively" if it is in service during half of the reviews. When computers or word processors are being used less than half the time, it's hard to justify additional equipment. When they are used more than half the time, you should check to see if people are waiting in line during periods the equipment is in use. A second unit might reduce the inefficiencies that come with waiting for busy equipment to become available.

When evaluating whether word processors will pay for themselves, consider the reduction in proofing that results when automation is introduced. Computers with word processing software might also be considered; they are more versatile and are not limited to word processing functions.

According to *Fortune* magazine,[1] "Many personal computers, especially machines bought during the PC boom of 1983 and 1984, sit idle much of the time." An idle computer won't pay for itself; it won't improve service, reduce errors or increase productivity. It is probable, however, that most of these "dusty" machines were purchased by people having no idea of what they were going to do with them. If you follow the procedures outlined in Problem 22-1, you should be able to avoid having dusty computers cluttering your office.

WHAT SUPPORT SERVICES ARE AVAILABLE?

With most medium- to large-sized organizations, their data processing department can provide the support that is needed. Small organizations with no data processing personnel often get support from workers with their own computers at home. If they don't have this resource, they can get training from computer schools, trade schools, junior colleges, community colleges and other night schools. This text, however, stresses in-house help.

Faced with the invasion of personal computers, many data processing departments have decided to join rather than fight the small computer movement. They realize that mainframe computers are needed for large projects like Payroll, Management Information Systems, Accounts Receivable and Accounting. They also realize that larger computers are difficult to program, resistant to change and too expensive for minor assignments. As an example, using a huge computer to handle simple linear regression analyses is like using a sledge hammer to kill a gnat. In the past, when approached with this type of statistical project, many computer departments procrastinated or diverted the work to time-share networks. Now, however, they often run the analyses with personal computers or help user organizations run them.

Many data processing departments seek responsibility for standardizing hardware and software within the company; this results in less duplication of effort. As an example, when I was at the Air Force Accounting and Finance Center the quality control people developed an excellent sampling program for use on personal computers. (There were no commercial sampling programs available at that time.) Once the computer hardware and operating systems in the Center were standardized by the data processing people, the program could be used by anyone in the facility. Additional help from the data processing staff came in the areas of computer security, training and programming.

IS COMMERCIAL SOFTWARE HANDY?

Today, when acceptable commercial computer programs are available, they are usually cheaper and more reliable than programs built within the company. This is particularly true for small organizations with limited data processing support. Spreadsheet programs like Lotus 1-2-3, for example, can cost over $100,000 to develop; high-volume sales, however, have kept the price of the program reasonable. On sale, it can be bought for less than $200. Most of the better word processing programs were also expensive to write; they, too, are inexpensive to buy. Working alone, it could take the average programmer years to develop a comparable program from scratch.

Ten years ago, the unavailability of cheap, reliable software was a major problem. The few commercial programs that were available were untried and expensive. David Moorman,[6] for instance, refers to a payroll program that had no decimal points and a scheduling system that had everyone taking breaks at the same time. He also wrote about a billing system that omitted names and addresses.

Now, however, there are innumerable proven programs on statistics, quality control, accounting, accounts receivable and just about any other common task. Most of them are easy to use and reliable. Prudent people, however, don't take chances; they try out the programs before buying them. If testing a program is not practical, they question current owners to determine how the programs work for them. Where do you find applicable programs? *Quality* magazine and *Quality Progress* make periodic lists of available quality assurance software.[7,8]

Most commercial computer programs have one disadvantage; it is difficult for *amateur* programmers to change or maintain them. Any attempt to customize a commercial program is apt to make it completely unusable unless the individual making the changes is a professional programmer. Although commercial programs can be customized by experts, this approach tends to be time consuming and expensive. Waiting for most system programmers to customize commercial software is like wishing on a star—and joining the waiting line behind Rip Van Winkle.

There is another hitch. Don't expect to master word processing, database, or spreadsheet programs overnight. They may be fast, accurate and efficient. Some are also complex, confusing and hard to understand. The term "user-friendly" doesn't apply to everything on the software market. Get a thorough demonstration of any software you expect to buy, using your own data. The program may not do the things you want and you may not be able to understand the instructions.

Another consideration is the protection of commercial software. A study by *Future Computing* showed that for every copy of purchased software in use, a pirated copy has been made.[9] When you buy a software package, you normally buy the right to use it on a single machine or in a single facility. You seldom buy the right to copy it and take it home.

For a while, software companies were able to control software thieves by using intricate copy protection devices. Customers, however, were inconvenienced by the side effects of copy protection. They complained, causing many software companies to back off. This decision was also influenced by the spread of copy-protection-breaking software. Once a copy-protection technique was developed, competition came up with a countermeasure.[10] Software companies are beginning to prosecute those who make unauthorized copies of their programs. As a consequence, many companies and government offices are taking steps to reduce unauthorized duplication.

SHOULD YOUR COMPUTER DEPARTMENT DO THE PROGRAMMING?

Do you have a computer department that is responsive to your needs? Have the computer professionals given you prompt and effective service in the past? Do they have enough personnel that they can work on your projects when you need them? Is your organization short on computer skills with no one capable of programming? Are your needs unique enough that you can't find commercial software that will do what you want? If your answer to these questions is yes, you should consider having the computer department do your programming.

Advantages of using professional programmers

- They understand the capabilities and limitations of computers. This is a major asset.
- They can begin as soon as personnel are available; they seldom need additional training before getting started.
- They may have experience on similar programs. They may even have access to an applicable program that is already available.
- They are accustomed to documenting their work.[11] Amateurs tend to make many undocumented changes. In time, they become fuzzy about the logic they used. If the author of an undocumented program gets promoted, is transferred or quits, no one can take over without wasting a lot of time.

- They are accustomed to configuration control. Configuration control involves keeping track of changes in programs. Most amateurs make so many modifications, they get confused about which version of the program is current.
- Many professionals can customize commercial programs. This is not a job for amateurs.
- If you understand computers, you can ask the professionals to do the right things in the right way; the result can be an outstanding program that requires no revisions. This is why computer literacy is so important.
- If you get your data-input people involved in the program design, the finished program can fit their needs more effectively; this leads to better efficiency and fewer input errors. In addition, your data-input people will learn more about computers. The more they know, the easier it is for them to come up with good suggestions on how to make automation more effective.

Professional programmers are trained to handle the details of programming that amateurs seldom think about. If you want things done right the first time, look to the professionals.

Disadvantages of using professional programmers

- With the data processing department, you may spend too much time justifying what you want.
- Professional programmers are often busy when you need them most.
- Professional programmers and analysts seldom understand your work area like you do. I once asked our computer department for a program that would take random audit samples from a million payroll checks. They balked, saying it couldn't be done. Within a month, however, our amateurs developed the program and had it working, using a small personal computer. We didn't know computers as well as they. We did, however, know sampling and statistics.
- If you don't understand computers, you often ask analysts to do the wrong things in the wrong way; the result can be messed-up programs requiring many revisions. That's why computer literacy is so important.
- If you don't get your data-input people involved in the program design, the finished program can contribute to inefficiency and high error rates.

SHOULD YOUR OWN DEPARTMENT DO THE PROGRAMMING?

Are your needs fairly simple? Do you want complete control of your programs? Do you want to change your programs on a moment's notice without writing lengthy letters of justification? Do you have unique needs that the programming department wouldn't understand without extensive indoctrination? Do you have engineers, technicians or clerks familiar with BASIC and capable of doing your programming for you? Do you want your data-entry personnel involved in developing input formats they can use efficiently? If so, and your data processing department won't address these needs, you should consider doing your own programming. When computer departments are not responsive, the inefficiencies of amateur programming will be tolerated by those who can't otherwise get what they need when they need it.

Advantages of doing your own programming

- Customizing your own programs is easier.
- Responses to change requests are quicker.
- Computer literacy within a department improves.[12-14] This knowledge helps if you start auditing computer operations of other organizations.
- Justifications are simplified. You know your needs better than anyone else. You shouldn't have to spend more time justifying proposed programs than the computer department spends developing them.

Disadvantages of doing your own programming

- Changes are hard to control. At times, they are made without the knowledge of management.
- Poor housekeeping often results in the users not knowing which version of the program is current.
- Amateurs' programs are not always properly documented. Without good documentation, assumptions, limitations and logic behind the programs get fuzzy.
- It is too easy to develop pride of "authorship" resulting in duplication of existing software; this is costly, time consuming and resembles "reinvention of the wheel."
- The cost of writing your own programs is seldom documented properly; in many cases no one knows how expensive they are.

SUMMARY

As managers and supervisors become better acquainted with computers, they often want one of their own. Purchase of a personal computer, however, should be justified. One common approach is to require that the computer pay for itself in less than three years. Adherence to this rule keeps computers from being status symbols instead of tools for providing quality service.

Part of the justification process involves determining where you will get your software and how much it will cost. If the programs are to be relatively simple, and someone in the department knows BASIC, in-department programming is often best—and often cheapest. If the computer department is cooperative, reliable and capable of timely service, have them do it. If the programs involve routine calculations such as regression analyses or quality control charts, commercial software is usually best.

FOOD FOR THOUGHT

Review your department's relationship with the data processing organization in your company. Then answer the following questions about their quality and responsiveness:
- Are they responsive or arrogant?
- How long does it take them to provide a simple program for your desktop computers?
- How long does it take them to make a simple change on one of your mainframe computer programs?
- On a scale of 1 to 10, how would you rate the quality of their service?
- How many departments in your company do their own programming?
- Do you see a relationship between quality of the data processing department's service and proliferation of amateur programming?
- Do they illustrate the theme "Quality Service Pays" or the theme "Poor Service Doesn't Pay"?

REFERENCES

1. William Bowen, "The Puny Payoff From Office Computers," *Fortune,* May 26, 1986, pp. 20–24.
2. Henry L. Lefevre, "Productivity—Microcomputers and the Government," *ASQC Quality Congress Transactions,* May 3–5, 1982, pp. 305–307.

3. Henry L. Lefevre, "One Personal Computer Boosts Accounting Productivity 1,000 Percent!" *Productivity Improvement Bulletin,* April 25, 1986, pp. 4–5.
4. Henry L. Lefevre, "A Computer in Every Office," *The Press,* July 1982, pp. 6–13.
5. William Kreykenbohm, "Processors Aren't Always Cost-Effective," *Government Computer News,* August 30, 1985, p. 72.
6. David L. Moorman, "Winning Quality Assurance in Software," *MIS Week,* December 8, 1986, p. 47.
7. "QA/QC Software Directory," *Quality Progress,* March 1987, pp. 35–66.
8. Frederick W. Miller, "Quality Software Update '87," *Quality,* June 1987, pp. 48–58.
9. Joe Diodati, "Software Duplication and How to Control It," *The Office,* February 1986, p. 20.
10. Jim Seymour, "Will Users Kayo Copy Protection?" *Today's Office,* June 1986, pp. 14–19.
11. Henry L. Lefevre, "Deliver Yourself From Documentation Devils," *Personal Computing,* June 1982, pp. 85–86.
12. Henry L. Lefevre, "Computer Literacy," *Quality,* September 1983, p. 90.
13. Henry L. Lefevre, "Love 'Em or Hate 'Em—Here Come the Computers," *Quality Control Supervisor's Bulletin,* June 25, 1985, pp. 1–2.
14. Henry L. Lefevre, "Computers—Are They QA's Patron Saint or Satan?" *Midwest Regional Quality Control Conference,* Minneapolis, 1970.

Chapter 23

Database Quality Control

Databases have large quantities of information stored in computer memory. This data can be enlarged, removed, changed, organized, manipulated, sorted, retrieved or selected for formal reports. Most databases are on line. The term "on line" means that users can work with the information at their leisure; they don't have to depend on programmers, analysts or computer operators to help them. Users have special codes that allow them to access the database directly via computer terminals; then they can add, look at, remove or manipulate the information.

As Robert M. Curtice[1] says, "the promise of a database is its ability to share consistent and timely data throughout the organization, to enable users to access that data directly without technical assistance, and to easily evolve so that it meets changing business requirements."

Jurnack,[2] on the other hand, looks at databases as tools for reducing paperwork. He says: "In addition to generating the routine reports which are issued on a periodic or regular basis, an effective system should lead to the elimination of many of these reports. More important, it should evolve into an exception reporting system that would allow each manager to ask questions and get answers in relatively short periods of time in order to improve his decision-making capability."

With databases, quality really pays. If the quality of their design and content is high, they can save a considerable amount of money; if their quality and security are poor, they can drive you out of business.

BENEFITS OF USING A DATABASE

Databases can be very large or very small. Both sizes can be used to reduce costs and improve quality. The quality organization at the Air Force Accounting and Finance Center had a small database;[3,4] its original hardware consisted of a personal computer, one floppy disk drive and a small printer. The users collected information from satellite organizations, summarized it, and fed analyses to interested parties. Savings netted by the report-generating part of this small $4,000 system were approximately $50,000 per year.

A typical large database is used by the American Association of Retired Persons.[5] It contains files on the organization's 23 million members and requires 37 full-time vendor employees including operators, tape librarians, production control staff, systems programmers, telecommunications specialists and a systems administrator. In one day it can handle 100,000 data transactions.

On the other hand, GE FANUC[6] has a moderate-sized database; benefits they accrued from it include:

- Improved productivity
- Better reports
- Reduced costs
- Identification of potential problems
- Speedier customer service
- Reduced paperwork
- Improved feedback

GE FANUC has their test-data-capture, quality-indicator and field-quality information systems connected to their business systems computer. This hookup makes communication between them easy and efficient; it helps them share data with sources that were previously independent. It also enables them to blend analytical and storage functions so they don't have to reinput data when analyzing information or printing charts.

One of the systems at the Republic National Bank of New York emphasizes budgets;[7] it uses small satellite computers tied into their mainframe. The previous year's budget figures go from the mainframe to the satellite units. Then department managers using spreadsheet programs develop budgets for the current year. The new numbers are sent to the budget officer via electronic mail. The budget officer consolidates the budgets and presents the results to the budget department. If revisions are required, the process is repeated.

POOR DATABASE QUALITY INVOLVES MAJOR RISKS

Databases can improve productivity and reduce costs. Database errors, on the other hand, can be quite expensive. How expensive? Consider the following.

- The government lost a $1.25 million suit because of poor data. Four lobster fishermen were killed when the National Weather Service called for fair weather and goofed. The fishermen encountered 100-mile-per-hour gusts and 60-foot waves. A factor in the poor forecast was the government's failure to repair an electronic data buoy. As a consequence, critical data was missing from the forecaster's database. Had the correct information been available, lives might have been saved.[8]
- Flawed information published by the Federal Aviation Administration (FAA) contributed to the crash of a World Airways plane during 1973. Families of the victims were awarded nearly $13 million.[8]
- Dun & Bradstreet lost a $350,000 libel suit to a Vermont construction company. They had sent out a credit report that incorrectly called the company bankrupt. The problem was due to a data-entry error by a part-time student.
- A motorist in Alaska spent a night in jail because a database showed him charged with traffic violations that should have been erased from his record.[9]
- Incorrect information in federal databases has resulted in law agencies getting over 12,000 inaccurate reports on suspects.[9]

Those who develop and maintain databases are at least partially responsible for the data they contain. The possibilities of poor quality are great—and so are the costs. Additional instances where poor data could cause extensive damage include:

- *Pharmaceutical databases.* If information on possible side effects is missing, a doctor's reliance on the database could contribute to a patient's death.

- *Military personnel databases.* Incorrect information could contribute to officers failing to get promotions they deserved—and eventually being discharged from the service.
- *Charge-account databases.* A department store charged my account for purchases made by another client. I promptly closed my account.
- *Stock-account databases.* A brokerage house gave me credit for the sale of someone else's stock. It took them weeks to straighten out the problem.
- *AIDS-testing databases.* Colorado requires mandatory reporting of positive tests for AIDS.[10] An error in that database could be devastating.

CONTROLLING DATABASE QUALITY— THE FIRST STEP

The first step in controlling database quality is to determine what the current accuracy is. One database manager reviewed the quality of information in his database every week. Proud of the results, he periodically submitted reports to upper management stating that the information was more than 99 percent correct. Being skeptical by nature, the quality analysis supervisor had his technicians check information in the database against the source documents. Their analyses showed that the true quality was close to 95 percent.

Why the difference?

The database manager used the computer to do his checking. This approach was fast, efficient and inaccurate. The manager had assumed that the only possible erroneous data would contain blanks, nines, z's or zeros. These entries represented unknown or missing information. Most of the errors found by the quality technicians looked like good data but were not.

TECHNIQUES FOR IMPROVING DATABASE QUALITY

Common techniques for improving database quality include:

- Running computer audits (automated inspection)
- Checking computer data against source documents (manual inspection)
- Monitoring rejected transactions
- Improving computer edits
- Using templates

- Testing alternatives to see which is best
- Coordinating database design
- Installing database security systems

The following sections provide more detail on each of these techniques.

Running Computer Audits

Although automated computer audits have their disadvantages, they also have their benefits.[11] They are fast, they can cover the entire database and they are predictable. An automated computer audit runs like the search function of a word processor. As an example, take the case of a typist who uses the word "to" in place of "too." The search function can find each use of the word "to." Then, the reviewer can decide whether the word was used properly.

In most cases, computers can also change the spelling of a word without the reviewer getting involved. If the computer was told to change the word "to" to "too" every time it occurred, however, new errors would be introduced; there are many places where "to" is an appropriate word or partial word. If direction given the computer is not adequate, the computer might even change the spelling of "today" to "tooday."

Similar changes have been made to databases; the results are often abysmal. One organization used the computer to "fill in" missing data in one of their data elements. The resulting data looked better, with fewer blanks and unknowns; the resulting quality, however, was worse. It is easy to find blanks and unknowns; it is difficult to find erroneous data that looks logical.

Using Source Documents to Verify Quality

Using source documents to verify database quality is slow, expensive and about 95 percent effective. Checks of computer data against source documents that I supervised caught about 95 percent of the errors; 5 percent went undetected.

Manual audits provide an excellent method for *determining* the quality of a database; they are a poor method for *improving* the quality. The current trend is toward error prevention. Inspection and error detection, however, can never be eliminated. Without them, you wouldn't know when error prevention programs were needed and whether they were successful.

Monitoring Rejected Transactions

Most computer databases require that the data-input clerks identify themselves when entering information. Some of these databases also identify rejected transactions. A rejected transaction is one identified as being wrong by a system edit; it would not be accepted by the computer.

Databases with search functions provide the error data. Then, control charts for the group can help identify problems and statistically out-of-control situations. Charts on individuals can be used to identify performance patterns when out-of-control situations are known to exist. In some instances, knowledge of the performance patterns helps supervisors initiate corrective action. As an example, data-entry clerks showing upward error trends throughout the day may be tiring. A more frequent change of assignments often helps; don't overwork tired eyes.

In many instances error distributions follow the Pareto principle, where 20 percent of the employees make about 80 percent of the errors. Once the 20 percent are identified, this information can be integrated into an error prevention program in the following ways:

- Discuss the problem with the error-prone employees. In many instances, they can contribute to the solution. They may ask for more training. On the other hand, they may indicate that the computer screen is giving them problems—or the lighting—or the noise—or the humidity—or the glare—or other variables.
- Discuss the problem with the error-free employees. How are they different? Are their eyes more resistant to the glare? Are they less affected by the environment? Do they have special techniques the others don't use? If so, can these techniques be taught to the error-prone workers? Should the error-free employees be used as trainers?

Improving Computer Edits

Edits are used to keep illogical data from entering the database. As an example, an edit might reject any Social Security number with the first three digits larger than 729. According to Raabe,[12] no Social Security number has its first three digits above 729 or between 587 and 699; these numbers have never been issued. The above edits can reduce the risk of fraud; they can also catch typing errors. The edit of Social Security numbers is simple, although it requires knowledge of the Social Security system.

Relationship edits are more complex. They are edits that check two or more variables to see if their relationship is logical. For example, the computer could question a Social Security number starting with 574 if the owner had never been in Alaska. The first three digits of a Social Security number identify where it was issued. 574, for example, had to be issued in Alaska. Numbers 575–576 were allotted to Hawaii. Numbers 545–573 were allotted to California.[12] Although it is possible to have a Social Security number starting with 574 without showing Alaska in the employee's work history, it is not probable. Exceptions can occur if the work history is incomplete or the individual received the Social Security number in Alaska without working there. Minors often get Social Security numbers for tax purposes.

Other relationship edits could include the following:

- A Payroll database should have salary limits for each job classification. Then if data-entry personnel try to enter a clerk's salary exceeding $5000 per month, an edit can trigger an investigation. This edit reviews the relationship between job classification and salary.
- An Accounts Payable database should include an Approved Vendor's List. Then, edits can ensure that vendors won't be paid unless they have been approved. This edit reviews the relationship between names on the payment vouchers and those on the Approved Vendor List.
- A Credit Card database should include credit limits. Then edits can ensure that credit is not extended beyond limits of the owner's credit line.
- Personnel databases can record age and years of experience. Then, edits can ensure that the two are compatible. As an example, years of experience should never exceed age.

Many of the best edits are developed by database users intimately involved with the information being recorded. Another way to select edits is to monitor errors detected during database audits; if the errors can be detected logically, develop an edit that will enable the computer to screen them out. Edits should not be left to programmers with no user involvement.

Using Templates

Templates are pieces of paper or cardboard with holes in them, allowing the user to see select data on the forms beneath. When placed over a source document, the important data can be seen through the holes; unimportant clutter is hidden by the solid parts of the template.

One data-entry clerk I worked with had a difficult time entering numbers into the computer. There was so much information on the source document that she became confused and entered the wrong data. In order to reduce the clutter, we developed a template with holes that matched the data to be copied. Then we noted that the data had to be entered out of sequence. This problem was reduced when we placed numbers under each of the holes in the template; the numbers identified the sequence to be used when making entries.

Both of these actions were stopgap measures. The ultimate solution involved changing the sequence used to feed data to the computer. This, however, required action by the programmers who were maintaining input screens for the databases.

Testing Alternatives

One problem with listening to everyone's suggestions is that you get many conflicting ideas. Some suggestions are great; they improve quality and productivity. Other suggestions are counterproductive; they make things worse. In order to separate the good from the bad, it can be helpful to use designed experiments and control charts (see Chapter 18). Here are typical system changes that can be evaluated before implementation:

- Test whether a specific data-input template helps quality.
- Test whether a specific template helps productivity.
- Determine which set of edits works best.
- Determine whether new input formats at the data-entry terminal help reduce errors.
- Evaluate the impact of different computer terminals on error rates.
- Compare the effect of different data-input terminal screen colors on error rates.
- Determine how long stretches of data-entry work affect error rates and productivity. Do data-entry clerks make more errors during their first, second, third or fourth hour at the terminal?

Coordinating Database Design

During the design phase, analysts should coordinate the needs of all users and potential users. In this way, they ensure common data elements have common definitions, agreeable to everyone using the system. Data input is a major contributor to the cost of maintaining databases. If you have a number of organizations feeding the same information into different computer files, you have redundancy. This often occurs because organizations left out of the original planning find the system doesn't fit their perceived needs.

When it is necessary to have more than one database using the same data, it is still desirable to have a single set of data definitions agreeable to all users. Many organizations have database managers who do the coordination, ensuring that there is just one "official" definition and source for each data element. A data element is information that fits into a single pigeonhole in the database. For example, a person's name is one element. Street address can be a second; city can be a third; state can be a fourth.

Database Security

Having the best database in the world with no security is like being in charge of the gold at Fort Knox and removing all safeguards. Without security, an outstanding database can become as useless as a computer struck by lightning. August Bequai,[13] when writing about computer-related thefts, claimed: "Annual losses are said to run as high as $1 billion. Every business and governmental agency with a computer is a potential target." By now, the losses are probably much higher.

During the 1960s and 1970s, "rings of defense" were used to protect corporate databases.[14] The idea was to keep "invaders" off company grounds. If they reach the grounds, use a pass system to keep them out of the building. If they enter the building, use more sophisticated identification to keep them out of the data processing area. If they get into the data processing area, depend on keys and more passwords to keep them out of the computer. Now, however, most databases are connected to phone lines; complex passwords, encryption and call-back systems are required for protection.

Passwords are much better security devices in theory than they are in practice. Many passwords are simple, such as a single letter or the programmer's name. Those that are complex get written down; I have even seen them taped to data-input terminals. Even well-devised, random passwords have limited value if they are not changed frequently.

The second method, encrypted or coded transmissions, make data transmission safer. The cost and inconvenience, however, keep this technique from becoming routine.

The third and possibly the best security technique is the call-back system. Some databases require that everyone needing to contact the computer from the outside have their phone numbers entered into the computer's system software. Then, when the computer receives a call, it automatically hangs up, verifies the phone number and then calls back. If the phone number is not on the computer's authorized list, security personnel are alerted—the computer never does call back. Call-back systems are fairly effective, unless compromised by an authorized user within the company.

Being safe from outsiders, however, is less than half of the security problem. According to Kurt Leuser,[15] "at least 30 percent of all business failures are the direct result of employee dishonesty, and no business is immune." He also notes: "Computer larceny deals in big dollars. The average computer theft nets $143,000. That is 80 times as much as the average 'take' of $1,800 in a bank robbery." How can a company protect itself? Leuser recommends:

1. Limiting each employee's computer access to scheduled work hours.
2. Developing a system for tracking transactions with an audit trail that records user activities.
3. Involving *informed* managers and supervisors throughout the company.
4. Changing passwords periodically.
5. Separating developmental and operational groups. Developmental personnel are most likely to have the skills for compromising the system; operational personnel are most likely to have the opportunities.
6. Running extensive security checks on potential workers before they are hired. According to Leuser, "One person in ten is a thief and should be kept out of any organizations."[15]

Additional tools include the following:[16]

- Remove all manufacturer-installed systems-access protocols that can compromise security like SYSTEMS, SYS, LIST, etc.
- Accept only prepaid calls from network users. According to Baird, hackers are notoriously reluctant to spend their own money on communications.
- Consider using unlisted telephone numbers for access to the database and change the numbers at least annually.
- Revoke the access authority of terminated employees as soon as termination has been initiated.

SUMMARY

Computer databases are versatile. They can be small enough to fit in a personal computer or large enough to require a mainframe. Regardless of size, however, the quality of their data is important.

Audits are only the first step in controlling database quality. Here are some other techniques for quality improvement and error prevention:

- Learn what your error-prone employees are doing wrong—and why.
- Learn what your error-free employees are doing right—and why.
- Have effective edits.
- Critique the format of source documents and the instructions provided by your computer's data-input screen. They can contribute to high error rates.
- Consider templates for stopgap help.
- Test alternatives before making permanent changes. The new ways may not be better.

FOOD FOR THOUGHT

Determine who is responsible for the quality control function within your company. Ask that individual:

1. "What is the quality level of the data?"
2. "How are the following tools being used?"
   a. Automated audits
   b. Manual audits
   c. Rejected transactions
   d. Computer edits
   e. Templates for data input
   f. Coordination during database design
   g. Database security systems

REFERENCES
1. Robert M. Curtice, "Getting the Database Right," *Datamation*, October 1, 1986, pp. 99–104.
2. Stephen J. Jurnack, "Achieving Productivity With Quality Information Systems," *Prepared for the 31st Annual Technical Conference of ASQC*, May 16–18, 1977 (a supplement to the transactions).
3. Henry L. Lefevre, "Productivity—Microcomputers and the Government," *ASQC Quality Congress Transactions*, May 3–5, 1982, pp. 305–307.
4. Henry L. Lefevre, "One Personal Computer Boosts Accounting Productivity 1,000 Percent!" *Productivity Improvement Bulletin*, April 25, 1986, pp. 4–5.

5. Wayne Haefer, "For Nation's Elderly: A Timely Information System," *The Office*, June 1987, pp. 32–39.
6. R. W. Butz and K. Sateesh, "QIS—A Vital Business Tool," *Quality*, June 1987, pp. 32–36.
7. Sam Dickey, "Banking on OA Integration," *Today's Office*, November 1986, pp. 42–47.
8. Peter Marx, "Information Databases—The Legal Risks," *MIS Week*, February 2, 1987, pp. 39, 46.
9. Tom Percey, "My Data Right or Wrong," *Datamation*, June 1, 1986, pp. 123–128.
10. Jeff Moad, "As AIDS Spreads, State PC Systems Are Reaching Limits," *Datamation*, August 15, 1987, pp. 43–53.
11. Henry L. Lefevre, "Quality Control and Database Management Systems," *ASQC Technical Conference Transactions*, May 8–10, 1978, pp. 371–374.
12. Steve Raabe, "Social Security Number Fraud Can Be Reduced," *Rocky Mountain Business Journal*, August 19, 1985, p. 4.
13. August Bequai, "What to Do About Crime in the Electronic Office," *The Office*, January 1985, pp. 101–104.
14. Emory L. Morsberger, "Computers and Corporate Data Security: A Twofold Problem," *The Office*, September 1984, pp. 17–21.
15. Kurt G. Leuser, "Security Programs: Only As Good As We Make Them," *The Office*, August 1984, pp. 91–100.
16. Lindsay L. Baird Jr., "Sensible Network Security," *Datamation*, February 1, 1985.

Chapter 24

Key 5: Involving People

Having the best tools in the world has limited value if only the elite are allowed to use them. Managers, statisticians and engineers can solve many problems by themselves; they can solve many more if they have input from other members of the organization. This is where participative management comes in; it helps get more people involved.

According to Edward E. Lawler III:[1] "Participative management is an idea whose time has come. But it is not a new idea. Indeed, for decades the management literature has been filled with arguments for better treatment of employees, more interesting work, and more democratic supervision." As Lawler observes, there is often a long pause between formulation of theory and general acceptance in the world of business.

Participative management requires letting people contribute to decisions that involve them. In *Managing to Keep the Customer,* Robert Desatnick supports this concept by writing:[2] "People make the best decisions when they use the collective wisdom of the group. It is only natural for people to want to participate in decisions that affect them. Participation reduces resistance to change and gives employees a sense of ownership."

Where you have participative management, you are more likely to find:

- Smiling, cooperative receptionists at the front desk enhancing the company's reputation
- Cheerful bank tellers who make few errors
- Data-entry clerks who maintain near-perfect databases
- Quality control supervisors who know what's going on and who provide objective personnel evaluations
- Vice-presidents who take time to learn the language of technical subordinates

The one thing you really need, however, is a company president who supports participative management and sets a favorable climate within the organization.

QUALITY CIRCLES

Currently, one of the most popular techniques for implementing participative management is the Quality Circle. Developed by the Japanese, Quality Circles were once considered the answer to all our quality problems. Some people asked, "If Circles worked for the Japanese and enabled them to surpass us in the field of quality, why not copy the technique and catch up?" The truth is that Quality Circles are not cure-alls. Latzko[3] notes that even authorities from Japan admit their Circles accounted for no more than 10 percent of the country's quality resurgence. Robert Cole[4] supports this contention: "One of the common misconceptions prevalent in American management circles is that QC Circles are primarily responsible for Japan's remarkable success in improving product quality." Even Deming[5] notes problems with Quality Circles: "We tried QC-Circles among the hourly workers, without first educating the management into their responsibilities to remove obstacles reported. We learned our lesson the hard way: our QC-Circles disintegrated."

Although Quality Circles are not perfect, they do have significant advantages; the most prominent are

- Savings for the company
- Improved communications
- Better training

The following paragraphs elaborate.

Savings for the Company

Where Quality Circles have been successfully implemented, the payback ratios range between 2:1 and 8:1.[6] Payback ratio is the ratio of dollars saved to the cost of getting the savings. If a Quality Circle implements programs that save $80,000 per year and the cost of getting the savings is $20,000 per year, the payback ratio is 80,000:20,000 or 4:1.

Improved Communications

It is easier to dislike someone you don't know and it is more difficult to communicate with people you dislike. When you are working on team projects, however, you start rubbing elbows with many people. This includes members of the team, facilitators, customers and those who serve you. The term "facilitator" is Quality-Circle jargon. It refers to those who train, advise and help the Circles get going, in other words, those who facilitate the development and work of the Circles without necessarily being members. With small companies, the job of facilitator is usually a part-time assignment sandwiched between other duties. With larger companies, most facilitators work with a number of Circles or teams; facilitating can be their only job.

Circle members work with facilitators and get to know them. When the Circle requires people with special skills, members rub elbows with them, also. When members make presentations to management, they get exposure to the brass. Soon, many of their excuses for disliking people disappear; they know each other too well. With familiarity, the ability to communicate improves.

In addition to meeting many individuals, Circle members get to know their problems. Many start asking: What are the customer's needs? How does their own work affect the customers? How can workers serve each other better? Why do some people produce data that can't be used without revision? How can they provide better service?

Better Training

The Air Reserve Personnel Center had an excellent Quality Circle program while I was working for the government. The training they received in troubleshooting, statistics and data presentation made them outstanding candidates for promotion. This was particularly true when openings occurred in the Quality Analysis, Statistics and Quality Assurance organizations.

Quality Circles, however, are only one way of benefiting from the team approach.

ALTERNATIVES TO QUALITY CIRCLES

Once American companies began to run into problems with Quality Circles, many of them made modifications and introduced new approaches to the team concept.

- Celestial Seasonings in Boulder, Colorado[7] introduced Work Teams, looking for ways to improve productivity and costs as well as quality. They also looked for bottlenecks in their operations. Unlike Quality Circles, however, participation in Work Teams was not voluntary; everyone was involved.
- Celestial Seasonings also used Adventure Teams that helped develop new products; membership was optional. An Adventure Team could be started by anyone with ideas for a promising new item. The originator sought co-workers to assist in the development phase whenever additional skills were needed. If the idea was good, the teams had no trouble getting participants. Secretaries and vice-presidents ended up in the same group when they had skills that were needed. The teams performed feasibility studies, formulation, design and preliminary marketing analyses. Raspberry Patch Tea, one of the company's best-selling beverages, was a worker-sponsored product.[7]
- Quality Technics had a concept called *Team* Approach to *Problem Solving* (TAPS). Although quite similar to Quality Circles, they were open to all levels of the organization ranging from management to shift workers. They were highly structured and stressed both planning and training.[8]
- International Packings Corporation used the SCAT © approach. The acronym SCAT was copyrighted by the company and stands for *Statistical Control Analysis Techniques*. SCAT teams differ from Quality Circles by being interdepartmental and by working on projects assigned by management. Service areas involved in the SCAT program included engineering, the corporate R&D lab, accounting, sales and customer service. The company also used Quality Circles on

projects that involved a single department—they could choose their own projects.[9]
- CalComp used supervisors to lead their teams; this put first-level management in the group. With traditional Quality Circles in the United States, supervisors often feel bypassed. How does CalComp classify their approach? They call it a grass-roots program for "people development."[10]
- Lana Chandler, of Kanawha Valley Bank NA, Charleston, West Virginia,[11] favored Quality and Efficiency Committees (QEC). Here, the main concept was to tap the ideas of middle management. According to Chandler, "Even managers, particularly those below the senior level, can find themselves lost in the same maddening maze as an entry-level employee when it comes to changing corporate policy." By stressing middle management participation, the QEC teams filled a niche that is usually ignored by Quality Circles.
- Not all participative-management innovations are successful. Rosabeth Kanter[12] wrote about a company that introduced skip-level meetings. Level A could skip Level B and meet directly with Level C. The idea was to shorten lines of communication and help managers find out what was going on. The end result, however, was that managers on the missing level were usually the scapegoats; they were blamed for most of the problems that were discussed.

TEAM SURVIVORSHIP—HOW MANAGEMENT CAN HELP

Helping teams survive is often more difficult than getting them started. Approaches for management to consider include the following:

- Show obvious management support.
- Have reasonable expectations.
- Provide rewards.
- Publicize awards.
- Help teams find meaningful problems.
- Acknowledge the new skills.
- Don't undercut supervision.

The following paragraphs elaborate.

Management Support

Management backing is critical. Without strong direction and support from the top, participative management and cooperative teamwork won't survive. The average worker is quick to determine whether management wants, or only tolerates, team activity. When management support is obvious, workers see potential benefits in helping a team. When management support is superficial, most workers shy away. It is something like helping out with the company picnic. In some companies, those who do all the work on company socials get favorable exposure to management; their efforts are appreciated and their promotion potential is enhanced. In other companies, people assigned to work on these functions are considered expendable—the bosses assign subordinates who won't be missed. Alert employees are quick to determine which kind of company they've joined.

Reasonable Expectations

Few participative management teams will solve all of the company's problems during the first year; many won't even seem to pay for themselves. There are, however, spin-off benefits that have to be considered. Improved morale is one such bonus; it is an intangible, but real, asset. Improved employee competence is another. Facilitators spend months training new members of a team. They often cover statistical process control, data analysis, data presentation and other skills that are used in troubleshooting; these subjects used to be foreign to most hourly personnel. Once the skills have been learned they are used, not forgotten. A 40-hour participative management program can be more valuable than a 40-hour college course in statistics; the students get to apply what they learn.

Provide Rewards

Workers seldom perform beyond the line of duty unless there is "something in it for them." In many cases, a little recognition will do. Bonuses and monetary awards also help. When teams include middle and upper management, however, it sometimes helps to let them keep part of the savings to invest in their department's activities.[12] That way they can spend money on training, computers, computer software, seminars or electronic mail systems without going through tedious justifications. In the end, there's something in it for them—their departments are able to do a better job; they look good and become more promotable.

Publicize Awards

Awards not only have to be given, they should also be publicized. Kanter[12] tells of a company that did such a good job of hiding its recognition program that few people knew it had one. The company actually gave many awards, but didn't publicize them. In some cases, a little cash was added to a paycheck or the boss would do something in private. The company didn't realize that publicity could be as important as the award itself. Those who are recognized for truly outstanding work become role models. Then, others try to attain similar levels of achievement.

Meaningful Accomplishments

Without meaningful accomplishments fairly early in the cycle, teams often disband. Here, facilitators generally hold the key; they help team members select projects that are both meaningful and possible. Supervisors can also be helpful, especially when working through the facilitators. In many cases, team members are supposed to choose their own assignments. The supervisors, however, often know which projects will do the company the most good. By working with the facilitators, supervisors can have their ideas considered without threatening the independence or leadership of the team.

New Skills

The training and education that quality teams give their members are outstanding intangible assets. Management needs to let the team members know that their increased capabilities improve their chances of promotion. One manager in a West Coast aerospace firm had the opposite approach. When a subordinate asked which courses would improve his value to the company, the boss discouraged him from going to school at all. Unfortunately, the subordinate heeded the advice and dropped out of graduate school. In the end, the employee, the manager and the company suffered.

Don't Undercut Supervision

When supervisors feel left out or bypassed, they find subtle ways of ensuring that quality teams don't work; no one wants their position or authority threatened. It is management's job to ensure this doesn't happen; managers who cancel meetings with their supervisors to make time for team members are hurting their teams. When supervisors see subordinates getting easier access to the boss, they usually develop strategies to correct the situation. Soon, the teams suffer. How? Ask the supervisors; they have their own ways of discrediting challengers.

SURVIVORSHIP—HOW TEAM MEMBERS CAN HELP

Supervision and management, like team members, seldom support a project unless there is "something in it for them" too. In Quality Circles and other team operations, it is up to the members to ensure that their bosses see the advantages of supporting the team. Here are typical ways of influencing supervision and management:

- Stress tangible benefits.
- Use graphics.
- Avoid overconfidence.
- Don't undercut supervision.
- Strive to meet management's expectations.

The following paragraphs elaborate.

Stress Tangibles

The president of a large company was very expressive; every time we showed him successful projects, he lit up like a sweepstakes winner. Other executives many not have such expressiveness, but they usually have similar attitudes; therefore, teams should stress tangible benefits in any presentation they make—honest, verifiable, tangible gains. This includes showing the cost of obtaining the benefits as well as the gross profits: $10,000 in claimed savings doesn't mean much if members of the team spent $35,000 achieving it.

Use Graphics

The old Chinese proverb, "One picture is worth more than a thousand words," is particularly true where management is concerned. Don't waste the boss's time. Use charts and graphs wherever possible, and try them out ahead of time. A confusing graph is no better than a two-hundred-word sentence.

Avoid Overconfidence

Team members often get more exposure to management than their peers. At first, this is scary. Soon, however, it can become expected. At times, a few successes lead to overconfidence and team members get careless. One thing to remember is that your reputation is seldom better than your last presentation. It's something like the star quarterback who becomes overconfident and starts throwing interceptions. The quarterback's performance last week doesn't mean much if he is throwing wild today. Even heroes can be booed by the fans.

Don't Undercut the Supervisor

When we were kids we used to say, "The bogeyman will get you if you don't watch out." So will supervisors, if you start trying to undercut them. Supervisors can make or break a team. Don't get overconfident; don't challenge them. When you do, everyone loses.

Management's Expectations

Meeting management's expectations is important for any operation. With Quality Circles and other forms of participative management, what does management expect? During 1981–82, Cole and Byosiere[13] conducted a survey to answer this question. Interviewees were "early adapters" of Quality Circles in the United States and Japan. Ranking of expectations, shown in order of importance for American companies, was as follows:

1. Increase worker satisfaction.
2. Increase quality.

3. Increase worker participation.
4. Increase productivity.
5. Develop worker skills.
6. Reduce turnover and absenteeism.
7. Increase flexibility.
8. Avoid unions.

It should be noted that only these eight options were offered. Therefore, it is possible that items not on the list could be even more important to management. The list does show, however, that worker satisfaction and quality were considered more important than avoiding unions and increasing flexibility.

IS TOTAL INVOLVEMENT NECESSARY?

According to Jim Harrington:[14] "We need to make effective use of all the talents that our labor force has to offer, both mental and physical. The employees want to participate in the decision-making processes that affect them."

Many employees do want to participate in the decision-making processes. Some don't. That is why a large number of participative management systems depend on volunteers. In the United States, most system initiators find that some employees are not interested. It is important, however, to provide opportunities for those who are.

SUMMARY

Quality Circles and other team concepts have been successful in both manufacturing and service industries. When properly planted and nurtured, they pay for themselves many times. When dumped on barren soil and left to fend for themselves, they seldom survive. Those planning to start teams or other forms of participative management should consider the following:

- Teams should be evaluated on their total accomplishments. This includes the projects they complete, the people they train and the communication barriers they remove.
- Management must benefit. One way or another, teams must contribute to the bottom line.

- Members must benefit—and know what the benefits are. Possible rewards include recognition, exposure to management, promotions, training and a sense of accomplishment.

FOOD FOR THOUGHT

Review the problem-solving approaches used in your department. Then answer the following questions.

1. Do they use teams?
2. If teams are used, are they open to everyone or just a select few?
3. Is morale better among team members or nonparticipants? Why?
4. Where teams are used in your company, are they paying for themselves?
   a. If they are paying for themselves, how are they doing it?
   b. If they are not paying for themselves, why?

REFERENCES
1. Edward E. Lawler III, *High-Involvement Management* (San Francisco, CA: Jossey-Bass, 1986), p. 1.
2. Robert L. Desatnick, *Managing to Keep the Customer* (San Francisco, CA: Jossey-Bass, 1987), p. 32.
3. William J. Latzko, *Quality and Productivity for Bankers and Financial Managers* (Milwaukee, WI: ASQC Quality Press, 1986), p. 143.
4. Robert E. Cole, "Common Misconceptions of Japanese QC Circles," *ASQC Quality Congress Transactions,* May 26–29, 1981, pp. 188–189.
5. W. Edwards Deming, *Out of the Crisis* (Cambridge, MA: Massachusetts Institute of Technology, 1986), p. 146.
6. Charles A. Aubrey, II, *Quality Management in Financial Services* (Wheaton, IL: Hitchcock Publishing, 1985), p. 52.
7. Henry L. Lefevre, "Teamwork Promotes New Products and Higher Productivity Levels," *Productivity Improvement Bulletin,* December 25, 1985, pp. 1–4.
8. Louis N. Jones and Ronald C. McBride, "Team Approach to Problem Solving, TAPS," *ASQC Quality Congress Transactions,* May 4–6, 1987, pp. 139–147.
9. Gary Johnson, "Chasing Quality Problems," *Quality Progress,* October 1984, pp. 57–59.
10. Nicholas J. Pennucci, "A New Approach to Quality Circles," *Quality,* April 1984, pp. 61–63.

11. Lana J. Chandler, "Want Employee Input? Try Forming a QEC," *The Office*, September 1985, pp. 241–247.
12. Rosabeth Moss Kanter, "Quality Leadership and Change," *Quality Progress*, February 1987, pp. 45–51.
13. Robert E. Cole and Philippe Byosiere, "Managerial Objectives for Introducing Quality Circles: A U.S.–Japan Comparison," *Quality Progress*, March 1986, pp. 25–30.
14. H. James Harrington, *The Improvement Process* (Milwaukee, WI: ASQC Quality Press, 1987), p. 85.

Chapter 25

Keep People Involved

People working with quality teams and quality programs generally believe "there's something in it for them." From time to time, this belief must be reinforced, and the benefits have to be real. In addition, team members need to be convinced that management is also committed. Expecting the workers to put company and quality first when top management sets a poor example is like expecting the tooth fairy to make billionaires out of underprivileged children. It would be nice, but . . . .

REASONS FOR KEEPING INVOLVED

Motivational theories for keeping people involved are very complex and difficult to prove. One of the best-known theorists, Abraham H. Maslow,[1] conceived a formal hierarchy of needs that has been quoted by psychologists, managers and personnel directors for years. Even Douglas McGregor, father of the X and Y-theory concepts, drew from Maslow's writings when formulating his own approach.[2] Maslow, however, admits that "the specific form that these needs will take will of course vary greatly from person to person."[1]

MASLOW'S HIERARCHY OF NEEDS

Despite its limitations, Maslow's Hierarchy of Needs will help many readers understand available incentives. According to Maslow,[2,3] the priority of needs of most people follows the progression from physiological needs—to security needs—to social needs—to ego or esteem needs—to self-actualization. Once you have the lower needs under control, you develop more interest in the higher levels. Let's explore how these needs keep people involved.

Physiological Needs

With a few exceptions, the physiological needs of most workers in the United States are being met; they are no longer prime motivators. Physiological needs are things needed for maintaining the body in a state of equilibrium. They include food, shelter, water, clothing, air and rest.

Security Needs

In the United States, security is still an important incentive; few get guaranteed lifetime employment. In addition, sickness and retirement worry many of us. Job retention, health care assistance, retirement benefits and insurance fall under the security umbrella. Union negotiations often stress these benefits over raises; they take worry off the worker's mind and they are seldom, if ever, taxed. Except for job security, these benefits are not strong incentives for motivating the individual; they are not related to performance. Iacocca[4] drew a strong correlation between performance and security when he wrote, "The only job security anybody has in this company (Chrysler) comes from quality, productivity, and satisfied customers."

Social Needs

Social needs involve acceptance by others; in the workplace, these needs can be productive or counterproductive. The productive aspect can come from the boss giving compliments for a job well done; this promotes a feeling of acceptance. Well-planned social activities can also help. Poorly planned activities and command performances are often counterproductive; so are peer pressures that discourage workers from exceeding quotas.

Ego (Esteem) Needs

Ego needs are met by accomplishment and reinforced by merit raises; across-the-board and constant percentage raises, however, don't help. Robert L. Desatnick, who held executive positions at McDonald's Corporation and Chase Manhattan Bank,[5] wrote: "I marvel at the naivete of organizations that fail to perceive what happens when all employees get the same annual birthday increase of 5 percent. The best performers are driven out and the worst performers are encouraged to stay." If nonperformers get the same raises as performers, there is little incentive to perform; the ego or self-esteem requirement is not being met.

Ego needs are best met when rewards and raises are based on performance and become public knowledge. Blake and Mouton[6] supported the performance concept when they wrote: "From a corporate point of view, wide agreement exists on the just basis of rewarding performance. The just way is when reward is based on merit. The idea is that people who contribute more than their colleagues are moving the corporation forward more." In addition, Blake and Mouton[7] attacked the secrecy surrounding wages: "It can be accepted that something so widespread as the silence that presently exists about salary treatment has come into being for specific reasons. The most obvious is to hide the perceived inequity that often results when one is aware of what one's colleagues earn in comparison with oneself." A second reason for silence is that too few managers can justify wage disparities with objective data. Proposed techniques for being objective are discussed toward the end of this chapter.

Self-Actualization Needs

Maslow[1] refers to self-actualization as "man's desire for self-fulfillment, namely, to the tendency for him to become actualized in what he is potentially." In the words of the military recruiters, this can be boiled down to "be all you can be." Bob Mornin, when he was president of the Coors Container Company, did an outstanding job of getting the impossible from subordinates. He furnished them with the tools to make the job possible and gave them the freedom to achieve. As a consequence, many of his subordinates had their self-actualization needs met well beyond their expectations.

OBJECTIVE EVALUATIONS

Few activities by management turn off people more quickly than subjective evaluations. Only the "fair-haired boys" condone favoritism—and few of them will admit they are being favored. In order to maintain objective evaluations it is necessary to measure performance; in order to measure performance properly, it is best to have standards. In *Managing to Keep the Customer*, Desatnick addresses this issue by writing: "The systems approach to customer service superiority is, in brief: first train to the exacting standards as defined, then continually audit performance against those standards to identify any possible slippage."[8] When you measure performance impartially, you are being objective; you can defend your position. When you don't measure performance impartially, you are being subjective; you are flying by the seat of your pants.

Quality vs Quantity

Two elements common to most objective evaluations are quality and quantity. A common complaint from quality professionals is "When the chips are down, production and schedule always come first; most evaluations ignore quality." Production personnel, however, tend to take the opposite viewpoint. According to them, "Quality control personnel, with no checks and balances, will nitpick the company out of business; their evaluations ignore production."

If one area of the company receives all of the attention, employees from other areas will become demotivated and drop out of any team effort; they will not stay involved. Rebecca Lee Huls addressed this issue when covering quality in the insurance industry. She wrote: "You can effectively monitor your responsiveness in terms of timeliness as well as quality. Often, if the emphasis is placed on timeliness, quality will suffer, if placed on quality, timeliness will suffer. By monitoring both elements simultaneously, you avoid placing emphasis on either one."[9]

In order to evaluate whether quality is getting a fair shake consider the following questions.

Who gets the promotions?

In production-first organizations, production personnel are on the fast track; people who want to get ahead stay out of quality assurance. In quality-first organizations, the opposite is true. In fair-and-neutral organizations, quality assurance personnel are promoted as fast as those from production.

What is stressed during evaluations?

I took over one service organization where the reviewers had never been inspected. Production was obviously being stressed; the previous chief had never measured anything else—and this was a "quality" branch.

Is the quality organization filled with misfits?

That occasionally happens. It shouldn't! Filling the quality assurance organization with weak personnel gives other workers the message "Quality doesn't count in this organization." A Midwestern company chose a weak production executive to head one of its quality divisions. He didn't last very long, but the damage he did was overwhelming; it took years to clean up the mess.

Quality/Quantity Rating Formula (QQR)

How can you make a fair trade-off of the quality and quantity of individuals or organizations? One technique developed in the service sector is the Quality/Quantity Rating Formula (QQR); it is also called the Quality/Quantity Index (QQI).[10-13] The formula is

$$QQR = (factor\ 1) \times (\%\ quality) + (factor\ 2) \times (\%\ quantity)$$

or

$$0.5 \times (\%\ quality) + 0.5 \times (\%\ quantity)$$

Factors are the constants used in the formulas. These constants should add up to 1.0. When quality and quantity get equal emphasis, both factors are the same; both are 0.5. Otherwise, the element with the largest factor gets the greatest emphasis—this is not always bad.

If Joe Brown's quality is 95 percent and his production comes to 95 percent of the standard, then his QQR is:

$$QQR = 0.5 \times 95 + 0.5 \times 95$$
$$= 47.5 + 47.5$$
$$= 95.0 \text{ percent}$$

PROBLEM 25-1

The statistical technicians in a government office had the following performance records during June:

Name	% Quality	% Quantity
Joe	95	100
Jerry	95	97
Jack	92	110
Jill	99	90

The 110% quantity figure for Jack means that the quantity of his work was 110 percent, which is 10 percent above the standard. Using the Quality/Quantity Rating (QQR) formula, rank the four technicians.

SOLUTION 25-1

Name	% Quality	% Quantity	Calculation	Result
Joe	95	100	$0.5 \times 95 + 0.5 \times 100 =$	97.5%
Jerry	95	97	$0.5 \times 95 + 0.5 \times 97 =$	96.0%
Jack	92	110	$0.5 \times 92 + 0.5 \times 110 =$	101.0%
Jill	99	90	$0.5 \times 99 + 0.5 \times 90 =$	94.5%

Based on these calculations, the ranking of the technicians would be

Rank	Name	Quality/Quantity Rating
1.	Jack	101.0 percent
2.	Joe	97.5 percent
3.	Jerry	96.0 percent
4.	Jill	94.5 percent

Jack's production was high enough to put him on top, even though his quality was relatively low. In order to avoid this type of situation, some supervisors place a bottom limit on both quality and quantity. In this instance, the bottom limits might have been set at 95 percent quality and 90 percent quantity. Then, Jack would be warned about his quality and Jill would be encouraged to speed up.

In Problem 25-1, quality and quantity of production were given equal weights. When the cost of poor quality is high, however, quality should get a heavier weighting. As an example, when evaluating bank personnel who transfer millions of dollars each day, the formula might become

$$\text{Q/Q Rating (QQR)} = 0.9 \times (\% \text{ Quality}) + 0.1 \times (\% \text{ Quantity})$$

Note that the two factors, 0.9 and 0.1, still add up to 1.0 in order to keep the ratings close to 100.

PROBLEM 25-2

This problem shows what happens when you place increased emphasis on quality instead of treating quality and quantity as equals. Use the same data as Problem 25-1, but change the formula to

$$\text{Q/Q Rating (QQR)} = 0.9 \times (\% \text{ Quality}) + 0.1 \times (\% \text{ Quantity})$$

Since the formula favors quality over quantity, assume the people involved are working with million-dollar transactions.

SOLUTION 25-2

Name	% Quality	% Quantity	Calculation	Result
Joe	95	100	0.9 × 95 + 0.1 × 100 =	95.5%
Jerry	95	97	0.9 × 95 + 0.1 × 97 =	95.2%
Jack	92	110	0.9 × 92 + 0.1 × 110 =	93.8%
Jill	99	90	0.9 × 99 + 0.1 × 90 =	98.1%

Based on these calculations, the ranking of the technicians would be

Rank	Name	Q/Q Rating
1.	Jill	98.1 percent
2.	Joe	95.5 percent
3.	Jerry	95.2 percent
4.	Jack	93.8 percent

Changing the relative emphasis caused the ranking to change dramatically. Jill, for example, has moved from the bottom of the ranking to the top. The factors used in the formula must be chosen carefully and known by everyone; they should reflect the relative importance of quality and quantity for the specific operation.

Adjusted-Productivity Formula

Another formula for expressing the trade-off between quality and quantity is the "adjusted-productivity formula."

A penalty system for errors has been used to balance quality and quantity ratings.[14] Using this approach, the formula becomes

$$\text{Adjusted Productivity} = (\% \text{ Quantity}) - 2 \times \% \text{ Errors}$$

Count the quantity of production; then impose a penalty for errors. If the cost of errors is high, the factor "2" can be increased to 3 or 4. If the cost of errors is low, the factor can be reduced to 1.5 or 1.1.

PROBLEM 25-3

Taking data from Problems 25-1 and 25-2, rank the technicians a third time using the adjusted-productivity formula. Assign a penalty factor of 2, eliminating rejections from the production count and penalizing production by an equal amount. A factor of 3 would increase the penalty.

The performance data was:

Name	% Quality	% Quantity (Good & Bad)
Joe	95	100
Jerry	95	97
Jack	92	110
Jill	99	90

SOLUTION 25-3

The first step is to calculate the error rate. The formula is

$$\% \text{ Errors} = 100 - \% \text{ Quality}$$

Now the table becomes

Name	% Quality	% Quantity	% Errors Calculation		% Errors
Joe	95	100	100 − 95	=	5
Jerry	95	97	100 − 95	=	5
Jack	92	110	100 − 92	=	8
Jill	99	90	100 − 99	=	1

The formula is

Adjusted productivity = (% Quantity) − 2 × (% Errors)

The calculations are shown in the following table.

Name	Calculation (% Quantity − 2 × % Errors)		Corrected Productivity
Joe	100 − (2 × 5 = 10)	=	90 %
Jerry	97 − (2 × 5 = 10)	=	87 %
Jack	110 − (2 × 8 = 16)	=	94 %
Jill	90 − (2 × 1 = 2)	=	88 %

Based on these numbers, the new ranking for the technicians is:

Rank	Name	Corrected Productivity
1.	Jack	94 %
2.	Joe	90 %
3.	Jill	88 %
4.	Jerry	87 %

Here, Jill is helped by her high quality. Jack is penalized by his low quality, but his output is high enough to compensate; he still ranks first.

More complex formulas are used in gainsharing programs like the Scanlon Plan, the Rucker Plan and Improshare.[15]

MANAGEMENT AND THE QUALITY MESSAGE

The above material stresses the negative effect of subjective evaluations on employee morale and team participation. The problem, however, goes much further. The climate set by top management has a major impact on the willingness of team members to participate in quality programs. A critical question is "Does top management set a good example?" If words were deeds, the answer would be a resounding "yes!" A large segment of management supports quality, apple pie and motherhood. To illustrate, a single issue of *Quality Progress* published the following pronouncements:

- Richard L. Thomas, president of First Chicago Corporation,[16] said: "At First Chicago, we are especially conscious of the importance of quality. We give it extremely close attention because it flows from our number one bank-wide commitment, which is that the customer is our highest priority."
- Claude I. Taylor, chairman of the board of Air Canada, said: "We at Air Canada realize that our products are so customer-sensitive that the quality imperative has to be our primary consideration, at every operating level, if we are to be world competitive."[17]
- Armand V. Feigenbaum, president of General Systems Company, Inc., said, "Quality-leveraged companies are likely to have a five-cents-on-the-sales-dollar advantage over their competitors."[18]
- Robert Tallon, president of Florida Power and Light Company, said: "The quality improvement imperative is not a fad .... I believe it's the most valuable management system ever employed by our company."[19]
- General Lawrence Skantze, commander of the Air Force Systems Command, said, "The military and industry team that produces low-quality weapons won't produce very many because the country won't be around long enough to need them."[20]

Has top management got the message, or are they giving lip service to the quality theme? Maybe both alternatives are true. Let's take a look.

The Message

The Japanese have done a good job of teaching us the catechism "Quality is crucial." A survey by Cole and Byosiere[21] showed that managerial objectives for introducing Quality Circles in the United States were ranked with "Increase quality" second only to "Increase worker satisfaction." An identical survey taken in Japan showed that "Increase quality" ranked first. In addition, the 1986 Gallup Survey of top executives showed that 57 percent of those responding claimed to consider quality more important than profit, cost or schedule.[22] Turning to the service industries, 40 percent of the service sector respondents claimed that quality was one of the "very critical" issues facing U.S. business today. The quality-first message seems to have impressed the upper echelon.

Lip Service

In some instances, however, lip service is all that quality is getting; when the chips are down, quality can become expendable. I worked with a vice-president of production who knew all the right words when it came to praising quality. When the pressures rose, however, he ran rough-shod over his quality assurance counterpart in order to cut short-term costs and make the schedule.

The true feelings of top managers become obvious when their own vested interests become involved; security and survival are on the second step of Maslow's Hierarchy of Needs.[1-3] The following stories point out the biases of some top executives.

- Peter Drucker, referring to corporations facing takeover, wrote that a targeted company often "pays ransom to the raider—which goes by the Robin Hood-like name of *greenmail*—and buys out the shares the raider acquired at a fancy price, way beyond anything its earnings and prospects could justify."[23] In many instances, greenmail does little more than save the hides of the top bosses. It doesn't provide additional tools to make the company more competitive. It doesn't improve quality or productivity. It doesn't improve morale. It seldom saves worker jobs. Quite the contrary—layoffs often result as the companies try to recoup losses. After Goodyear paid greenmail to Sir Goldsmith, the company had to sell off 12 percent of its revenue producers; they also took on a $2.6 billion debt.[24] Is greenmail more important than quality? Does the corporate hierarchy deserve half the responsibility for these fiascos, or are they right in placing all the blame on the corporate raiders? Do the employees get a fair shake? Does quality suffer?
- In another case, a defense contractor lost some 20 senior engineers and engineering managers; some had 25 years of service in the company. Their reason for quitting was that they were held to a three percent raise because "any more would be inflationary." At the same time, "nine people in the top management group voted themselves bonuses and additional stock options amounting to a 25-percent to 30-percent increase in their compensation."[25] Could this management be trusted? Did they expect to build company loyalty? Did quality suffer? Were team players motivated?
- In a third case, *The Chief Executive* magazine reported that a division manager in a large chemical company added $60,000 to his bonus; his technique was to hold back on expenditures and price reductions, improving the division's short-term profits. His economies qualified

him for an inflated bonus, but his division suffered; a competitor hit the market with a better product six months before his company.[26] Is this unusual? Not really. Executives and senior managers are often given bonuses based on short-term results. Only long-term results, however, enable companies to survive.

The above illustrations are not intended to blame top management for all morale, motivation and quality problems. Some company presidents have taken derelict companies and turned them into industrial giants; some have taken industrial giants and turned them into derelicts. The performance of most is in between.

SUMMARY

Keeping people committed to quality and participative management programs involves showing them what they have to gain. When people perceive they are being treated fairly and recognized for their efforts, they tend to stay on the team. Disillusionment, however, sets in when evaluations are subjective and when top executives feather their own nests at the expense of their subordinates—and the company.

The problem of irresponsible management can be corrected by the government (the cure can be worse than the ailment) or by a stockholder majority (throw the rascals out). The problem of subjective evaluations can be corrected by using the Quality/Quantity Rating, the adjusted-productivity formula or other tools that facilitate objective evaluation.

FOOD FOR THOUGHT

Review the last performance evaluation you have either received or given. Then answer the following questions:

1. Did the reviewer stress quality, quantity or some other performance factor?
2. Was the review subjective (seat of the pants) or objective (concrete and verifiable)?
3. Did the review address physiological, security, social, ego or self-actualization needs?
4. If the review were challenged, would the challenge hold up? Theoretically, challenges can come from the person being reviewed

(because the rating was poor) or that person's peers (because the rating was inflated).

REFERENCES
1. Abraham H. Maslow, *Motivation and Personality* (New York: Harper & Row, 1970), p. 46.
2. C. W. Tribett and R. J. Rush, "Theories and Motivation: A Broader Perspective," *Quality Progress,* April 1984, pp. 38–42.
3. Maslow, *Motivation and Personality,* pp. 35–46.
4. Lee Iacocca, *Talking Straight* (New York: Bantam Books, 1988), p. 249.
5. Robert L. Desatnick, *Managing to Keep the Customer* (San Francisco, CA: Jossey-Bass, 1987), p. 27.
6. Robert R. Blake and Jane S. Mouton, *The Versatile Manager: A Grid Profile* (Homewood, IL: Dow Jones-Irwin, 1980), pp. 106–107.
7. Blake and Mouton, *The Versatile Manager: A Grid Profile,* pp. 114–115.
8. Desatnick, *Managing to Keep the Customer,* p. 65.
9. Rebecca Lee Huls, "Dedication to Quality Spans All Industries," *ASQC Quality Congress Transactions,* May 4–6, 1987, pp. 90–95.
10. Henry L. Lefevre, "Quality and Quantity in Productivity," *Nationwide Careers,* December 5, 1984, p. 7.
11. Henry L. Lefevre, "A Quality/Quantity Index," *Quality,* August 1978, p. 33.
12. Henry L. Lefevre, "Evaluations Made Easy: Go With Hard Numbers," *Supervisor's Bulletin, Bureau of Business Practice,* October 15, 1986, p. 1–3.
13. Henry L. Lefevre, "Integrating Quality and Quantity," *ASQC Technical Conference Transactions,* May 20–22, 1980, pp. 624–627.
14. Based on procedures similar to those used at Rocky Mountain Orthodontics, Denver, CO, during 1976.
15. Edward E. Lawler III, *High Involvement Management* (San Francisco, CA: Jossey-Bass, 1986), pp. 157–166.
16. Richard L. Thomas, "Bank on Quality," *Quality Progress,* February 1987, pp. 27–29.
17. Claude I. Taylor, "No Boundaries to Quality," *Quality Progress,* February 1987, 30–31.
18. Armand V. Feigenbaum, "ROI: How Long Before Quality Improvement Pays Off?" *Quality Progress,* February 1987, pp. 32–35.
19. Robert Tallon, "How Long Before Quality Improvement Pays Off?" *Quality Progress,* February 1987, pp. 36–37.
20. General Lawrence Skantze, "Quality and National Defense," *Quality Progress,* February 1987, pp. 40–42.
21. Robert E. Cole and Philippe Byosiere, "Managerial Objectives for Introducing Quality Circles: A U.S.–Japan Comparison," *Quality Progress,* March 1986, pp. 25–30.

22. "Gallup Survey: Top Executives Talk about Quality," *Quality Progress,* December 1986, pp. 49–54.
23. Peter F. Drucker, *The Frontiers of Management* (New York: Truman Talley Books, 1986), p. 232.
24. Iacocca, *Talking Straight,* p. 95.
25. Drucker, *The Frontiers of Management,* p. 139.
26. Robert Heller, *The Supermanagers* (New York: E.P. Dutton, 1984), p. 119.

Chapter 26

Key 6: Knowing Where and How To Use the Other Keys

There are times when students learn their lessons so well they surpass their teachers. The Japanese "quality masters" provide one illustration; they learned about quality from the Americans—and then surpassed us. The case of the manufacturing gurus provides a second; they learned many Statistical Quality Control techniques from the service sector—and then surpassed them. Statistical Quality Control pioneers, coming from the service sector, include:

- **W. Edwards Deming.** He developed statistical procedures for the Department of Agriculture and the Bureau of the Census prior to World War II, long before he became a national authority on quality assurance.[1]
- **A. C. Rosander.** He developed statistical procedures for the federal government for over 30 years.[2] He is now consulting in many areas.
- **Harry G. Romig.** He prepared the original Military Standard 105D calculations for the government[3] long before Statistical Quality Control was popular.
- **Edward M. Schrock.** He developed quality control procedures for the

government during World War II. He ended his career as a consultant in manufacturing.

Quality in the service sector is hard to define and easy to ignore. People dropping defective TV sets on the customer service desk must be dealt with. Missiles that blow up on the launching pad get everyone's attention. But when insurance adjusters underpay claims, "quality" is harder to pin down; the average customer doesn't know the difference. In some cases, the adjusters save the company's money; in others, they lose customers. Disgruntled people seldom suffer in silence; they tell a "chain" of friends. Phone customers who are put on hold may not complain; they do, however, evaluate the service. In time, they may look for a company that treats them better.

It brings to mind the familiar situation of the chicken and the egg: Without chickens, there are no eggs; without eggs, there are no chickens. Similarly, with few quality "missionaries" in the service sector, there are few success stories; with few success stories, quality assurance in the service sector is hard to sell.

Many executives are like cannibals; they would rather eat the quality control missionaries than listen to them. Despite the problems, however, some progress is being made. Service organizations making the most headway include

- Government
- Banking
- Insurance
- Hospitals
- Service sectors of manufacturing companies

QUALITY ASSURANCE IN GOVERNMENT

Many techniques for service sector quality were developed by people in the government. Deming's improvements in the Census Bureau's sampling strategy were particularly significant. One-hundred-percent sampling of the country's entire population is impractical and early sampling procedures were questionable.

Deming developed sound ways of getting reliable information with known confidence limits; they are valid today. Deming's techniques are known by many names including probability sampling, random sampling, scientific sampling and statistical sampling. Much of his work was statistical but he also looked at the practical side of things. As an example,

Key 6: Knowing Where and How to Use the Other Keys

he observed that "a probability-sample will send the interviewer through mud and cold, over long distances, up decrepit stairs, to people who do not welcome an interviewer."[4] This insight highlights a problem that will always be with those doing survey and census work. Analyses are no better that the data. If individuals doing the leg work avoid the mud, cold, long distances and decrepit stairs, the data and the analyses will be biased. The field crews have to follow the sampling program if the analyses are to be meaningful.

Does quality sampling pay? Yes! A national magazine found this out the hard way. They conducted a preelection poll using faulty sampling techniques. Their conclusion was that Franklin D. Roosevelt would lose the presidency. He won in a landslide and the magazine soon folded.

Rosander, like Deming, did extensive work in the field of sampling. In one instance,[5] he took samples to profile those most likely to have errors in their income tax returns. An audit of 160,000 returns showed these results:

1. Within the sample, payments were off by $1.5 billion; 90 percent favored the taxpayer.
2. On the average, higher income returns showed larger shortages.
3. Businesses tended to make more errors than individuals.
4. Unreported income, underreported income, personal deductions and exemptions were common.

Information of this nature has helped the Internal Revenue Service audit efficiently.

Other original work coming out of the government includes:

- The Air Force Accounting and Finance Center was among the first to use microcomputers to expedite service, reduce errors and cut costs. Using a microcomputer costing around $4,000, they saved the government over $200,000 the first year: $150,000 of the savings came from a program that eliminated the need for field office forecasts of funds requirements.[6,7] The program not only saved money, it also improved the quality of the forecasts: $50,000 additional savings came from computerizing routine statistical reports. This program made the reports more timely, improved their quality and cut their cost.[6]
- The Air Reserve Personnel Center developed sampling techniques for improving the quality of information in their databases.[8] Additional information on the procedures they used is contained in Chapter 23.
- The Bureau of Labor Statistics has an extensive quality improvement program. Their accomplishments include reducing data-entry errors by 40 percent, increasing data-entry productivity by 29 percent and

reducing their process discrepancy rates from 18.5 percent to 10.6 percent over a six-year period.[9] Tools incorporated into their quality planning include process capability studies, flow charts, surveys, checklists, computer edits and trend analyses.
- The City of Los Angeles, California, under Mayor Tom Bradley, formed a Productivity Advisory Committee with a charter to reduce costs while still maintaining or improving the quality of city services. Members of the committee were executives from local businesses, service companies, unions and consulting organizations. Working with city agencies, they came up with 156 projects and potential savings approaching ten million dollars.[10] Membership on the committee is essentially public service since compensation is limited by statute to $100 per person per month.[11]

One of the federal government's greatest weaknesses in the area of service quality involves their cumbersome procurement operation. Their bulky specifications are intended to ensure that they receive the best product at the lowest possible price. This program, however, has hurt as much as it has helped. During the late 1970s a request for floppy disks received "tender loving care" for almost six weeks before being processed. The claim was that procurement wanted to make sure they received the best price and the best product. Attempts to expedite the purchase, however, resulted in the rebuttal "Regulations state that we don't have to touch the request for 45 days." They took the full period. When the floppy disks arrived, they cost the government about 50 percent more than "off the shelf" floppies.

The government is valiantly trying to improve the quality and timeliness of their purchases. Now, common items, like floppy disks, can be stocked; this improves timeliness of the purchases. In addition, acquisitions costing less than $10,000 can be purchased without so much red tape.[12]

The government is also trying to simplify and standardize federal specifications.[12,13] Simplification is paying off. In one instance a 22-page specification for a set of socket wrenches resulted in a single bid of $145.75 per unit. After boiling the specification down to one page, they received seven bids; the lowest "responsive" bid was $82.52 per unit.[12] Congress has cited a large number of cases where the military paid excessive amounts for items that should be "off the shelf." In many instances, the high cost comes from the confusing and complex federal specifications. Some people in government are aware of the problem. Some improvements are being made.

During my seven years in the federal government, I worked with some of the most dedicated professionals in the quality assurance community. I also worked with incompetents who wouldn't last a week in the outside world.

Government regulations protect the underachievers; they also make it risky to fire nonperformers. On the other hand, they have elaborate procedures for rewarding the competent; sometimes these incentives help, despite their complexity. The government also gives some innovators time to develop new quality control procedures—time that would not be made available by most industrial organizations. Because of this dichotomy, the government is in the forefront of some quality developments; they are bringing up the rear in others.

QUALITY CONTROL IN BANKS

While at the First National Bank of Arizona, Eugene Kirby set up a quality control organization responsible for coordination of quality functions, standards, procedures, performance evaluations (hardware and software), quality monitoring, monthly reports, computer security, MICR quality control and project reviews.[14,15] During this period he was also active in organizing the Banking Committee of the Administrative Applications Division (now the Quality Management Division) of the American Society for Quality Control (ASQC). Sickness, however, forced him out of his leadership role.

Bill Latzko, while working for Irving Trust Company, was also a dynamo in the banking quality assurance area. Although many of his early publications were on MICR quality,[16,17] he also developed a clerk-oriented quality improvement plan (QUIP),[18] a plan for reducing clerical quality costs[19] and a program for measuring productivity in banks.[20] Most of Latzko's contributions to quality assurance in the banking industry are documented in his book, *Quality and Productivity for Bankers and Financial Managers*.[21]

Charles A. Aubrey, II, of the Continental Illinois National Bank of Chicago has been stressing the worker motivation and customer perception of quality. His book *Quality Management in Financial Services*[22] includes quality planning, standards, measures, costs, productivity, Quality Circles, motivation and customer surveys.

Thurmon Sutcliffe of the Chemical Bank, New York, stresses predelivery sampling of purchased checks, random sampling of operations personnel, development of quality indicators and random customer surveys.[23] He also uses histograms, attributes control charts, quality cost studies, and payback analyses.[24]

At Marine Midland Bank, Janet S. Waksman uses flow charts and trend analyses to monitor the bank's market research operation.[25] The objective is to "be able to explain and even anticipate shifts in customer attitudes toward quality service and . . . adjust your product performance to meet the real needs of your customers."

On the other hand, Anyonu and Bajaria[26] contend that "banks are beginning to look at a quality control discipline as an aid toward productivity improvement, with major emphasis being on data processing quality control." After conducting a study at the Bank of the Commonwealth in Detroit, Michigan, they recommended using process control, Pareto analysis, design of experiments, failure-mode-and-effects analyses, process capability studies, quality information systems and motivation programs. Those impressed by this advanced thinking, however, should be cautioned that programs of this magnitude need to evolve slowly so that program costs don't exceed proven savings.

At Manufacturers Hanover Trust Company, quality-oriented personnel are working on reducing the cost of the float. According to Cejka,[27] float is "non-earning assets that are not invested for profit because they represent cash items in process of collection, or items available for collection that did not get into the collection systems." For large banks, a reduction of the money "in float" can be extremely profitable—especially when more prompt collections are involved. As Cejka explains, "The check recipient wants to have all checks collected as soon as possible to maximize the use of these funds."[27] Techniques developed for Statistical Quality Control are excellent tools for attacking this potentially profitable project.

INSURANCE COMPANY QUALITY ASSURANCE

The drive for quality assurance programs in the insurance industry has been encouraged by the cost of correcting errors, consumerism and the government. It was also influenced by a study of data quality in the insurance industry commissioned in 1976 by the Insurance Services Office (ISO).[28] The ISO is a nonprofit association of insurance companies where resources are pooled to obtain more accurate actuarial data (used for calculating insurance rates). The ISO helps member organizations by supervising special studies, performing inspections, identifying innovative actuarial ideas, discovering progressive underwriting concepts and calculating average insurance rates for different types of policies.[29]

In the insurance industry, errors can put a company out of business. Philip D. Miller of the Insurance Services Office (ISO) in New York indicates that the cost of correcting a coding error, for example, can be five to ten times the cost of the original coding entry.[29] The cost of not catching the error, however, can be much higher.

Why?

First, the errors don't often cancel each other; there is a bias against the company. According to Miller: "When a company shortchanges an insured or an agent, the company hears about it. Rarely are overpayments brought to the company's attention."[29]

Second, errors can lead to improper decisions on insurance rates. If the rates are too low, the company loses money. If they are too high, the company loses customers.

Third, once errors are identified, the company is subjected to closer scrutiny by the government as well as by the customer. Once the government's monitoring bodies identify problems, they increase their audits. Putting it another way, once they see smoke, they keep manning the fire lines for a long time—long after the fire's out.

The ISO[29] developed a system for consideration by the Data Quality Officers of member companies that included

- Documenting the way data flows through the company
- Documenting controls for data transfer, change, translation and reproduction
- Identifying critical data elements (types of data)
- Identifying who is responsible for each segment of data handling
- Establishing performance standards
- Monitoring performance against the standards
- Establishing edits to check the validity of data before it is accepted by the computer
- Conducting periodic audits

United States Fidelity & Guaranty Co. (USF&G), an ISO member, developed a quality control program that includes quality guidelines, sampling, trend analyses, flow charts and Pareto analyses.[28,30] They take sample size and acceptance criteria from Military Standard 105D and use interval sampling with a random start. They don't, however, stop inspecting when an error is found; they continue looking for all the defects.[28]

Rebecca Lee Huls of the United Services Automobile Association (USAA), a full-service, member-owned insurance and financial services association, stresses Statistical Quality Control.[31,32] USAA runs either control charts or trend charts on administrative functions such as

- Minutes that phone-in customers were put on hold
- How many callers hung up after being put on hold
- The speed of response to mail requests
- Quality of responses to customer requests

- Whether transactions were properly documented
- Whether bills were accurate

Expanding beyond the traditional area of quality, Huls also suggests monitoring

- Sales
- Backlogs
- Work produced

These charts help forecast work loads so that staffing can be adjusted to meet customer needs. In most organizations, the quality department has the skills for doing these analyses. By supplying this information to management, the quality department shows their responsiveness and value to the company.

At Paul Revere Insurance Group in Worcester, Massachusetts, Patrick Townsend stresses the participative management route to quality improvement. Their program is called "Quality Has Value" and involves quality teams, value analysis and surveys. Their surveys "are used both as measuring devices and as sources for ideas."[33] Their quality teams are similar to Quality Circles but require 100-percent participation. In addition, they don't give presentations to management; this removes some of the resistance that often comes from first-level managers who feel undercut. In line with most participative management programs, the quality teams include an extensive recognition system.

While working with The Hartford Insurance Group, Frank Scanlon has been quite active in developing quality assurance programs for the service sector.[34-36] The need is great; according to Scanlon, "17 to 25 percent of all the paperwork is being reprocessed due to errors."[35] The main elements of his program include commitment, sampling, checking, recording, analyzing and corrective action. Orientation of the program stresses participative management. As Scanlon says, "The heart of a quality program is recognition—recognition of deserving employees."[35]

QUALITY ASSURANCE IN HOSPITALS

The quality of service in hospitals is often a life-and-death matter. Is the proper medicine being dispensed? Are the best surgical procedures being used? Are unnecessary tests being given? Has the patient been given too many X-rays? Or as Bill Cosby might say, "Has the stethoscope been in the refrigerator too long?" A program for the nurses, housekeeping staff and maintenance crew is fairly easy to implement—just follow the conventional quality assurance procedures. Checks on the doctors, however, will seldom be initiated unless the quality assurance effort has strong support from the very top; many doctors think quality control involves second-guessing.

Despite obvious difficulties, however, formal quality assurance programs are alive and well in many medical facilities; the Graduate Hospital in Philadelphia, Pennsylvania, is a good example.[37] Key elements of their program include

- Quality assurance education programs
- Audits
- Classification of inspection categories
- Trend charts
- Reports
- Supplier quality assurance (vendors)

Education Programs

When people know nothing about quality assurance, they tend to resist formal quality programs. According to Werner,[37] "hospitals have been primarily managed by individuals who have not worked in other types of industries . . . they do not have a basis of comparison for evaluating hospital systems against the standard systems that exist in most businesses." As a consequence, the Graduate Hospital developed "an educational program to orient management, employees and medical staff to quality and productivity control principles to gain both an understanding of and support for the program."[37]

Audits

Werner[37] favors frequent unannounced audits. He observes that announced audits often lead to "temporary" corrections being initiated before the audit. Those favoring announced audits want the cooperation of organizations being reviewed. With doctors, this is often necessary.

At Graduate Hospital, the auditors used extensive checklists. Typical "yes or no" questions that were asked included the following:

- Did the nurse interview/observe patient within 24 hours of admission?

- Was the patient positioned for optimal body alignment?
- Did the nurse discuss plans for the patient with other disciplines who were working with the patient?
- Did the physician and the nurse in charge discuss current plans for the patient daily?

The hospital also had audits covering infection control procedures, length of hospital stays, use of standard treatments and equipment calibration.

Classification of Inspection Categories

The Graduate Hospital in Philadelphia[37] classifies inspection categories. A typical weighting system might be

Category	Relative Weight
Procedural rating	20.0
Service rating	20.0
Records rating	10.0
Equipment maintenance rating	20.0
Bacteriological measurement rating	10.0
Public relations rating	10.0
Physical environment rating	10.0
Total	100.0

These ratings are similar to the classification of defects used in most industrial quality assurance systems. Here, however, the classifications have numeric weights and involve rating categories instead of specific defects. In addition they add up to 100, giving users an easy-to-understand scale for rating shifts, departments and hospitals.

Trend Charts

Once a standard rating system is developed, trend charts often follow. Trend charts used by Werner[37] include goals or targets to shoot at. These goals are not statistical quality control limits; the goals are negotiated by the supervisor being reviewed and that supervisor's boss. The goal-setting is monitored by the Management Systems Engineering Department. The advantage of this approach is that the people feel committed to goals they helped set. Additional information on trend charts is contained in Chapter 13.

Reports

The reporting system at Graduate Hospital in Philadelphia integrated "quality measurement with productivity measurement so the optimum balance could be found between maintaining the quality of care provided and the labor costs of that care."[37] Each level in the company received reports on their own activities every four weeks; their bosses also received copies. Reporting levels within the organization were:

- Hospital
- Division
- Department
- Cost center

Vendors

Although receiving inspection systems are common in manufacturing organizations, they were scarce in hospitals. Werner[37] highlighted this problem when he observed: "A Request for Quotation (RFQ) was developed which included perhaps for the first time in the hospital industry, questions regarding the supplier's quality assurance program. This RFQ was submitted to two suppliers and their reactions to the questions regarding their quality assurance program were identical—they had never had these kinds of questions asked before and they did not know how to reply."[37]

Graduate Hospital in Philadelphia has a thorough, well-documented program; it is not, however, alone. There are other quality systems in the health-care field.

- Col. Michael Scotti, Jr., M.D., Director, Quality Assurance, Office of the Surgeon General,[38] stated:

    Quality Assurance initiatives demand that we measure the care we provide. Each inpatient record is examined for serious events such as post-operative infections, unexpected returns to intensive care units, small or weak newborns, and 15 other such occurrences. Each of these events is reviewed by the physician's peers and opportunities for improvement are seized. More than two dozen of our most significant operations have been measured against expected complications and deaths to provide early identification of possible difficulties in health care delivery. Outpatient review is done on a random basis in every clinic and department. Summary problem lists and current medication records are required in all. Every instance of possible difficulty with the provider, the facility or the equipment is followed up officially.[38]

- Part of the program for the Humana hospital chain includes measuring quality against goals; stipulations range from having the emergency room respond to patients within 60 seconds to maximum patient waiting times.[39] Humana also requires technicians to notify a supervisor if they miss a vein twice.[40]

Are all of these quality assurance programs expensive? Jan O'Neill and Mary Zimmerman say "No!" According to them,

> Employees at Meriter Hospital (Madison, Wisconsin) are discovering that the quality/cost balance need not involve sacrificing one for the other. Indeed, they are finding that in focusing on improving quality—as defined by customers—cost reduction follows. The most effective approach to delivering top quality care and service at lower costs entails unprecedented levels of teamwork, cause-driven problem solving, and a never-ending commitment to quality which focuses on meeting—and if possible, exceeding—customer needs and expectations.[41]

The program they developed at Meriter emphasizes training, team building and problem solving in the administrative part of the hospital. They cut in half the number of problems occurring in orientation, bypass admits, and hardware in the registration area. They reduced potential revenue losses from $63,702 to $9,652 per year in the billing area.

SERVICE SECTORS OF MANUFACTURING COMPANIES

In his book *Total Quality Control*,[42] Armand Feigenbaum describes the "hidden plant" as "the proportion of plant capacity that exists to rework unsatisfactory parts, to replace products recalled from the field, or to retest and reinspect rejected units." The service side of the building has an equally wasteful section called the "hidden office." It exists to retype letters, recalculate specification limits, explain subjective personnel evaluations, redo design blunders and correct engineering errors. As Dr. Al Endres explains it, "In most cases, the cost of the hidden office is at least 20 percent of your cost of operation."[43] If this estimate is accurate, quality service must really pay!

Key 6: Knowing Where and How to Use the Other Keys 327

Sponsors of the hidden office that are currently receiving the most attention include

- Procurement
- Engineering and design
- Clerical services
- Personnel

Procurement

Hospitals are not the only organizations needing cooperation between their procurement and quality assurance teams. All buyers should consider quality when making purchases—especially when using Ship-To-Stock[44] and Just-In-Time[45] systems. Both systems save company funds by reducing the cost of inventories; both require close liaison between vendors, purchasing agents, and quality assurance personnel. When you have small inventories, you'd better have a competent, cooperative vendor. You need to communicate and be aware of supplier problems before an unacceptable shipment is delivered to your door. The alternative is to run out.

William Stoner of Hewlett-Packard attacked the procurement problem by making vendors part of the company team.[46] His approach was to

- Select the best vendors available
- Share information with the vendor
- Train vendor personnel
- Help vendors solve their problems

When selecting the best vendors, Stoner suggests being wary of those with excessive Accounts Receivable; they may go out of business. He also suggests avoiding vendors with piles of scrap in their back rooms; they generally have high production costs. He favors those close to his plant: "This precaution saves travel time and helps expedite corrective action."[46] Dick Laford, when interviewed for *Productivity Improvement Bulletin*,[47] identified the best vendors as having the fewest rejections in Receiving Inspection. He also favored those who caused the least difficulty during processing and who contributed to the fewest customer complaints.

Initial price should not be the first consideration. Bill Latzko documented a case where purchase of bargain MICR ribbons resulted in his bank observing "a sudden decrease in encoding productivity."[48] Most likely the ribbons were improperly manufactured—or had been on the shelf too long. MICR ribbons tend to deteriorate with age and cause flaking of the "ink."

McCabe[49] reviewed a purchasing operation where many departments were involved and no one was taking charge: "Since the accuracy of the system was not a purchasing responsibility, there was no thrust by purchasing to fix the problem." When the purchasing manager took ownership of the process, he found that part of the problem was "errors in the purchase orders . . . . The responsibility for these was totally contained within the purchasing department. Data on errors in POs were collected and a P-chart established with an average error rate of almost 6 percent. A team of buyers reviewed the data. Process changes were instituted and some additional training given. A 40 percent improvement was achieved in a few weeks as evidenced by the P-chart."

The above case study brings out the following points:

- Managers shouldn't spend all their time monitoring the manufacturing sector; the service sector can be eating up the profits.
- If no one takes charge of an operation, quality will normally suffer.

Engineering and Design

The concept of bringing engineering and design personnel under the scrutiny of a quality assurance review is relatively new. Design engineers, like computer programmers, tend to be fiercely independent. The current trend, however, is to have quality, reliability, marketing, customer service and production personnel review designs early in the game.

- Quality and reliability personnel can help verify design concepts with planned experiments like those of Taguchi.[50,51] Even simple experiments, like those discussed in Chapter 18, help optimize products and processes. Hewlett-Packard used extensive testing during the design of a new oscilloscope. The result was to improve reliability (reduced failure rates) by a factor of three.[52]
- Marketing and customer service personnel can help the design department identify what the consumers want and don't want. As an example, developing the ideal insurance policy for people over 80 would be useless if no one over 80 wanted it.
- Production personnel can help ensure that the design makes sense from a productivity standpoint. Data-entry personnel, for instance, should review data-entry screens before computer programmers "freeze" them into the system. Statistical technicians should review

Key 6: Knowing Where and How to Use the Other Keys 329

statistical forms they are expected to use before 10,000 copies have been ordered. It pays to have the users review the product before it goes on the market—even if the user is someone who works for you.

In addition, control charts can be used to monitor the quality of the designers. Variables and attributes that can be monitored include errors caught during design review, changes required after the original design and undocumented design changes. Design may be an art but it can still be monitored and evaluated.

Clerical Services

All organizations have some clerical services. Otherwise, correspondence would never reach the customer, supplies would always be short and workers would not be paid. When workers are not paid, business comes to a screeching halt. Only owners and volunteers work without regular paychecks, and few companies can survive with nothing but volunteers. Tools frequently used to improve clerical quality include flow charts, control charts, Pareto charts, computer edits and audits.

- Thornton[53] documents procedures he used to analyze problems in a complaint-handling operation; 10 percent of the observations contained errors. Flow diagrams were used to identify the key variables. A Pareto chart was used to display the relative frequency of different types of errors. Then, a fishbone (Ishikawa) diagram was used to provide detailed information on the causes of the most common error. Since it appeared that operations (customer service representatives) might be the most important variable, their error rates were plotted on a modified p-chart. The p-chart showed an "out-of-control" situation; there was a significant difference between operators. Thornton's conclusion was "The study indicated not only the need for training but where that training should be directed."[53]
- Latzko stresses the need for flow charts, specifications, capability studies, independent checking, training and leadership for good clerical quality.[54] Latzko's Quality Improvement Program (QUIP) involves running capability studies and keeping records on each employee's performance. The record, he says, "is the manager's tool for helping his clerks achieve better quality. Over a period of time, the form enables a manager to ascertain whether mistakes are increasing or decreasing—and if the former, what the nature of those mistakes is."[55] The QUIP program, according to Latzko,

"causes internal failures to decrease by 25 percent or more almost at once, and within a short period of time, by 50 percent or more."[55]
- Setting meaningful standards is more difficult than many people realize. Karl Albrecht and Ron Zemke in *Service America* refer to a large West Coast city where the managers wanted to improve the service level. The bosses had concluded: "We're not doing somebody a favor when we provide a permit to build an addition to a house, we're doing a service. We must treat them like customers, not like naughty children."[56] They wanted to be customer oriented, but they had trouble identifying "customer-oriented service." Was it a friendly clerk? One that was fast? One providing personal treatment? To answer these questions, they initiated a customer research program that identified the key needs and expectations of the people they served.

Personnel

The personnel function, like almost any administrative activity, can be evaluated. Hershauer, Ruch and Adam[57] went to great pains to develop ways of measuring competence in this field. A few of the "deviations" they proposed measuring were:

- Employees incorrectly assigned
- Employee skill mismatched to job
- Salary adjustment to wrong employee
- Employees inappropriately compensated
- Errors in posting or reporting guidelines
- Salaries not in line with market
- Incorrect claim processing
- Departments not adequately staffed

The above errors or deviations are specific to the personnel function. Specialized lists, however, can be developed for almost any job. Then, supervisors can evaluate subordinates objectively and identify areas needing attention. Once the measurements are developed, trend analyses, control charts and other statistical procedures can be used to identify which areas need to be monitored. Given this information, management can clear some of the hurdles that keep employees from doing better work.

WHERE DO WE GO FROM HERE?

Desatnick, in *Managing to Keep the Customer*,[58] claims that 60 percent of all employed individuals work in a service capacity. In reality, that number is 40 percent too low; we are all in the business of serving someone. If we aren't, we should be. Faced with this ever-increasing need for service, how do we succeed? The following suggestions are submitted as initial guideposts; they will help you start the journey. Unless you take the initial step, you'll never arrive at Shangri-la.

1. Find out who your customers are. We all serve.
2. Find out what your customers want.
3. Determine what you need to do to satisfy your customer's perceived wants and needs.
4. Develop written standards around the actions you need to take.
5. Meet those standards.
6. Monitor your performance to ensure that you continue to meet those standards.
7. Get continuous feedback from your customers. When your customers or their perceptions change, start the cycle over at step 1.

If you follow these steps, you should continue to get better, you should survive during changing times and you should experience the elation of self-actualization. There is no thrill like reaching for a star—and catching it.

SUMMARY

The body of this text concentrates on methods of improving quality in the service sector. Most of the tools used on the production lines can be used in the service side of the plant; most of the methods developed by the service sector have been used in manufacturing.

"Success stories" covered in this chapter should help you see the similarity between problems faced by banks, insurance companies, hospitals, clerical pools and personnel offices; the tools for resolving these problems are also similar.

Quality service pays and the potential profits are huge. With the service sector accounting for more than half of most expenditures, this mother lode lies waiting for the innovative and the adventurous. You can keep chipping away at manufacturing operations to save pennies or you can address the untapped service side of your company and multiply your achievements manifold. I've worked in both arenas; I've seen how far the service sector has to go.

FOOD FOR THOUGHT

Review the case studies in this chapter. Then answer the following questions:

1. How much similarity can you find in problems faced by different kinds of companies?
2. How much similarity can you find in the techniques the two sectors use in solving problems?
3. Once you've mastered the tools used by one industry, could *you* apply them to another?

REFERENCES
1. "W. Edwards Deming, A Mission Pursued on Two Continents," *Quality Progress,* October 1986, pp. 78–79.
2. A. C. Rosander, *Washington Story* (Boulder, CO: Johnson Publishing, 1985).
3. "Harry G. Romig—Statistical Quality Control Pioneer," *Quality Progress,* May 1983, p. 4.
4. W. Edwards Deming, *Some Theory of Sampling* (New York: Dover Publications, 1966), p. 10.
5. A. C. Rosander, *Applications of Quality Control in the Service Industries* (Milwaukee, WI: ASQC Quality Press, 1985), pp. 45–46.
6. Henry L. Lefevre, "Productivity—Microcomputers and the Government," *ASQC Quality Congress Transactions,* May 3–5, 1982, pp. 305–307.
7. Henry L. Lefevre, "Time Series Forecasting for Non-Mathematicians," *ASQC Quality Congress Transactions,* May 27–29, 1981, pp. 1029–1034.
8. Henry L. Lefevre, "Quality Control and Database Management Systems," *ASQC Technical Congress Transactions,* May 8–10, 1978, pp. 371–374.
9. John F. Early and William D. Lockerby, "Applying Process Management in a Service Organization," *ASQC Quality Congress Transactions,* May 9–11, 1988, pp. 2–8.
10. Letter from Roger L. Rasmussen, Chairperson, Productivity Advisory Committee, to Tom Bradley, Mayor, City of Los Angeles, March 30, 1987.

Key 6: Knowing Where and How to Use the Other Keys

11. Administrative Code, City of Los Angeles, Chapter 19, Productivity Advisory Committee, D8–117, Rev. January 31, 1986.
12. Calvin Stevens, "Eliminating Federal Specifications," *ASQC Quality Congress Transactions,* May 3–5, 1982, pp. 313–318.
13. John M. Wyatt, "Government-wide Approach to Food Quality Assurance," *ASQC Technical Congress Transactions,* May 20–22, 1980, pp. 49–52.
14. Eugene Kirby, "MICR Quality Control—A Technique for Banking," *ASQC Technical Congress Transactions,* June 7–9, 1976, pp. 362–369.
15. Eugene Kirby, "Quality Control in Banking," *Administrative Applications Division Yearbook, 1975,* pp. 53–57.
16. William J. Latzko, "Statistical Quality Control of MICR Documents," *ASQC Technical Congress Transactions,* May 16–18, 1977, pp. 117–123.
17. William J. Latzko, "Quality Control of MICR Input," *Long Island ASQC Conference Transactions,* 1974.
18. William J. Latzko, "QUIP—The Quality Improvement Program," *ASQC Technical Congress Transactions,* 1975, pp. 246 ff.
19. William J. Latzko, "Reducing Clerical Quality Costs," *ASQC Technical Congress Transactions,* 1974, pp. 185 ff.
20. William J. Latzko, "Quality Productivity Measures—Participative Management," *ASQC Technical Conference Transactions,* May 26–29, 1981, pp. 389–395.
21. William J. Latzko, *Quality and Productivity for Bankers and Financial Managers* (Milwaukee, WI: ASQC Quality Press, 1986).
22. Charles A. Aubrey, II, *Quality Management in Financial Services* (Wheaton, IL: Hitchcock Publishing, 1985).
23. Thurmon Sutcliffe, "The Role of Quality in Banking, *ASQC Technical Congress Transactions,* May 8–10, 1978, pp. 326–327.
24. Thurmon Sutcliffe, "Tutorial—Banking and Financial Institutions," *ASQC Technical Congress Transactions,* May 14–16, 1979, pp. 695–702.
25. Janet S. Waksman, "Using Market Research to Meet the Challenge, *ASQC Quality Congress Transactions,* May 9–11, 1988, pp. 876–880.
26. K. E. C. Anyanonu and H. J. Bajaria, "Quality Control in Banks—Why, Where and How," *ASQC Technical Conference Transactions,* May 20–22, 1980, pp. 307–312.
27. Mirek R. Cejka, "Quality Improvement Towards Float Management," *Annual North East Quality Control Conference Transactions,* October 9–11, 1985, pp. 129–134.
28. Randolph L. Rohrbaugh, "One Company's Approach to Data Sampling and Audits," *ASQC Technical Conference Transactions,* May 14–16, 1979, pp. 297–305.
29. Philip D. Miller, "Quality Control in the Insurance Industry," *ASQC Technical Conference Transactions,* May 14–16, 1979, pp. 311–320.
30. Charles D. Zimmerman, III, "USF&G's Quality Control Program," *ASQC Technical Conference Transactions,* May 14–16, 1979, pp. 306–310.

31. Rebecca Lee Huls, "Control Charts for Service Companies," *Quality Control Supervisor's Bulletin,* November 25, 1987, pp. 1–2.
32. Rebecca Lee Huls, "Dedication to Quality Spans All Industries," *ASQC Quality Congress Transactions,* May 4–6, 1987, pp. 90–95.
33. Patrick L. Townsend, "Quality is Everybody's Business," *ASQC Quality Congress Transactions,* May 19–21, 1986, pp. 31–35.
34. Frank Scanlon, "Cost Improvement Through Quality Improvement," *ASQC Quality Congress Transactions,* May 26–29, 1981, pp. 385–388.
35. Frank Scanlon, "Cost Reduction Through Quality Management," *ASQC Technical Conference Transactions,* May 20–22, 1980, pp. 270–273.
36. Frank Scanlon and John T. Hagan, "Quality Management for the Service Industries—Part I," *Quality Progress,* May 1983, pp. 18–23.
37. John P. Werner, "Application of a QA Program in a Hospital Facility," *ASQC Technical Conference Transactions,* May 20–22, 1980, pp. 313–322.
38. Col. Michael Scotti, Jr., M.D., "Surgeon General Quality Assurance," *Army Echoes.*
39. Humana, "Report on Medical Excellence," excerpt from the *1982 Annual Report* of Humana Inc.
40. John R. Dorfman, "Batting .857," *Forbes,* October 25, 1982, pp. 145–146.
41. Jan O'Neill and Mary Zimmerman, "Roadmap for Quality: One Hospital's Approach," *ASQC Quality Congress Transactions,* May 9–11, 1988, pp. 440–448.
42. Armand V. Feigenbaum, *Total Quality Control* (New York: McGraw-Hill, 1983), pp. 46–47.
43. "Improving Quality in Support Functions," *Quality Control Supervisor's Bulletin,* July 25, 1986, pp. 1–3.
44. Richard J. Laford, *Ship To Stock,* (Milwaukee, WI: ASQC Quality Press, 1986).
45. Richard J. Schonberger, "Just-in-Time Production—The Quality Dividend," *Quality Progress,* October 1984, pp. 22–24.
46. "Put Vendors on the Home Team," *Quality Control Supervisor's Bulletin,* September 10, 1986, pp. 1–3.
47. Henry L. Lefevre, "Cut Inspection Costs and Improve Vendor Quality with Ship-to-Stock," *Productivity Improvement Bulletin,* March 25, 1986, pp. 1–3.
48. Latzko, *Quality and Productivity for Bankers and Financial Managers,* pp. 40–41.
49. William J. McCabe, "Quality Methods Applied to the Business Process," *ASQC Quality Congress Transactions,* May 19–21, 1986, p. 434.
50. Thomas B. Baker, "Quality Engineering by Design: Taguchi's Philosophy," *Quality Progress,* December 1986, pp. 32–42.
51. Raghu N. Kackar, "Taguchi's Quality Philosophy: Analysis and Commentary," *Quality Progress,* December 1986, pp. 21–29.
52. Roy E. Wheeler, "Quality Starts With Design," *Quality,* May 1986, pp. 22–23.
53. Manly P. Thornton, "SPC For Administrative Systems," *ASQC Quality Congress Transactions,* May 4–6, 1987, pp. 287–292.

Key 6: Knowing Where and How to Use the Other Keys   335

54. William J. Latzko, "Measuring Clerical Quality," *ASQC Quality Congress Transactions,* May 9–11, 1988, pp. 114–121.
55. William J. Latzko, "Quality Control for Banks," *The Bankers,* 1977, pp. 64–68.
56. Karl Albrecht and Ron Zemke, *Service America* (Homewood, IL: Dow Jones-Irwin, 1985), pp. 116–117.
57. James C. Hershauer, William A. Ruch and Everett E. Adam, Jr., "Quality Measurement for Personnel Services," *ASQC Technical Conference Transactions,* May 20–22, 1980, pp. 262–269.
58. Robert L. Desatnick, *Management to Keep the Customer* (San Francisco, CA: Jossey-Bass, 1987), p. xi.

Chapter 27

Quotable Quotes

Basic concepts in this book are highlighted by the following quotations. They are intended to intrigue those who read this part first; they are meant to summarize for those who read it last.

PREFACE

"Quality departments in the service industries are like orphans waiting for adoption. Almost everyone proclaims their right to live. Few, however, want to acknowledge their legitimacy or pay for their maintenance."

"Many service industries have hired consultants from manufacturing companies as 'foster parents' in order to gain insight into raising baby quality assurance departments. To date, however, few have been willing to sign lifelong contracts for the infant departments' nursery care."

"Governmental agencies were leaders in the field of service sector quality."

"Most manufacturing organizations have clerical operations and use computers. These activities involve either service quality or administrative quality control and fall under the service sector umbrella."

"A good illustration is more helpful than pages of directions."

CHAPTER 1

"Providing poor quality in the service sector is like fielding a 'sand lot' team in the World Series play-offs; it gives the company a bad name and hurts profits."

"Some people worry if part of the work isn't inspected. They are like compulsive housekeepers who dust the furniture four times per day in fear that neighbors might drop in."

"To many people, computers are austere, argumentative, unbending robots that never make mistakes. To most data processing professionals, computers are friendly servants that are never moody, do what they are told and provide challenges."

"Most administrative, clerical and service organizations use computer databases. Some of these electronic file cabinets, however, are treated like 20-acre, hutchless rabbit ranches; the contents are hard to confine and difficult to control. In addition, they proliferate until they've used up all the allotted space."

CHAPTER 2

"Quests for quality and beauty are eternal and evasive. Once you think you have found them, perceptions change."

"A frown is an attitude defect if there is a requirement for a smile. A misspelled word is a product defect if there is a spelling requirement."

"Tools and facilities have a major impact on customers' perceptions. With fast-food operations, for instance, appearance and cleanliness are critical."

"Quality in the service sector has much in common with quality in manufacturing. Both services and products should be free of defects."

"Talk to your customers and evaluate their comments. Many of them will be happy to tell you what they expect."

"Combine ideal attitudes, perfect timeliness, the best available tools and good facilities with a service that is free of defects. Then, customer satisfaction usually follows."

CHAPTER 3

"Starting a service company with no knowledge of the potential customers is like swimming in the Gulf of Mexico with a broken leg, a bleeding cut and no shark repellent. Neither risk-taker can keep above water very long."

"Poor quality often has a ripple effect; one instance of poor service may hurt many people."

"Determining customer requirements takes extensive research; depending on intuition can be risky."

"Few companies can afford to develop the 'perfect' service that no one wants."

"Writing takes time and effort on the part of the buyer. As a consequence, the feedback you get generally comes from people who are either irate or very happy with services they received."

"Toll-free hot lines are a good way to solicit customer information with minimum effort on the part of the buyer."

"Customer feedback should be cherished; don't allow this valuable information to die in the files of the marketing department."

"Surveys are popular for measuring customer satisfaction and customer satisfaction is a key to success."

"The price of ignorance can be failure."

"Feedback is hard to obtain; if you don't ensure that your customers have something to gain from being cooperative, you get little response. When they benefit from filling in the forms, they are more apt to cooperate."

"To some, phone interviews are similar to high-pressure sales pitches. If they are not performed with finesse, interviewers may get dubious responses."

"Personal interviews are a helpful but expensive way of identifying specific customer needs."

"If you had the wisdom of King Solomon and the statistical skills of Dr. Deming, you could control bias within reasonable limits. But you could not eliminate it."

"Evaluation of survey responses has a lot to do with the value of a survey; inconsistencies between what customers say and what they mean must be addressed."

"Aging data, biases, inconsistencies and sampling errors should all be considered before you commit major resources based on customer feedback."

CHAPTER 4

"Managers who don't know what's going on are like climbers in the Himalayas with no map, no guide, no compass and little chance of survival. There's the possibility that they might stumble on Shangri-la, but the odds are poor."

"Many managers believe they know what is going on because they study the reports received from subordinates. Without direct feedback, however, the chance of being sandbagged is greater than any knowledgeable manager should risk."

"Early exposure to the workings of a company is not enough; frequent refresher courses are needed."

"Management By Wandering Around (MBWA) describes a practice used by 'hands on' managers for decades."

"A large number of management controllable errors result from workers having equipment, procedures, designs, tooling or facilities that are not compatible with error-free work. Inadequate training also falls into this category."

"Open rap sessions are similar to MBWA but they require even more finesse."

"Customer-centered audits use typical customers on the audit team; the object is to identify what satisfies and what dissatisfies the customer."

"Some organizations prefer having unannounced audits. This is particularly popular in areas where fraud or theft is possible."

"Audit reports should help good operations look good and help substandard operations improve. When outstanding work is identified during an audit, it should be documented."

"The admonition 'know thine own business' includes knowing what quality costs. Armed with this knowledge, executives can initiate corrective action; without it, they are tilting at windmills."

"Money spent preventing errors usually results in reduced total error costs because the total number of errors is reduced."

"If you can't prevent errors, the next priority is to catch them before they do more damage."

"Customers are your final inspectors—errors and defects caught by them can be very expensive."

"A manager who doesn't have a firm understanding of what is going on is apt to be blind-sided as often as a rookie quarterback with a weak offensive line playing his first game in the National Football League."

CHAPTER 5

"Verbal instructions . . . tend to be inconsistent; trying to keep them from changing is like trying to keep drunken drivers from shifting lanes."

"In the service sector, quality standards usually specify what is acceptable service or performance; they identify the target and acceptable limits surrounding it (the target zone)."

"If the standards and specifications are too tight, the workers won't even try to meet them; if they are too loose, quality can suffer."

CHAPTER 6

"As an art, sampling is practiced by almost everyone."

"Without formal training in statistics, good cooks learn to take representative samples, checking the quality of their products before serving."

"Sampling clerical records is similar to sampling stews and cars. The primary differences are in the materials being tested, not in sampling fundamentals."

"Redundant inspection may be justified on a short-term basis; system improvements, however, usually provide a better long-term solution."

"Subjective sampling is like shopping; you inspect the units that you like."

"Subjective sampling and grab sampling are generally inaccurate and subject to error or bias; these procedures should be avoided."

"Interval sampling, interval sampling with a random start, random sampling and stratified sampling are the preferred procedures; their results are less apt to produce inaccurate conclusions."

CHAPTER 7

"Outstanding communications and exceptional quality control programs are needed to make the Just-In-Time and Ship-To-Stock programs work."

"A common alternative to receiving inspection is the squeaky wheel system. Purchasing agents may continue to buy the cheapest product on the market until the users start to squeak, holler and revolt."

"Sample plans can be used in a production environment, even when the 'product' is a stack of travel vouchers, a pile of hospital admission reports, a batch of case studies or a day's worth of statistical calculations."

"When a worker's quality is controlled by supervision, the worker normally gets prompt feedback from someone who has a direct impact on that person's career."

"By sampling and performing internal quality audits, supervision can identify who needs additional training, who needs motivation and who needs clearer instructions."

"For maximum benefits, it is best to have both internal and external sampling, auditing and review. That way, feedback can be both quick and free of bias."

CHAPTER 8

"Although known for its applications in high volume manufacturing operations, Military Standard 105D can also be used in the service sector."

"When everything is going well, the risks are less and you can take smaller samples. When problems arise, the risks are higher and you should sample more. The idea is to have the most inspection when the risks are greatest."

"Choosing sampling systems is a little like choosing computers; people tend to prefer systems they understand."

"The AQL identifies the average level of quality you are willing to live with over a period of years. It doesn't, however, identify whether garbage can slip through the screening process."

"Military Standard 105D is the most frequently used set of governmental sample plans in the United States. It helps you select the proper sample size and tells you when to accept the batch being tested."

CHAPTER 9

"It's not enough to measure the production of workers. The quality of their efforts should also be reviewed."

"In the service sector, Military Standard 105D is not used as much as it should be. In addition, many who use it don't use it properly."

"When defects are detected, they should be returned to their source. This concept is not always clear to those being inspected. Many believe that it is OK to send known defects to the customer."

"Many sample plans allow acceptance of batches after defects have been found—as long as the acceptance number is not exceeded. To remove this source of confusion, many supervisors try to stick to sample plans where the acceptance number is zero."

"When problems develop and rejections become frequent, tougher sample plans are required. They may also be used where the cost of accepting bad work is high or the people being inspected have not proven themselves."

CHAPTER 10

"Dodge & Romig sampling tables stress Lot Tolerance Percent Defective (LTPD) and Average Outgoing Quality Limit (AOQL); they help identify consumer risks. You might call them tools of the consumer advocate."

"The assumption of 100-percent inspection being 100 percent effective is not limited to the Dodge & Romig tables. It is also hidden in Military Standard 105D and many other sampling systems."

"Harold F. Dodge and Harry G. Romig were pioneers in quality control through sampling. Their sample plans stressed protection of the consumer rather than the producer."

"The Dodge & Romig sampling tables are effective at catching poor work (LTPD) and identifying the worst average level of quality that will reach the customer after screening (AOQL)."

CHAPTER 11

"Continuous sampling is a technique for inspecting vouchers, records, transactions, cases and materials as they are produced. As an example, continuous sampling can be used for auditing a technician who is working on expense accounts, statistical calculations, data-entry work, hospital records, bank transactions, travel vouchers or insurance claims."

"Intuitive judgments about whose quality is best can result in supervisors being challenged and subordinates being disillusioned."

"Continuous sampling is usually economical where the time spent inspecting each unit exceeds two minutes."

"The greatest advantage of continuous sampling is that it helps you put your inspection dollars where your problems are. Why use the same level of sampling on all employees? Those doing quality work require less auditing."

CHAPTER 12

"Those unfamiliar with the proper tools are like clerks with mechanical calculators trying to compete with those using personal computers. The first group may do a creditable job, but they have a hard time keeping up, and they usually make more errors."

"Managers who haven't investigated capability studies are like amateur aviators plowing through visibility-zero fog with no knowledge of instrument flying. First, they are not using the best available training. Second, their ignorance can be costly."

"Those who can take the tools that others developed and adapt them to their own unique situation have an edge on their less adventurous competition."

CHAPTER 13

"The higher up you go in the organization, the more systems you have to monitor and the more you must depend on visual aids. Trend charts are excellent visual aids."

"Capability studies help determine whether the goal, standard or specification is reasonable. They can also be used to find out whether high variability is due to a few poor workers or the group as a whole."

"When procedures are changed, quality often drops until the workers become accustomed to the new way of doing things."

"An investigation of a 'freak' point often gives you added insight into your process."

CHAPTER 14

"Variation can be good or bad. With no variation, the world would be dull and monotonous. With too much variation, the world would be a celestial madhouse with nothing in control."

"Equipment variation in the service sector includes different typewriters, word processors, computers, data-entry keyboards, calculators and many other items. Any time you change a worker's typewriter, for example, you will probably change the individual's productivity and error rate."

"Environmental variation can also influence service quality. In some cases, quality and productivity are hampered by abnormal temperatures, excessive humidity, noise or smoke."

"Analyses of 'abnormal' points often provide information on how to improve a process."

"In the utopia of some idealists, all work would be perfect; neither errors nor variability would exist. In the service sector, as in manufacturing, errors do occur—and so does variability."

"Most factors contributing to error rates are management controllable; managers, however, must be shown the problem before they can be expected to initiate corrective action."

CHAPTER 15

"Variables involve measurements like time, number-of-records-processed, backlog or volume-of-incoming-work; these data usually follow the normal curve. Attributes involve right-or-wrong, defect-or-no-defect judgments; they seldom follow the normal curve."

"Average-and-range charts are often associated with manufacturing operations; production plants have used them for decades. Now, they are becoming popular in the service sector."

"Being in 'statistical control' indicates that the system is running smoothly; it doesn't mean that improvements can't be made."

"In some cases, data that is 'in statistical control' lulls organizations into complacency even though system improvements are needed to make the organization competitive."

CHAPTER 16

"What can attributes control charts tell you? Assume that ABC Airline's upper control limit for late flights is five percent. If six percent of their flights are late this month, they are statistically out of control. When this situation is discovered, management should be alerted and reasons for the problem should be investigated."

"The main disadvantage of np-charts is they require a constant sample size. With np-charts, allowing sample sizes to fluctuate would be like giving all college students the same math proficiency exam without considering the student's major or class level."

"P-charts, p-charts, np-charts and c-charts are all attributes control charts. The choice of which to use is often dictated by the personal preferences of the people involved."

CHAPTER 17

"Capability studies are being discovered by the service sector; they help blind managers see."

"When managers set standards and specifications without knowing the capability of their process, they're flying blind like injured bats with damaged radar."

"When you know the natural process limits, you know the capability your process has after all 'unnatural' sources of variation are removed—in other words, you know your process capability under the conditions of the study."

"In the past, standards and specifications have been set by a multitude of criteria ranging from scientific wild guesses to capability studies. The latter is preferable."

"In the service sector, variation in the capability of individuals often has a greater impact on quality than it does in the manufacturing sector."

"Capability studies reveal the capability of people, equipment, processes and procedures—under the conditions of the test."

CHAPTER 18

"Choosing the right process or product can be an art or a science. Normally, it's in between."

"Some managers have a wealth of experience and an outstanding memory; they know what worked in the past and are able to apply this knowledge to current problems."

"Subjective decisions are allowable when indecisiveness can be costly or fatal. They should not be relied on, however, if other timely options are available."

"Control charts help evaluate process adjustments. They also help detect unexpected changes."

"When the sequence of the tests is randomized, the probability of excessive influence from extraneous or time-related changes is reduced."

"Ends testing is a simple technique for selecting the better of two systems, processes, procedures, tools or materials. Conditions, however, have to be rigidly controlled and conclusions should not be extrapolated beyond the items and conditions of the test."

CHAPTER 19

"Efficient quality assurance is similar to efficient reading. If you're working on the wrong projects, having phenomenal speed and superior tools won't solve your problems; it will only help you waste time more efficiently."

"It seldom pays to spend a million dollars to solve a nickel-and-dime problem. Efficient problem solving involves identifying the problems that are likely to provide the best payoff—or the biggest bang per buck."

"Tools can be explained by books; they can't be mastered, however, unless they are used."

CHAPTER 20

"Computers are here to stay. Those who don't understand them are like tug boat captains trying to race a speed boat—they don't have the right equipment."

"The era of tedious calculations and repetitive number crunching is reminiscent of the days of Charles Dickens, Ebenezer Scrooge and *A Christmas Carol*. At that time, according to Dickens, low-paid clerks with green eyeshades handled the payroll, accounting and routine statistical calculations. Now, computers do most of the number crunching."

"Those who want to make computers into status symbols will waste time and money. Those who buy first and plan later will have similar problems."

"Having system programmers solely responsible for the accuracy of their database is similar to having football coaches referee championship games when their own teams are playing."

CHAPTER 21

"Computers . . . are not cure-alls; they can be abused, misused and forced to hurt your profits. Knowledge of the potential risks and rewards of automation is vital."

"Negotiating with programmers and analysts without learning their language, 'computerese,' is like ordering a five-course meal in France without understanding French."

"Those who leave computers and computer software to the specialists generally get what the specialists are willing to give them. Those who understand computer basics have a better chance of getting what they need."

"Many computer specialists insist on speaking in their own tongue. If you can't understand them, you had better learn their dialect. Your future may be at stake."

CHAPTER 22

"Unless managers have objective guidelines for justifying equipment, they often find desktop computers easier to request than to use."

"Until you identify potential applications, you shouldn't think of automating."

"Waiting for most system programmers to customize commercial software is like wishing on a star—and joining the waiting line behind Rip Van Winkle."

"When computer departments are not responsive, the inefficiencies of amateur programming will be tolerated by those who can't otherwise get what they need when they need it."

CHAPTER 23

"The first step in controlling database quality is to determine what the current accuracy is."

"Edits are used to keep illogical data from entering the database."

"Many of the best edits are developed by database users intimately involved with the information being recorded."

"One problem with listening to everyone's suggestions is that you get many conflicting ideas. Some suggestions are great; they improve quality and productivity. Other suggestions are counterproductive; they make things worse."

"Having the best database in the world with no security is like being in charge of the gold at Fort Knox and removing all safeguards. Without security, an outstanding database can become as useless as a computer struck by lightning."

CHAPTER 24

"Having the best tools in the world has limited value if only the elite are allowed to use them. Managers, statisticians and engineers can solve many problems by themselves; they can solve many more if they have input from other members of the organization."

"Management backing is critical. Without strong direction and support from the top, participative management and cooperative teamwork won't survive."

"The training and education that quality teams give their members are outstanding intangible assets."

"When supervisors feel left out or bypassed, they find subtle ways of ensuring that quality teams don't work; no one wants their position or authority threatened."

"At times, a few successes lead to overconfidence and team members get careless. One thing to remember is that your reputation is seldom better than your last presentation."

"Quality Circles and other team concepts have been successful in both manufacturing and service industries. When properly planted and nurtured, they pay for themselves many times. When dumped on barren soil and left to fend for themselves, they seldom survive."

CHAPTER 25

"People working with quality teams and quality programs generally believe 'there's something in it for them.' From time to time, this belief must be reinforced, and the benefits have to be real."

"If nonperformers get the same raises as performers, there is little incentive to perform; the ego or self-esteem requirement is not being met."

"Few activities by management turn off people more quickly than subjective evaluations."

"When you measure performance impartially, you are being objective; you can defend your position. When you don't measure performance impartially, you are being subjective; you are flying by the seat of your pants."

"If one area of the company receives all of the attention, employees from other areas will become demotivated and drop out of any team effort; they will not stay involved."

"The true feelings of top managers become obvious when their own vested interests become involved; security and survival are on the second step of Maslow's Hierarchy of Needs."

"Keeping people committed to quality and participative management programs involves showing them what they have to gain. When people perceive they are being treated fairly and recognized for their efforts, they tend to stay on the team."

CHAPTER 26

"Phone customers who are put on hold may not complain; they do, however, evaluate the service. In time, they may look for a company that treats them better."

"Many executives are like cannibals; they would rather eat the quality control missionaries than listen to them. Despite the problems, however, some progress is being made."

"When people know nothing about quality assurance, they tend to resist formal quality programs."

"Managers shouldn't spend all their time monitoring the manufacturing sector; the service sector can be eating up the profits."

"The concept of bringing engineering and design personnel under the scrutiny of a quality assurance review is relatively new. Design engineers, like computer programmers, tend to be fiercely independent."

"Statistical technicians should review statistical forms they are expected to use before 10,000 copies have been ordered."

"All organizations have some clerical services. Otherwise, correspondence would never reach the customer, supplies would always be short and workers would not be paid."

"Quality service pays and the potential profits are huge. With the service sector accounting for more than half of most expenditures this mother lode lies waiting for the innovative and the adventurous."

Index

A

A2 factor, 179
Acceptable Quality Level (AQL), 92
  normal inspection and, 100-112
Acceptance number (Ac), 92, 114
Accessibility sampling, 72
Accomplishments, 295
Adam, Everett E., Jr., 335
Administrative Code, City of Los Angeles, (Productivity Advisory Committee), 333
Adolph Coors Company. *See* Coors
Adventure teams, at Celestial Seasonings, 292
Aerojet General Corporation, 257
Affourtit, B., 156, 178, 190, 228, 240
Aging data, 35
Agriculture Canada, 12
Aid to Families with Dependent Children, 47
Air Canada, 310
Air Force Accounting and Finance Center (AFAFC), 56-57, 73, 127, 141-43
  computers used at, 258

Air Force Accounting and Finance Center (*continued*)
  database benefits at, 278
  trend charts used at, 141-56
Air Force Systems Command, 310
Air Reserve Personnel Center, 217, 291
Albrecht, Karl, 330, 335
American Association of Retired Persons, 278
American National Standard ANSI/ASQC, 79, 225
American Society for Quality Control, 12, 61
  ASQC-Gallup Survey, 12-21, 34-35, 47-48
  41st AQC Congress in Minneapolis, 30
  State University of Iowa Section, 190, 212
  Technical Conference (1973), 56
American Telephone and Telegraph (AT&T), 12
Analysts (computer), 259
ANSI/ASQC Standard, 79, 225
Anyanonu, K.E.C., 320, 333

351

AOQL (Average Outgoing Quality Limit), 114, 118-20, 124
Appraisal costs, 48-49
AQL (Acceptable Quality Level), 90-92
    normal inspection and, 100-111
Artinian, H.L., 178, 190, 204, 212
ASQC-Gallup Survey, 12-21, 34-35, 47-48
Assembler language, 259
Attitudes (types of)
    customers don't count, 16
    grumpy, 17
    I'm the expert, 17
    know it all, 16
    we're the good guys, 16-17
    you're the expert, 17
Attributes control charts, 138, 191-212
    abbreviations, 193
    applications, 193-95
    np-charts, 204-07
    p-charts, 194-204
    what they tell you, 195-96
    why they require larger samples, 192
Aubrey, Charles A., II, 32, 37, 61, 65, 141, 156, 245, 252, 299, 319, 333
Audit types
    computer, 281
    customer-centered, 45
    Management by Wandering Around, 40-42
    presidential, 43-44
    system, 40, 44-45
    tour-of-duty, 40
    unannounced, 46
Audits
    areas to be audited, 45
    auditors, 45
    corrective action details, 47
    frequency of, 45-46
    reporting results, 46-47
    scheduling of, 45-46
    scope of, 46
Austin, Nancy, 41, 53

Automation, 253-55
    as key to quality service, 7
Automobile sampling, 68-69
Average and range charts, 175-81
    calculations, 182-87
    definitions associated with, 179-81
    vs. trend charts, 187-88
    where used, 178-79
Average and standard deviation charts, 182
Average Outgoing Quality Limit (AOQL), 114, 118-20, 124
Awards, 295

B

Bailie, Howard H., 248, 252
Baird, Lindsay, L., Jr., 288
Bajaria, H.J., 193, 212, 320
Baker, E.M., 178, 190, 204, 212
Baker, Thomas B., 65, 334
Banks, quality service in, 319-20
BASIC computer language, 260
Batch, definition of, 92
Baumback, C.M., 28, 37
Bell Laboratories, 142
Bequai, August, 285, 288
Berger, John A., 252
Bias
    intentional, 73
    in surveys, 34
Bimodal populations, 164-66
Bingham, R.S., Jr., 86, 112, 121
Binomial distributions, 166
"Biscuits With Billy", 43
Blake, Robert R., 303, 313
Bowen, William, 275
Box, George E.P., 65
Bradley, Tom, 318, 332
Branst, Lee, 13, 21
Brooks, Roger, 86
Brown, Bradford S., 240
Burington, Richard S., 37

Butz, R.W., 288
Byosiere, Philippe, 297, 300, 310, 313

C

c-charts, 207-10
Capability studies, 61-62, 215-25
  attributes, 218-20
  defined, 215-16
  groups, 217, 220-21
  individuals, 217, 221-23
  preparation for, 218
  reasons for running, 215-16
  test cases, 223-24
  variables, 224
Caplan, Frank, 33, 37, 44, 48, 53-54
Cathode ray tube (CRT), 260
Cause-and-effect diagrams, 248-50
Cejka, Mirek R., 320, 333
Celestial Seasonings, 33, 292
Central processing unit (CPU), 260
Chandler, Lana J., 293, 300
Chart patterns, 143-55
  Déjà Vu pattern, 153-54
  Early Warning pattern, 145-46
  Freak pattern, 152-53
  Get Well pattern, 146-47
  Happy Days pattern, 143-44
  Jump-Shift pattern, 150-52
  Oddball pattern, 152-53
  Sad Sack pattern, 147-48
  Total Chaos pattern, 154-55
  Why Plot? pattern, 148-50
  Yo-Yo pattern, 144-45
Chart types
  attributes, 138, 191-212
  average and range, 175-81
  c-charts, 207-10
  flow charts, 242-46
  np, 204-07
  p, 196-204
  Pareto, 241-42
  range, 188-89
  trend, 141-56

Chart types (*continued*)
  variables, 138
Chunk sampling, 72
Clearance number, 124
Clerical records, 69
Clerical services, quality service in, 329-30
COBOL computer language, 260
Cole, Robert E., 290, 297, 299, 310, 313
Communications, 291
Computer(s)
  audits with, 281
  basics, 257-65
  Cathode ray tube (CRT), 260
  central processing unit (CPU), 260
  commercial programs for, 271-72
  computerese, 259
  costs, 268-70
  database, 260, 277-87
  definitions associated with, 259-64
  floppy disk drives, 261
  languages, 259
  as liabilities, 258
  literacy, 267-75
  productivity, 257-58
  programming, 272-74
Consumer's risk, 92-93
Continental Illinois National Bank of Chicago, 141, 319
  see also Aubrey, Charles A., II
Continuous sampling (CSP-1), 58, 123-34
  advantages of, 84, 125-27
  choosing a plan, 128-32
  defined, 124
  definitions associated with, 124-25
  disadvantages of, 127-28
  evaluating different plans, 133
Control charts, 58, 138
  attributes, 138, 191-212
  defect prevention, 189
  plotting, 201-02
  variables, 138, 175-90
  see also specific chart types

Control systems
  continuous sampling (CSP-1), 58
  control charts, 58
  Dodge & Romig, 113-21
  local systems (Latzko's), 58
  Military Standard 105D, 57
Controlling quality, 57-62
Coors, Bill, 27
Coors, Joe, 27
Coors (Adolph Coors Company and Coors Container), 26, 40, 45, 303
Copp, R.P., 193, 212
Corrective action, in audits, 47
Correspondence, and customer satisfaction, 27
Cost analyses, 47-52
  appraisal, 48-49
  external failure, 49-52
  internal failure, 49
  prevention, 48
Covington, Michael, 266
CPU (central processing unit), 260
Crosby, Philip B., 24, 37
Cross utilization, at Walt Disney Company, 26
Cross-Functional Analysis (CFA), 250-51
Cross-functional management, 250-51
CRT (cathode ray tube), 260
CSP-1. *See* Continuous sampling
Curtice, Robert M., 277, 287
Customer satisfaction, 23-36
  correspondence and, 27
  customer surveys, 28-36
  face-to-face contact and, 26-27
  knowing your customers, 24
  techniques for determining customer needs, 26-36
  toll free hot lines and, 27-28
  what customers want, 25-26
Customer-centered audits, 45

D

D3 factor, 179
D4 factor, 179
Database(s), 260
  AIDS-testing, 280
  benefits of using, 278-79
  charge-account, 280
  coordinating design, 284-85
  military personnel, 280
  pharmaceutical, 279
  quality control, 277-87
  security, 285-86
  stock-account, 280
Defect(s)
  definition of, 93
  prevention of, 19-20, 189
Defectives, definition of, 93, 114
Déjà Vu chart pattern, 153-54
Deluxe Check Printers, Inc., 82
Deming, W. Edwards, 20-21, 25, 31, 34, 36-37, 69, 72, 77, 79-80, 141-42, 156, 158, 173, 299, 332
  contributions of, 315
Desatnick, Robert L., 289, 299, 303-04, 313, 331, 335
Dickey, Sam, 288
Diodati, Joe, 276
Discrepancy prevention, 62-63
Disk drive, 260
Disneyland, 13, 15, 40
Dmytrow, Eric D., 178, 190, 217
Dobbins, Richard K., 17, 21
Dodge, Harold F., 69, 79, 86-87, 116, 121, 134-35
Dodge & Romig sample plans, 113-21
  AOQL sample plans, 118-20
  definitions associated with, 114-15
  LTPD sample plans, 116-18
Dorfman, John R., 334
Downing, Douglas, 266
Drucker, Peter, 35, 37, 310, 314
Dual populations, 164-66
Duncan, Acheson J., 134, 193, 212

E

Early, John F., 178, 190, 332
Early Warning chart pattern, 145-46
Edits, 260, 282-83
EDP, 260-61
Efficiency and problem solving, 241-51
   cross-functional management, 250-51
   flow charts, 242-46
   Ishikawa diagrams, 248-50
   Pareto charts, 241-42
   Why-Why diagrams, 246-48
Ego needs, of workers, 303
Electronic Data Processing (EDP), 260-61
   see also Computer(s)
Endres, Al, 326
Ends Test, 230-36
   critique of, 236
   running the test, 230-36
   sample sizes for, 230
Engineering, 328-29
Environmental variation, 159
Equipment variation, 158-59
Esteem needs, of workers, 303
Evaluations
   objective, 304-09
   of quality, 55-57
   subjective, 61
   supplier quality evaluation, 63
Evans, A. Randall, 32, 37
External failure costs, 49-52

F

Face-to-face contact, and customer satisfaction, 26-27
Facilitating, by management, 42
Facilities. *See* Tools and facilities
Federal Aviation Administration, 279
Feedback, 28
Feigenbaum, Armand V., 50, 212, 225, 310, 313, 326, 334
Firmware, 261
First Chicago Corporation, 310
First National Bank of Arizona, 319
   see also Kirby, Eugene
Fishbone diagrams, 248-50
Floppy disk drives, 261
Florida Power and Light, 310
Flow charts, 242-46
   in computer programs, 261
Food sampling, 67-68
FORTRAN computer language, 261
Fraction of production (continuous sampling), 124
Freak chart pattern, 152-53

G

GE FANUC, 278
General Dynamics, 141
General Systems Company, 50, 310
Get Well chart pattern, 146-47
Girard, Joe, 27
Goodyear, 311
Government,
   quality service in, 316-19
   standards, 61
Grab sampling, 72
Graduate Hospital (Philadelphia), 323-25
Grand average, 179
Grant, Eugene L., 121, 134, 158, 162, 174, 182, 190, 192, 199, 212-13, 225
Graphics, 297
Gryna, Frank M., Jr., 65, 86, 112, 121, 174
Guyton, D.A., 142, 156

H

H106 (and H107) sample procedures, 134
Hacquebord, Heero, 252

Haefer, Wayne, 288
Hagan, John T., 334
Hall-Sheehy, James, 266
Happy Days chart pattern, 143-44
Hard disk drive, 261
Hardware (computer), 261
Harrington, H. James, 47, 54, 252, 298-99
Hartford Insurance Group, 47
   see also Scanlon, Frank
Hawthorne effect, 229
Hays, H.C., 141, 156
Health Care Financing Administration (HCFA), 61
Heller, Robert, 314
Hershauer, James C., 335
Hewlett-Packard, 23, 327-28
Hierarchy of Needs (Maslow), 302-03
Higgins, Brian K., 252
Histograms, 162-69
   dual populations, 164-66
   meeting specifications, 167-69
   normal populations, 163-64
Hospitals
   audits, 323-24
   education programs, 323
   quality service in, 322-26
   trend charts, 324
   vendors, 325-26
Hot lines, 27-28
Huls, Rebecca Lee, 15, 64, 141, 156, 178, 190, 212, 252, 304, 313, 321, 334
Humana (hospital chain), 326
Humer, Don, 37
Hunter, J. Stuart, 65
Hunter, William G., 65
Hurayt, Gerald, 87

I

Iacocca, Lee, 313-14
IBM, trend charts at, 141
Improvement, 63-64

In Search of Excellence, 23, 27
Industrial Solid State Control, Inc. (ISSC), 24, 27
Innovative Management Technologies, Inc., 12
Input (computer), 261
Inspection. *See* Sampling
Insurance companies, quality service in, 320-22
Insurance Services Office (ISO), 320-22
Intentional bias, 73
Internal failure costs, 49
International Packings Corporation, 292-93
International Standards Organization (ISO), 61
Interval sampling, 73-75
Interviews, 33
Involvement, of people, 8
   total, 298
Irving Trust Company, 224, 319
   see also Latzko, William J.
Ishikawa, Kaoru, 53, 65, 252
Ishikawa diagrams, 248-50

J

Japanese Union of Scientists and Engineers (JUSE), 61
Johnson, Gary, 299
Jones, Lewis N., 252, 299
Judgment sampling, 72-73
Jump-Shift chart pattern, 150-52
Juran, J.M., 62-65, 86, 112, 121, 134, 174
Juran's Quality Control Handbook, 62-63
Jurnack, Stephen J., 277, 287
Just-In-Time programs (JIT), 82

K

Kackar, Raghu N., 65, 334
Kanawha Valley Bank N.A., 293

Kanter, Rosabeth Moss, 293, 295, 300
Kennedy, David A., 252
Keypunch, 261-62
King, Carol A., 25, 37
King, Joseph H., 141, 156
Kirby, Eugene, 319, 333
Krentz, Shirley, 37
Kreykenbohn, William, 269, 276

L

Laford, Richard J., 71, 79, 86, 121, 327, 334
LAN (Local Area Network), 262
Languages, computer, 259
  see also specific computer languages
Latzko, William J., 42, 47, 53-54, 59, 61, 65, 69, 71, 79, 82, 86, 121, 152, 156, 215, 224-25, 252, 299, 319, 333-35
Lawler, Edward E., III, 289, 299, 313
Lawson, Barry, 194, 212
Lawsuits, 52
Lawton, Robin L., 12, 21
LCL (averages), 179-80
Leavenworth, Richard S., 121, 134, 158, 162, 174, 182, 190, 192, 199, 212-13, 225
Lefevre, Henry L., 21, 64, 80, 86, 156, 173, 225, 256, 265, 275-76, 287, 299, 313, 332, 334
Leuser, Kurt G., 286, 288
Liabilities, computers as, 258
Lip service, 311-12
Listening, as management skill, 41
Literacy, computer, 267-75
Local Area Network (LAN), 262
Local systems (Latzko's), 58
Lockerby, William D., 332
Los Angeles, Productivity Advisory Committee, 318, 332
Lot, 93
Lot Tolerance Percent Defective (LTPD), 93, 113-18

Lotus 1-2-3 program, 271
Lower control limits (LCL), 179-80
LTPD, 93, 113-18

M

McBride, Ronald C., 252, 299
McCabe, William J., 178, 190, 194, 208, 212-13, 228, 240, 328, 334
McCay, James T., 252
McGregor, Douglas, 301
MacLean, Julie, 23, 61
Magnetic Ink Character Recognition (MICR), 82, 262
Mail questionnaires, 31-32
Mainframe, 262
  see also Computer(s)
Malpractice, 52
Management
  -controllable improvements, 42
  cross-functional, 250-51
  and quality message, 309-12
  wandering around management style (MBWA), 26-27, 40-42
Management Analysis Company, 31
Management support, 39-53
  audits, 43-47
  awards, 295
  expectations, 297-98
  facilitating skills of managers, 42
  listening, 41
  Management by Wandering Around (MBWA), 40-42
  open rap sessions, 43
  presidential audits, 43-44
  reasonable expectations, 294
  rewards, 294-95
  teaching by managers, 41-42
  for teamwork, 294
  tours of duty in the trenches, 40
Managing to Keep the Customer (Desatnick), 289, 304, 331
Mandall, M.I., 28-29, 37

Manufacturing companies, quality service in, 326-30
Marine Midland Bank, 319-20
Marr, Jeffrey W., 28, 35
Martin, William B., 49-50, 53-54
Marx, Peter, 288
Maslow, Abraham H., 301-02, 311, 313
  Hierarchy of Needs, 302-04
May, Donald C., Jr., 37
MBWA (Management by Wandering Around), 26-27, 40-43
Measurement of service quality, 59-60
Memory (computer), 262
Meriter Hospital (Madison, Wisconsin), 326
MICR (Magnetic Ink Character Recognition), 82, 262
Microcomputer, 262
Military Standard 105D, 57, 83-84, 89-97, 99-112, 121
  advantages of, 90-91
  defined, 90
  definitions applicable to, 92-95
  disadvantages of, 91-92
  normal inspection, 100-104
  process stability, 111
  reduced inspection, 107-11
  tightened inspection, 104-07
Military Standard 1235B sampling procedures, 135
Military Standard 414, 84, 86
Miller, Frederick W., 276
Miller, Philip D., 276, 320
Moad, Jeff, 288
Modem, 262
Moore, Bill, 43
Moorman, David L., 276
Mornin, Bob, 26-27, 303
Morsberger, Emory L., 288
Motivation, for keeping people involved, 301-13
Mouton, Jane S., 303, 313
Multi-Vari analysis, 169-72
Multiple sample plans, 93
Murakami, Inamura, 87

Murakami, Kishii, 87
Murphy, D.K., 87

N

n, 180
National Weather Service, 279
Natural process limits (NPL), 216
Needs, Maslow's Hierarchy of, 302-04
Negotiated standards, 62
Network (computer), 263
New-product review, 63
Nickell, Warren L., 24, 37
Normal inspection, 100-104
Normal populations, 163-64
Normal sample plans, 93, 96
np-charts, 204-07
NPL, 216

O

Objective evaluations, 304-09
O'Brien, Walter J., 25
OC Curve, 93-94
OCR (Optical Character Recognition), 232-34, 263
Oddball chart pattern, 152-53
Olson, James E., 12, 21
100 percent sampling, 70-71
O'Neill, Jan, 334
Operating Characteristic Curve (OC), 93-94, 96
Optical character recognition (OCR), 232-34, 263
Ott, Ellis R., 37, 65, 89, 96, 112, 173, 190, 212, 240
Outliers, 62
Output (computer), 263
Overconfidence, 297

P

p-charts, 193-204
    calculating averages, 197-99
    calculating control limits, 199-201
    calculating proportions, 196-97
    plotting control charts, 201-02
    working with percentages, 202-04
P-charts, 193, 194, 196, 202-04
Pareto, Vilfredo. *See* Pareto charts
Pareto charts, 241-42
Patterns. *See* Chart patterns
Paul Revere Insurance Group, 332
Pennucci, Nicholas J., 299
People involvement, 8, 289-99
    communications, 291
    graphics, use of, 297
    management support, 294-96
    overconfidence, 297
    quality circles, 290
    survivorship, 296-98
    training, 291-92
Percey, Tom, 288
Peripherals, 263
Person-to-person variation, 158
Personal computer, 263
Personnel, quality service in, 330
Peters, Thomas J., 23, 36, 41, 53
Pharmaceutical databases, 279
    see also Database(s)
Phone surveys, 32-33
Physiological needs, of workers, 302
Pitt, H., 215-16, 225
Presidential audits, 43-44
Prevention,
    costs of, 48
    of discrepancies, 62-63
Problem solving. *See* Efficiency and problem solving
Procedures, 60
Process average, 115
Process control, 63
Process planning, 63
Process stability, 111
Process variation, 159
Processes, control charts for evaluation, 228-39
Proctor & Gamble, 24, 27
Procurement, 327-28
Procurement sampling, 82-83
Producer's risk, 94
Production, in the service sector, 83-84
Productivity, computers and, 257-58
Productivity Advisory Committee (Los Angeles), 318, 332
Programmers (computer), 263
Programming, computer, 272-74
Project-to-project variation, 158
Punched cards, 263
Puri, Subhash C., 12, 21
Pyzdek, Thomas, 112

Q

Quality circles, 290, 292-93
    alternatives to, 292-93
Quality control, 57-62
    see also Quality service
Quality Customer Service (Martin), 49-50
Quality evaluation, 55-57
Quality excellence, 55-64
Quality improvement, 63-64
Quality planning, 63
Quality and Productivity for Bankers and Financial Managers (Latzko), 319
Quality service, 3-21
    ASQC-Gallup Survey, 12-21
    attitude types, 15-17
    basic tools of, 6-7
    customer satisfaction, 23-36
    defined, 11-14
    ideal, 14-20
    nature of, 4-5
    people involvement in, 8
    timeliness and, 17-19
    understanding automation, 7
    understanding sampling, 5-6

Quality service (*continued*)
  variables used in assessment of, 12
Quality in the service sector, 23-36, 59-62, 81-86, 316-32
  banks, 82, 319-20
  clerical services, 329-30
  government, 316-19
  hospitals, 322-26
  insurance companies, 320-22
  manufacturing companies, 326-30
  personnel, 330
Quality Technics, Team Approach to Problem Solving at, 292
Quality techniques, 58-62
  measurement, 59-60
  procedures, 60
  sampling, 62
  standards, 60-62
Quality vs. quantity, 304-08
Qualityservice Group, 25
Questionnaires, 31-32

R

R, 180
Raabe, Steve, 288
RAM, 263
Random Access Memory (RAM), 263
Random sampling, 75-77
Random sequence, 229
Range, 159-60
Range charts, 188-89
  see also Average and range charts
Rap sessions, as management tool, 43
Rasmussen, Roger L., 332
Rath & Strong, 230
Re (rejection number), definition of, 94
Read Only Memory (ROM), 263
Recognition Equipment, 43
Reduced inspection level, 94, 107-11
Reduced sampling, 124-25
  CSP-1, 123-34
    Military Standard 105D, 83-84, 89-96, 99-112

Redundant sampling, 70
Rejectable Quality Level (RQL), 94
Rejection number, 94
Reports, audit, 46-47
Republic National Bank of New York, 278
Rewards, 294
Rinderknecht, David M., 225
Rocky Mountain Orthodontics, 313
Rohrbaugh, Randolph L., 79, 333
ROM, 263
Romig, Harry G., 69, 79, 86, 116, 121, 332
  contributions of, 315
Rosander, A.C., 21, 65, 69, 71, 74, 77-80, 86, 121, 142, 156, 158, 162, 173, 178, 190, 208, 212-13, 332
  contributions of, 315
Rosenberg, Jerry M., 266
RQL, 94
Ruch, William A., 335
Rush, R.J., 313
Ryan, John, 21, 54, 252

S

s, 180
Sad Sack chart pattern, 147-48
Sample plans, 83-84
  Dodge & Romig, 113-21
  LTPD, 116-18
Sample sizes, 115, 181-82
  for Ends Test, 230
  for evaluating quality, 62
  for Tukey-Duckworth Test, 237
Sampling, 62, 67-79, 81-86
  accessibility, 72
  of cars, 68-69
  chunk, 72
  clerical records, 69
  continuous, 123-34
  external vs. internal samples, 84-85
  of food, 67-68

Sampling (*continued*)
  grab, 72
  interval, 73
  interval with a random start, 73-75
  judgment, 72-73
  as a key to quality service, 5-6
  100 percent, 70-71
  procurement, 82-83
  random, 75-77
  redundant, 70
  sample plans and service sector production, 83-84
  stratified, 77-78
  subjective, 71-72
  survey errors, 34-35
  systematic, 74
  300 percent, 70
  see also Reduced sampling
Sarazen, J. Stephen, 25
Sateesh, K., 288
Scanlon, Frank, 47, 54, 334
SCAT © Approach, at International Packings Corporation, 292
Scholtes, Peter, 252
Schonberger, Richard J., 86, 334
Schrock, Edward M., 173, 225
  contributions of, 315
Scotti, Col. Michael, Jr., 325, 334
Security, for databases, 285-86
  needs of workers, 302
Seder, Leonard A., 168, 174
Self-actualization needs, of workers, 303
Service problems, main causes of, 12-14
Service sector, quality in, 23-36, 59-62, 81-86, 316-32
  sample plans and, 81-86
  see also Quality in the service sector
Seymour, Jim, 276
Shainin, Dorian, 230, 240
Shertz, Robert S., 252
Ship-To-Stock programs, 82
Simulated sampling sequences, 130-32
Skantze, General Lawrence, 310, 313
Social needs, of workers, 302-03

Software, 263, 271-72
Special inspection levels, 95
Specifications, 167-69
Spencer, Donald D., 265
Spreadsheet programs, 271
Squeaky wheel system, 83
Squires, Frank H., 71, 80, 121
Staab, Thomas C., 56, 64
Standard deviation, 162, 182
Standards, 60-62
  based on capability studies, 61-62
  government, 61
  negotiated, 62
  subjective evaluations, 61
  trade organization, 61
State University of Iowa Section, American Society for Quality Control, 190, 212
Stephens, Kenneth S., 86, 96, 134
Stern, Nancy, 265
Stern, Robert A., 265
Stevens, Calvin, 333
Stoeger, Kenneth J., 252
Stoner, William, 327
Strategic Solutions, 29
Stratified sampling, 77-78
Subjective evaluations, 61
Supervisors, 297
Supplier quality evaluation, 63
Surveys of customers, 28-36
  aging data, 35
  disseminating results, 35-36
  inconsistencies, 35
  mail questionnaires, 31-32
  personal interviews, 33
  phone surveys, 32-33
  problems associated with, 34-36
  tabletop customer surveys, 30-31
  types of, 29-33
Survivorship, 296-98
Sutcliffe, Thurmon, 319, 333
Syntex Corporation, 43
System audits, 44-45
Systematic sampling, 74

T

Tabletop customer surveys, 30-31
Taguchi, Genichi, 328
Tallon, Robert, 310, 313
Tang, J., 142, 156
Tangibles, stressing, 296
Tanis, Elliot A., 174
Tape drives (computer), 264
TAPS (Team Approach to Problem Solving), 292
Tatge, Mark, 37
Taylor, Claude L., 310, 313
Taylor, Frank J., 53
Teaching, by management, 41-42
Team Approach to Problem Solving (TAPS), 292
Teams, 293-96
Templates, 283-84
Terminals, computer, 264
Thomas, Richard L., 310, 313
Thornton, Manly P., 252, 329, 334
300 percent sampling, 70
Tightened inspection level, 95, 104-07
Time-sharing systems, 264
Time-to-time variation, 158
Timeliness, 17-19
Toll-free hot lines, and customer satisfaction, 27-28
Tools and facilities, 137-40
  as keys to quality service, 6-7, 14, 19
  service industry vs. manufacturing tools, 139-40
Torrey, M.N., 135
Total Chaos chart pattern, 154-55
Total Quality Control (Feigenbaum), 326
Townsend, Patrick L., 322, 334
Trade organization standards, 61
Training, 63, 291-92
Traver, Robert W., 158, 173
Trend charts, 138, 141-56
  vs. average and range charts, 187-88
  defined, 142
  in hospitals, 324

Trend charts (*continued*)
  how to use, 142-43
  patterns, 143-55
Tribett, C.W., 313
Tukey, John W., 240
Tukey-Duckworth Test, 236-39
  sample sizes for, 230

U

UCL (averages and ranges), 180-81
Unannounced audits, 46
Union Oil Company, 40, 253
United Services Automobile Association (USAA), 15, 321
  see also Huls, Rebecca Lee
United States Fidelity and Guaranty Company (USF&G), 13, 74
Upper control limits (UCL), 180-81

V

Variables control charts, 138, 175-90
  average and range charts, 175-79
  range charts, 188-89
  sample sizes, 181-82
Variables measurements, 160-62
Variation, 138, 157-73
  environmental, 159
  equipment, 158-59
  measures of, 159-62
  person-to-person, 158
  process, 159
  project-to-project, 158
  sources of, 157-59
  time-to-time, 158
Vendors, 325-26

W

Waksman, Janet S., 319-20
Walker Research, 28

Walt Disney Company, 26
Walt Disney World, 15
  see also Disneyland
Wandering around management style, 26-27, 40-41
Waterman, Robert H., Jr., 23, 36, 53
Welch, C.M., 25
Welty, Earl M., 53
Werner, John P., 323, 334
West, Jack, 33
Western Electric Company, 121, 134, 156, 190, 225
Wheeler, Roy E., 65, 334
Why Plot? chart pattern, 148-50
Why-Why diagrams, 246-48
Windsor Export Supply, 178
Word processing, 264
Work teams, 293-96
Wyatt, John M., 333

X

x, 181

Y

Yo-Yo chart pattern, 144-45
Young, Barbara J., 62, 252

Z

Zemke, Ron, 330, 335
Zimmerman, Charles D., III, 13, 21, 333
Zimmerman, Mary, 326, 334
Zwissler, Lew, 31, 33